Glasgow Boys

Masterpieces of Art

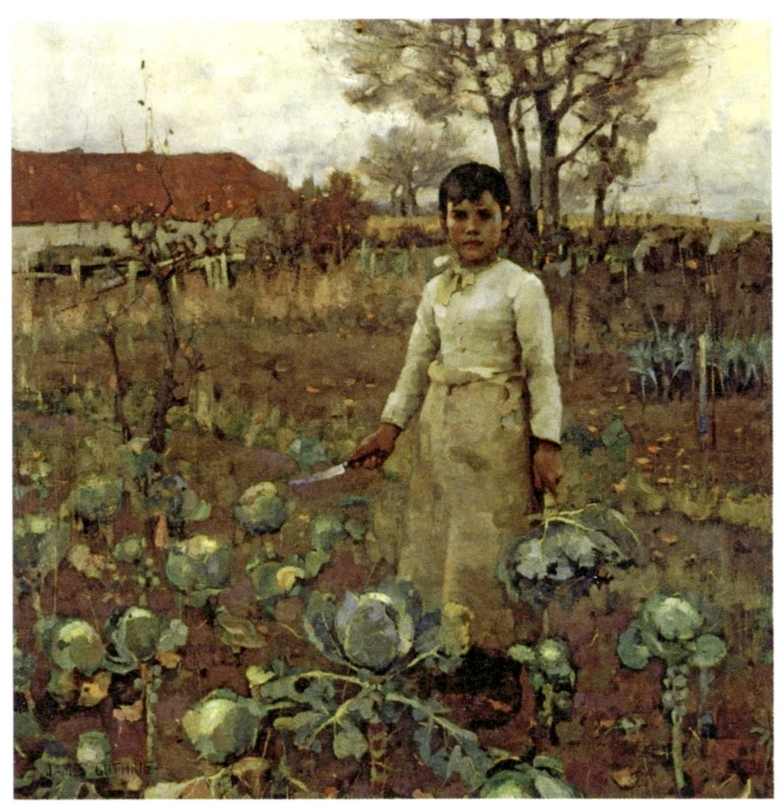

Publisher and Creative Director: Nick Wells
Commissioning Editor: Polly Prior
Senior Project Editor: Catherine Taylor
Art Director & Layout Design: Mike Spender
Copy Editor: Katharine Davies
Proofreader: Dawn Laker
Indexer: Helen Snaith

Special thanks to Tilly Lawton and Magdalena Pszuk.

FLAME TREE PUBLISHING
6 Melbray Mews
Fulham, London SW6 3NS
United Kingdom

www.flametreepublishing.com

First published 2018

25
5 7 9 10 8 6 4

© 2018 Flame Tree Publishing Ltd

Front cover: *In the Orchard*, 1886, by James Guthrie (1859–1930)
Courtesy of Paul Fearn / Alamy Stock Photo

Back cover: *Autumn Sunshine* (detail), 1883–84, by Edward Arthur Walton (1860–1922)
Courtesy of The Hunterian, University of Glasgow, Scotland / Bridgeman Images

Every effort has been made to contact image copyright holders. We apologize in advance for any omissions
and would be pleased to insert the appropriate acknowledgement in subsequent editions of this publication.

A CIP record for this book is available from the British Library upon request.

Image Credits: Courtesy **Alamy Stock Photo**/Paul Fearn 67 (& front cover); **Bridgeman Images** and the following: 1 & 56, 79, 108, 120 National Galleries of Scotland, Edinburgh; 3 & 111, 11 & 32, 14 & 77, 15 & 54, 18 & 28 & 40, 62, 119 Art Gallery and Museum, Kelvingrove, Glasgow, Scotland; 4 & 86, 10 & 50 & 65, 26 & 60, 69, 72, 81, 114 The Ellis Campbell Collection; 6 & 47, 125 Private Collection / Photo © Peter Nahum at The Leicester Galleries, London; 7 & 78, 20 & 44, 24 & 92, 36, 46, 66, 96, 101 The Fleming-Wyfold Art Foundation; 8 & 80 Laing Art Gallery, Newcastle-upon-Tyne, UK / © Tyne & Wear Archives & Museums; 9 & 42 Art Gallery and Museum, Kelvingrove, Glasgow, Scotland / © Tyne & Wear Archives & Museums; 12 & 57 Smith Art Gallery and Museum, Stirling, Scotland; 13 & 61, 19 & 112, 25 & 34, 41, 53, 64, 70, 89, 97, 110 Private Collection / Photo © The Fine Art Society, London, UK; 16 & 95, 84, 106 & 113, 118 Art Gallery and Museum, Kelvingrove, Glasgow, Scotland / © CSG CIC Glasgow Museums Collection; 17 & 55, 82, & 94, 85, 87, 98, 99, 116, 117 Private Collection / Photo © Christie's Images; 21 & 45, 39, 76 Yale Center for British Art, New Haven, USA / Gift of Isabel Kurtz in memory of Charles M. Kurtz; 22 & 122 Private Collection / Photo © The Maas Gallery, London; 23 & 49 Harris Museum and Art Gallery, Preston, Lancashire, UK; 27 & 73, 31 The Hunterian, University of Glasgow, Scotland; 30 The Higgins Art Gallery & Museum, Bedford, UK; 33, 48 Glasgow Museums, UK / © CSG CIC Glasgow Museums Collection; 35 The Fine Art Society, London, UK; 38 Private Collection / Courtesy of Manya Igel Fine Arts, London; 52 & 128 Falmouth Art Gallery, Cornwall, UK; 58, 104 Museum voor Schone Kunsten, Ghent, Belgium / © Lukas - Art in Flanders VZW; 59, 123 Private Collection / Photo © The Fine Art Society in Edinburgh, Scotland; 68 Berwick-upon-Tweed Borough Museum and Art Gallery; 71, 115 City of Edinburgh Museums and Art Galleries, Scotland; 74 Yale Center for British Art, New Haven, USA; 75 Museum of New Zealand Te Papa Tongarewa, Wellington, New Zealand / Gift of John Newton and Son, Kaiwharawhara, 1939; 88 Collection of Andrew McIntosh Patrick, UK; 90 Aberdeen Art Gallery and Museum, Scotland; 93 Private Collection / Photo © Whitford & Hughes, London, UK; 100 Victoria & Albert Museum, London, UK / The Stapleton Collection; 102 Bradford Art Galleries and Museums, West Yorkshire, UK; 103 Photo © Christie's Images; 105 Manchester Art Gallery, UK; 109 Laing Art Gallery, Newcastle-upon-Tyne, UK; 121 Yale Center for British Art, Paul Mellon Collection, USA / Gift of Isabella S. Kurtz in memory of Charles M. Kurtz; 124 The Fine Art Society.

ISBN 978-1-83964-996-7

Printed in China I Created, Developed & Produced in the United Kingdom

Glasgow Boys

Masterpieces of Art

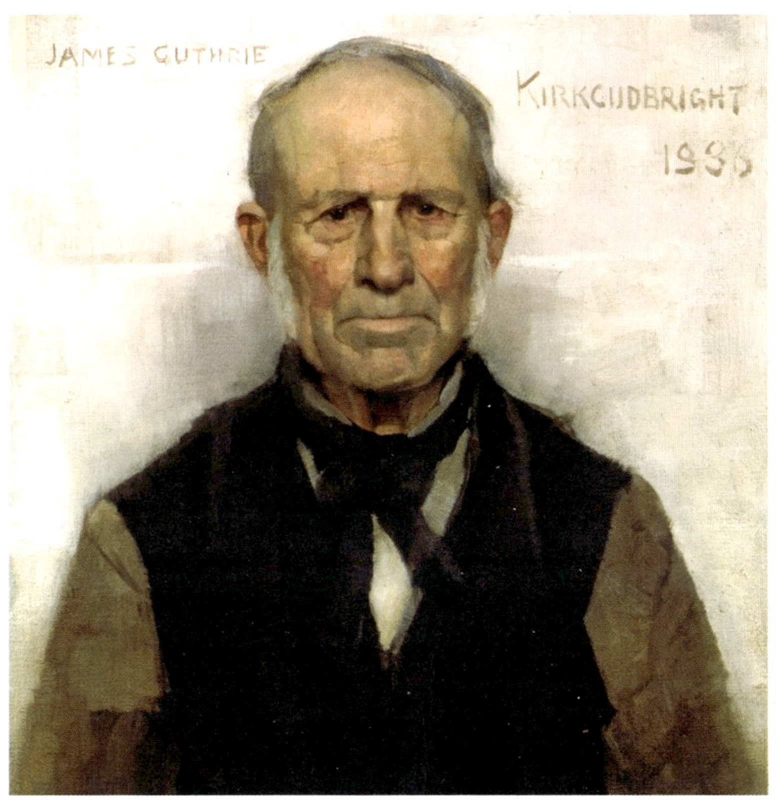

Susie Hodge

FLAME TREE
PUBLISHING

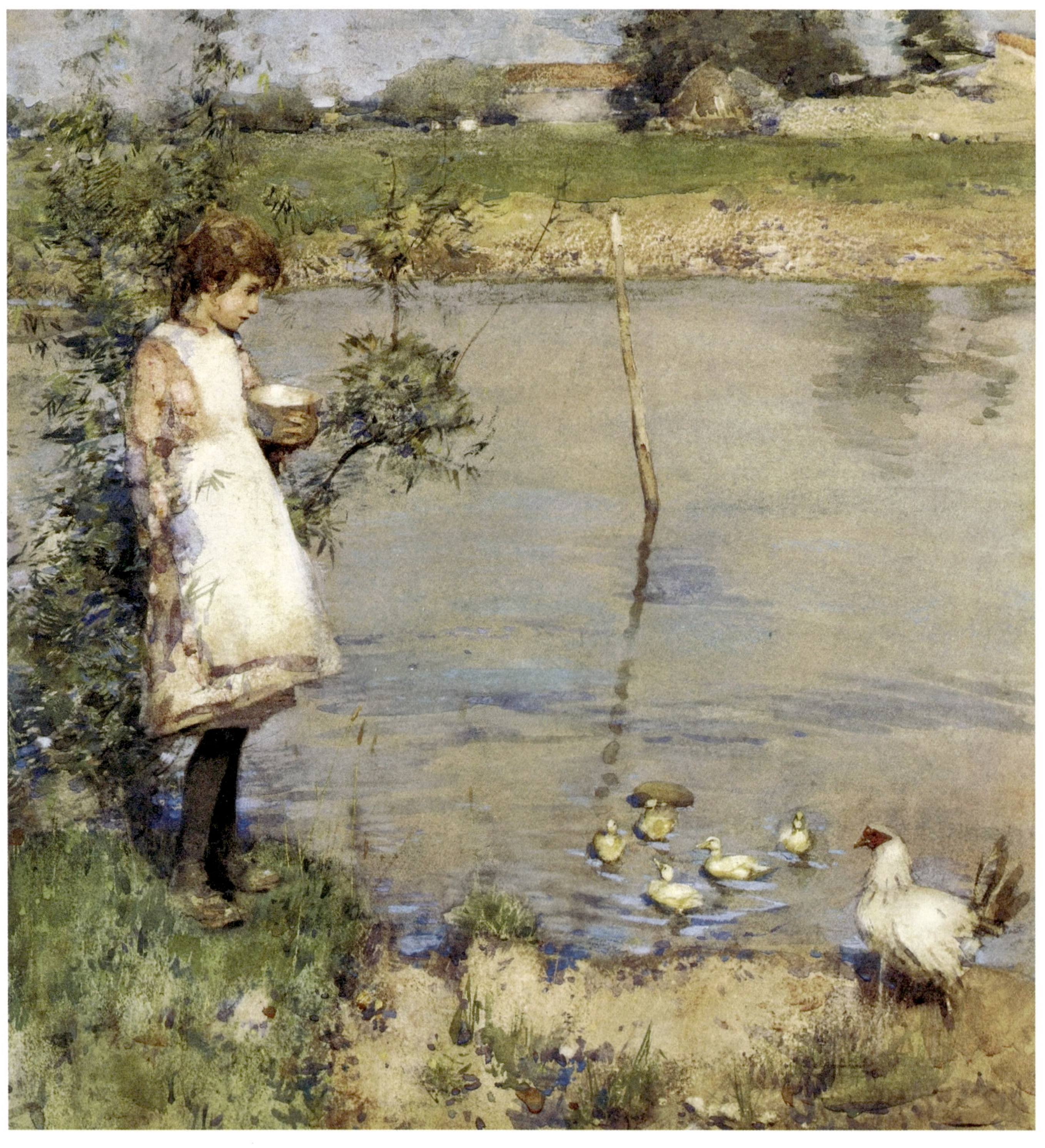

Contents

The Glasgow Boys: Defying Conventions

Flourishing from the 1880s until approximately 1914, the Glasgow School of Painters was a circle of young Scottish-based artists who mixed artistic activity with friendship, and challenged traditional Scottish art. Under the Glasgow School label were smaller groups, including The Four (also known as the Spook School), the Glasgow Girls and the Glasgow Boys.

Influenced by a range of art styles, including Realism, Impressionism, Post-Impressionism, English and Dutch landscape painting, and some Japanese art, the Glasgow Boys' colourful paintings of Scottish people, life and landscapes revolutionized Scottish art. They opposed the highly finished and often overly sentimental landscapes, genres and narrative paintings that were expected by the Royal Scottish Academy (RSA) in Edinburgh, instead developing a distinctively colourful, naturalistic and informal style of painting. They had no rules and no official membership or annual exhibition, but they all had similar ideals. Many of them trained at the Glasgow School of Art, the Slade in London or the Académie Julian in Paris, and all had a passion for naturalism, for painting *en plein air* (in the open air) and for fresh colours.

In absorbing and amalgamating naturalistic ideas from other parts of Europe, each of them created original paintings that defied contemporary artistic conventions in Scotland. To a degree, their highly coloured, naturally lit paintings resembled Impressionist works, but in other ways, they contrasted with them, and after the mid-1880s, the Glasgow Boys became recognized for their fresh, realist views of rural life, local landscapes, portraits, animals and flowers.

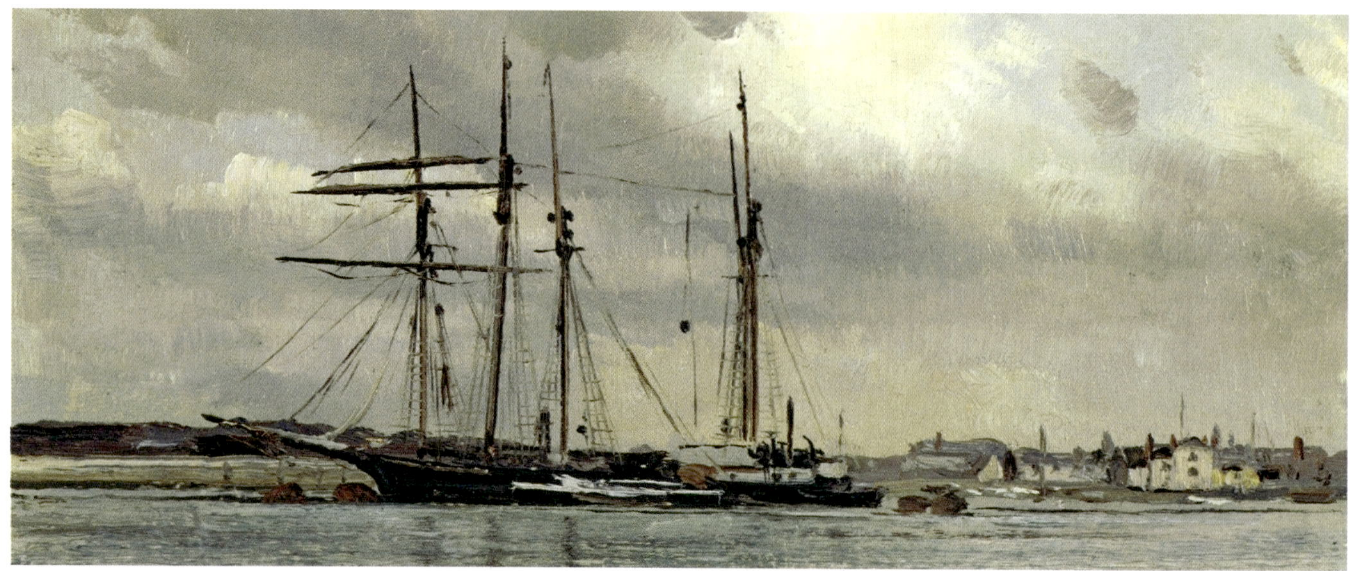

Glasgow at the Turn of the Century

Glasgow had become the leading industrial city of the British Empire by the 1880s. With the River Clyde providing access to the rest of Scotland, and the close proximity of the Atlantic, it was ideally placed for trade and industry. Vast local reserves of coal were advantageous and it became the world's leading shipbuilding centre. The largest Scottish railway companies established workshops there. Merchants based in Glasgow imported cotton, tobacco and sugar from America, and many successful industries developed.

Alongside this was an outburst of creativity. In 1888 and 1901, two huge International Exhibitions attracted visitors from all over the world, and art clubs and galleries were opened. As migrants moved in from other parts of Scotland, Ireland and England, Glasgow expanded to over twice the size of Edinburgh. Slums jostled for space, and the newly prosperous middle classes commissioned architects to build them luxurious homes, which they adorned with art. Some began collecting artworks, and most supported local artists, which was how Glasgow also became recognized internationally as a centre for avant-garde movements.

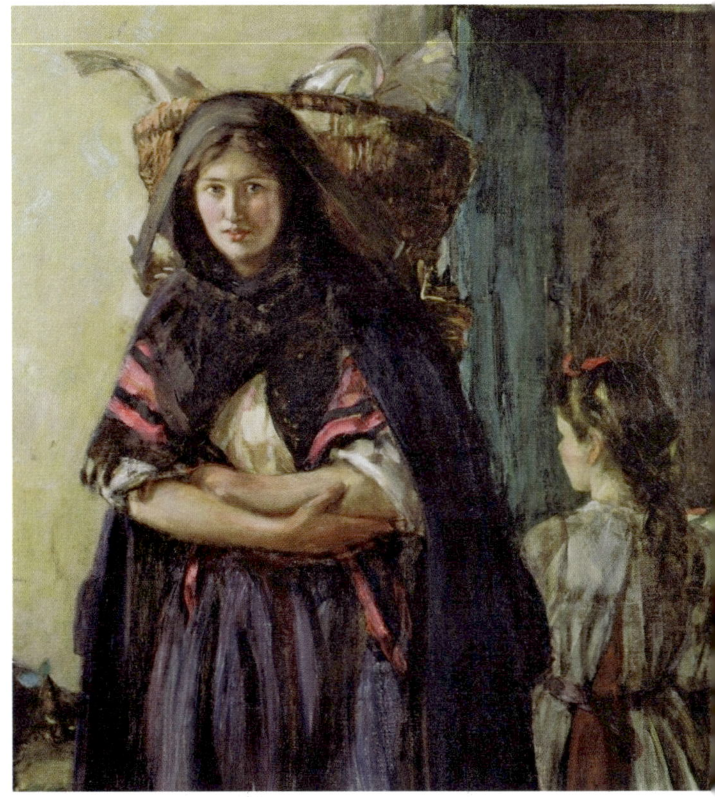

Scottish Art in the Late Nineteenth Century

To provide opportunities for artists to exhibit, the Institution for the Encouragement of the Fine Arts in Scotland was founded in 1819, in Edinburgh. Seven years later, it became the Scottish Academy of Art, its aim being to advance art across Scotland. In 1838, it was granted a Royal Charter and became known as the Royal Scottish Academy (RSA). Its members helped to found the National Gallery of Scotland in Edinburgh, which opened in 1859. Yet from the start, the RSA rejected any art that did not meet its criteria, and many artists from outside Edinburgh found it difficult to exhibit there. So, in 1861, the Glasgow Institute of the Fine Arts was formed to provide exhibiting opportunities for all, but especially Glaswegian artists. It opened its own gallery in 1879, and in 1896, it also received a royal charter, becoming known as the Royal Glasgow Institute of the Fine Arts.

The Glasgow Government School of Design had been established in 1845, changing its name to the Glasgow School of Art in 1853. It was soon over-subscribed, and in 1885, a new director was appointed. Francis H. Newbery (1855–1946) made several changes, including moving the School to new buildings designed by Charles Rennie Mackintosh (1868–1928). Mackintosh, his wife Margaret Macdonald (1864–1933), her sister Frances Macdonald (1873–1921) and Herbert MacNair (1868–1955) made up the Glasgow School group known as The Four, or the Spook School.

A group of amateur artists founded the Glasgow Art Club in 1867, to meet once a month and discuss each other's paintings. Its membership grew, professional artists joined, and exhibitions and annual dinners were held. It became Glasgow's major institution for painters, setting the standards and expectations of art across the city. However, several younger painters who were not admitted criticized its staid attitude, and in 1874, they founded their own art club, the St Mungo Society (after Glasgow's patron saint). Some of these later became the Glasgow Boys.

Who Were the Glasgow Boys?

The Glasgow Boys comprised a number of artists who became informally associated with each other through their shared artistic beliefs, friendships and their initial exclusion from Edinburgh's and Glasgow's official art institutions. Although they formed a Glasgow Boys' Society for a short time in 1887, it was never official. They all rejected the tight brushwork, polished finish, sentimental approaches and heavy use of brown varnish of the older generation of Scottish painters.

The Glasgow Boys included Thomas Millie Dow (1848–1919), Alexander Mann (1853–1908), James Paterson (1854–1932), William York Macgregor (1855–1923), Arthur Melville (1855–1904), John Lavery (1856–1941), George Henry (1858–1943), James Nairn (1859–1904), Thomas Corsan Morton (1859–1928), William Kennedy (1859–1918), James Guthrie (1859–1930), James Whitelaw Hamilton (1860–1932),

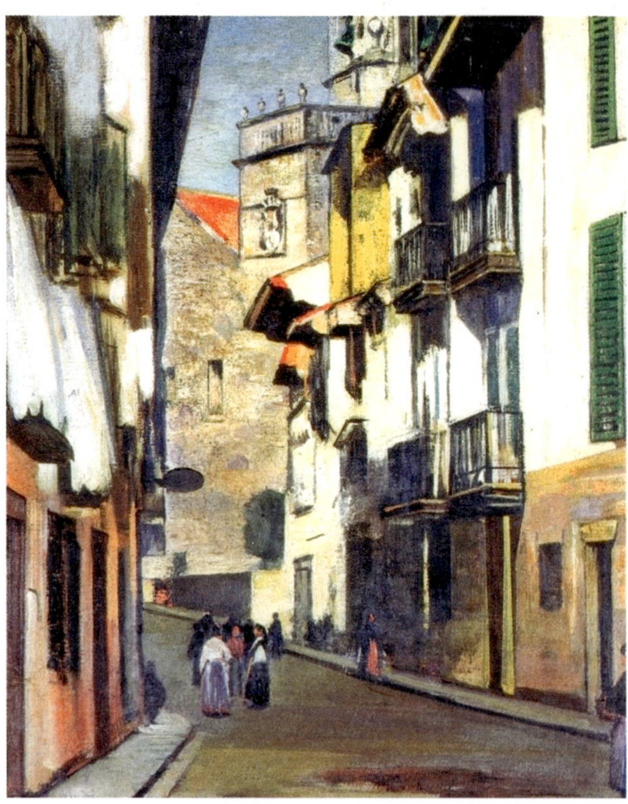

Edward Arthur Walton (1860–1922), Alexander Ignatius Roche (1861–1921), Joseph Crawhall (1861–1913), James Stuart Park (1862–1933), George Pirie (1863–1946), Edward Atkinson Hornel (1864–1933), John Quinton Pringle (1864–1925), Harrington Mann (1864–1937), David Gauld (1865–1936), William Page Atkinson Wells (1872–1923) and, more loosely associated, David Young Cameron (1865–1945).

Most came from Glasgow or spent time there, some initially met where they trained, or at the St Mungo Society, or on painting trips. They all shared common aims, including wanting to be accepted and recognized in Scotland as serious artists. They initiated *plein-air* painting in Scotland, creating effects of natural light and shade with patches of paint, and borrowed approaches and methods from the Hague and Barbizon Schools of painting, Japanese prints and French Realism, Symbolism, Impressionism and Post-Impressionism. Most were especially inspired by the paintings of the acclaimed master of naturalism, Jules Bastien-Lepage (1848–84), and James Abbott McNeill Whistler (1834–1903), and some also drew inspiration from the English Pre-Raphaelite Brotherhood and medieval painting.

For years, however, they were derided. Even after many of them had won accolades, had paintings bought by wealthy patrons or exhibited internationally, their work was still often censured or ridiculed. For instance, in February 1890, George Henry's *A Galloway Landscape* was written about in the *Helensburgh and Gareloch Times*: 'It may be clever but it is not art. It is utterly destitute of perspective, atmosphere and poetry, three very serious defects, as we take it, in a landscape picture.'

How Did They Come Together?

Apart from William York Macgregor and Harrington Mann, who were supported by their families, the Glasgow Boys had to earn a living, so they aspired to be accepted by any of the official Scottish art institutions. During the 1870s and 1880s, several applied for membership of the Glasgow Art Club, but most were refused, due to their youth and because they had ridiculed established members' paintings. So, although Glasgow's art scene was growing, many young artists were frustrated. They were aware that, elsewhere, artists were trying new ideas, but they could not progress at home.

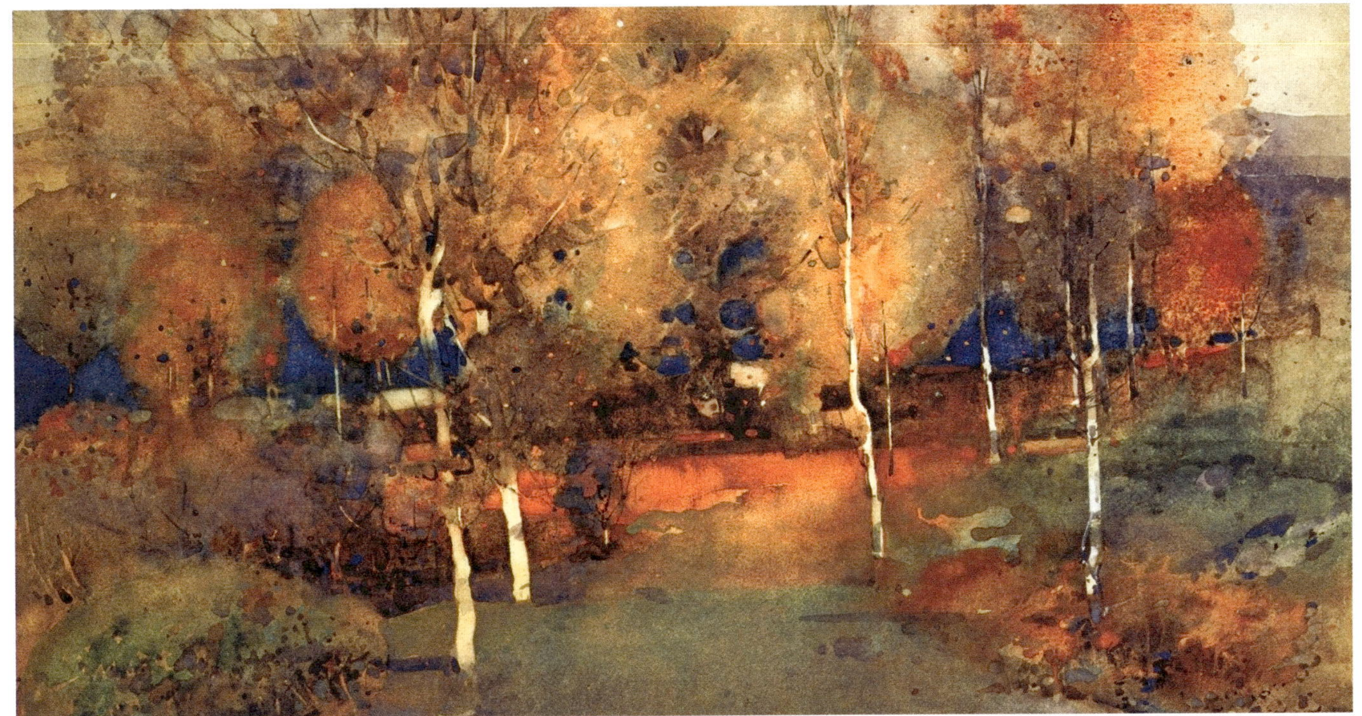

After 1879, the slightly older, financially independent Macgregor invited artists to his Glasgow studio, where he offered life classes and shared his materials. This tended to happen during winter, as several artists spent their summers working in the countryside, returning to Glasgow in the colder months to complete paintings that they submitted to galleries. These included London's Royal Academy and the Glasgow Institute, but rarely Edinburgh's RSA, which they disparagingly referred to as merely the 'Edinburgh Academy'. Within a short time, Macgregor's unofficial art club became packed with people who discussed the artists they admired, and developed their ideas and painting approaches. Although they had no official title or mandate, Macgregor became the natural leader. The only Glasgow Boys who did not meet at his studio were James Guthrie and Arthur Melville, who met members of the group on painting excursions.

At first, 'the Boys' were simply perceived as a group of exuberant young artists seeking to make their marks on Scottish art. It was only several years later, when their work had become well known beyond Scotland, that they became referred to as the Glasgow Boys.

The Glasgow Boys' Style

Although each of the Boys had his own style, their art had many elements in common. Many had trained in the same places – over half at the Glasgow School of Art, some at the Slade School of Fine Art in London or the Académie Julian in Paris, while a few had attended other Parisian or rural French ateliers. Even those who trained elsewhere had comparable outlooks, and especially after meeting at Macgregor's, they all evolved similar approaches to painting. At his studio gatherings, Macgregor advised them to: 'Hack out the subject as you would were you using an axe, and try to realize it; get its bigness. Don't follow any school, there are no schools in art.'

Sketching and painting outdoors was the Boys' major departure from the usual Scottish practice of painting in the studio; their use of realism and naturalism over sentimentality was also different, as was their application of loose, wide, often square brushmarks, and the build-up of the effects of light and shade with patches of subtly changing colour. Painting life around them, the Boys depicted their subjects objectively, but also captured atmosphere, such as still air in a winter woodland, a hazy dusk, a storm gathering over the sea, or sunlight playing on a figure.

This naturalistic approach continued for several years, but as Art Nouveau styles emerged, some of the Boys began painting in a more decorative and sometimes Symbolist style. As interests and experiences evolved, each artist's work developed slightly divergently, often subsequently influencing each other. For instance, David Gauld worked in oils and stained glass, which inspired bolder work among some of the others, and Hornel and Henry developed new ideas by spending time in Japan. Consequently, others became inspired by their new, more decorative colours and compositions.

The Glasgow Boys' Inspiration

The Glasgow Boys were inspired by a range of sources. Naturally, many were influenced by their teachers, and those who studied in France or attended some of the modern European art exhibitions in Glasgow were

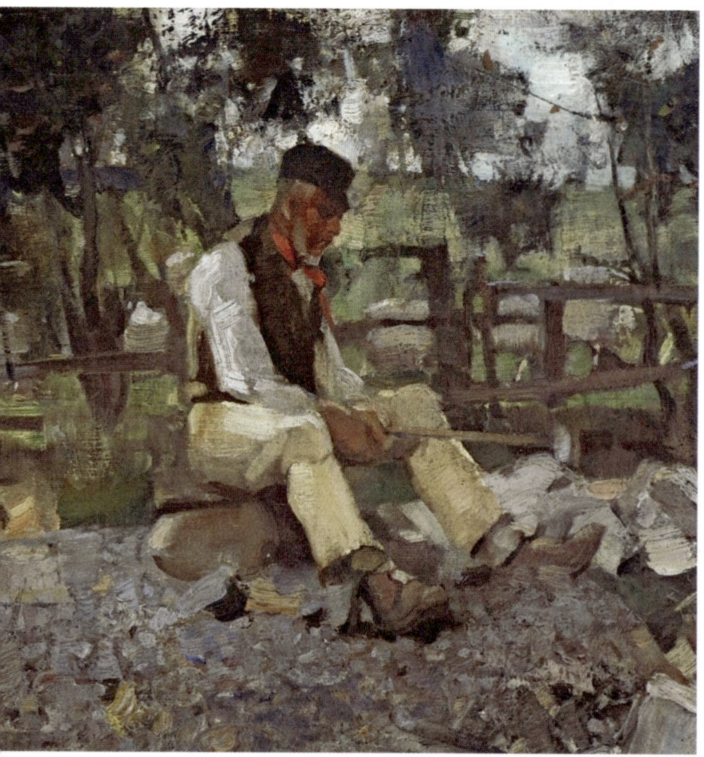

inspired by what they saw. In direct emulation of a community of artists who had painted outdoors in the village of Barbizon, near the French Forest of Fontainebleau, between 1830 and 1870, several painted in the artists' colony of Grez-sur-Loing, on the northern edge of the forest. Following the English landscape painter John Constable (1776–1837), whose work had been exhibited in Paris in 1824 to widespread approval, the Barbizon painters were among the first to paint outdoors from nature, rather than in the studio. Théodore Rousseau (1812–67), Jean-François Millet (1814–75), Charles-François Daubigny (1817–78) and Jean-Baptiste-Camille Corot (1796–1875) were the main Barbizon painters to influence the Glasgow Boys, as well as the Impressionists and artists of the Hague School.

Working in The Hague between 1860 and 1890, the Hague School was another naturalistic movement, which recorded Dutch rural life. Influenced by their own heritage of seventeenth-century Dutch painting, as well as the Barbizon painters, the Hague artists depicted landscapes and figures in muted, atmospheric tones. Among those who were particularly influential to the Glasgow Boys were Jozef Israëls (1824–1911), Anton Mauve (1838–88), Willem Roelofs (1822–97) and Matthijs Maris (1839–1917). Other individual artists whom the Boys admired included J.M.W. Turner (1775–1851), Jules Bastien-Lepage, J.A.M. Whistler, Gustave Courbet (1819–77), Richard Parkes-Bonington (1802–28) and Adolphe Monticelli (1824–86).

Bastien-Lepage and Whistler were the most profoundly influential. A French naturalist, Bastien-Lepage inspired them with his *plein-air* approach and square brushstrokes, while Whistler, a London-based American of Scottish-Irish ancestry, introduced them to Japanese art and evoking misty, atmospheric imagery. After four years in Paris, he moved to London in 1859 with his collection of Japanese *ukiyo-e* prints, and befriended some of the Boys. His sinuous contours, minimal design and reduced palette exuded an Oriental appeal, which was hated by some but greatly admired by the Glasgow Boys. By the time of their first group exhibition in 1885, Japonism – an admiration of all things Japanese – had already been expressed by the Impressionists and Post-Impressionists, but it was still unexpected when it appeared in the Glasgow Boys' paintings.

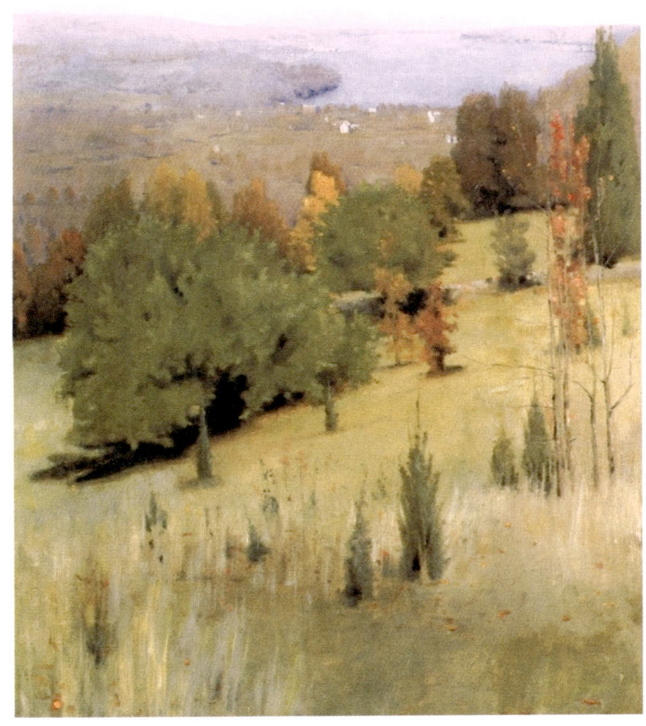

The First Exhibition

In 1861, the Glasgow Institute of the Fine Arts was founded by some of the city's most eminent figures, including the sculptor John Mossman (1817–90) and the painter and art collector John Graham-Gilbert (1794–1866), to provide exhibiting opportunities for contemporary artists. From its inaugural exhibition in 1862, it was successful, attracting nearly 40,000 visitors. In 1879, new premises were opened on Sauchiehall Street in Glasgow city centre, designed by John James Burnet (1857–1938), with a frieze created by Mossman, who taught the poet and sculptor Pittendrigh Macgillivray (1856–1938), the only sculptor to be associated with the Glasgow Boys.

By the early 1880s, the Institute had become renowned as the main venue in Glasgow for the public to see works of art by modern European artists. Among the artists whose paintings were exhibited

there during that decade were John Everett Millais (1829–96), Frederic Leighton (1830–96), Edward Burne-Jones (1833-98), Corot, Millet, Israëls, Maris, Bastien-Lepage, Whistler and Monticelli. Graham-Gilbert also loaned paintings by Turner and Constable.

Seeing works by these and others had a profound effect on the Glasgow Boys, and in 1885, they held their first collective exhibition at the Institute, including paintings such as Dow's *The Hudson River* (1884, *see* page 32) and *The Tennis Party* (1885, *see* page 90) by Lavery. With their bold use of colour, natural subject matter, dynamic compositions and naturalistic light, their paintings created a sensation.

First Phase: Social Realism

The combination of economic stability and a rise in interest in contemporary art was essential to the development of the Glasgow Boys' art. Over the years, their style and approach evolved, and in retrospect, it is often described as falling into three phases. The first began in the late 1870s, unofficially led by James Paterson and William York Macgregor, who began sketching together a couple of years before Macgregor held his life classes.

The style is naturalistic and often described as social realist, because many of the artists depicted the everyday lives and conditions of the poor, with unembellished realism and no moralizing or sentimentality. Vigorously applying paint with square brushes or palette knives, they portrayed their human subjects in Barbizon- and Hague School-inspired muted tones. Their most vital period, this first phase evolved when small groups of the Boys sketched together in rural locations over several summers. Back in their studios, they worked with their oil sketches and watercolours to produce finished paintings.

Painted in Cockburnspath, a small village near the Berwickshire coast, *Autumn Sunshine* (1883–84, *see* page 31) by Edward Arthur Walton shows his method of painting in full sunlight. A range of brushstrokes conveys textures in the landscape, which is the subject of the painting. *Hop-Pickers Returning* (1883) by Alexander Mann is another example of the group's earliest phase, demonstrating the refreshing lightness of his *plein-air* approach. Produced while Mann was studying in

London with the French artist Alphonse Legros (1837–1911), the work was based on sketches he made at Romney Marsh, in Kent, of a girl walking home from the fields after a day's work, and shows strong influences of Bastien-Lepage, Israëls and Millet.

Moniaive (1885–86) was James Paterson's rendition of the village of Moniaive in Dumfries and Galloway, where, from his first visit in 1879, he painted *en plein air* and took photos. He moved to the village in 1884, and he painted this view using several techniques borrowed from the Barbizon School, including a high viewpoint, varied brushstrokes, atmospheric perspective and a detailed foreground. Two more examples of the Boys' first phase include Macgregor's *Crail, Fife* (1883, *see* page 57), with its Impressionistic broad handling of colour, and George Henry's strongly lit *The Hedgecutter* (1886).

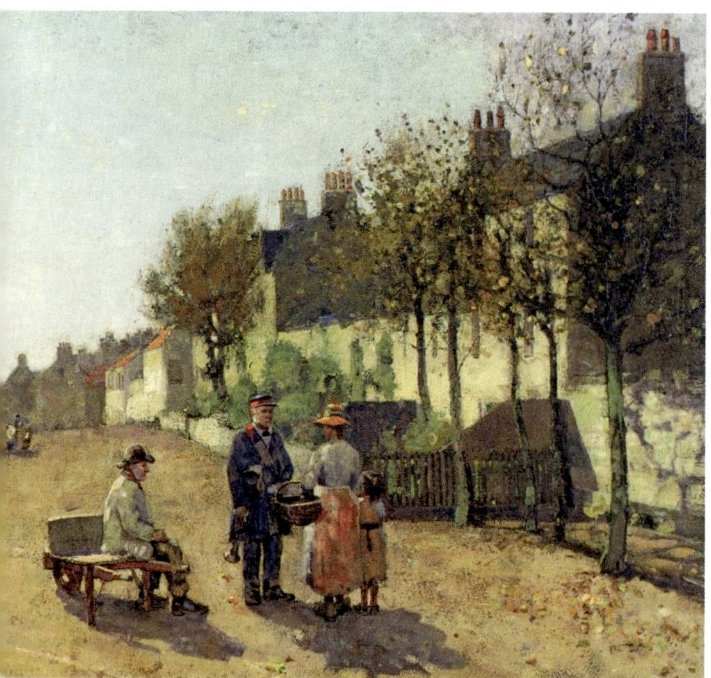

Second Phase: Decorative

During the late 1880s, a decorative aspect began to emerge in many of the Boys' paintings, which became seen as their second phase. It developed while Art Nouveau was evolving in parts of Europe, in

parallel with the influence of Japanese *ukiyo-e* paintings and prints. *Ukiyo-e* art was produced in parts of Japan from the seventeenth to nineteenth centuries, often featuring beautiful girls, landscapes or flowers in asymmetrical compositions and flat-looking colour.

To draw attention to Glasgow's achievements in science, industry and art, and to raise funds to build the Kelvingrove Art Gallery and Museum (which opened in 1901), Glasgow held an International Exhibition in 1888. The art section displayed works by artists including Constable, Turner, Corot, Bastien-Lepage, Courbet, Millet, Maris and Israëls. Meanwhile, exhibitions at the Glasgow Institute and La Societé des Beaux-Arts, a Glasgow gallery owned by the influential art dealer Alexander Reid (1854–1928), also provided opportunities for the public to see works by modern European artists.

Among many exhibitions in 1889, Reid held one of *ukiyo-e* prints, which heightened the craze throughout Glasgow and beyond for Japanese art. The Glasgow Boys had already been introduced to Japanese *ukiyo-e* art through Whistler's work, and his 1885 Ten O'Clock Lecture, which outlined his ideals, was printed in 1888. Guthrie's *The Morning Paper* (*c.* 1890–91, *see* page 97), a pastel of a young woman reading, demonstrates obvious influences of Whistler and Japanese art. Similarly, the stylized, flat-looking 1891 work by Hornel, *Children Dancing Around a Tree* (*see* page 98), conveys a stronger sense of pattern than realism.

The White Horse by Walton (*c.* 1898, *see* page 46) is another example of the influence of Whistler and Symbolism on the Boys. After training briefly in Düsseldorf, Walton had returned to study at the Glasgow School of Art, where he met and began painting with Guthrie and Crawhall, and later also with Henry and Lavery. In 1890, Henry and Hornel collaborated on *The Druids – Bringing in the Mistletoe* (*see* page 95), a stylized painting of druids in ceremonial robes, on a moonlit snowy hillside, depicting an ancient Celtic rite. Their use of gold leaf over incised gesso enhances the painting's ornamental quality, presenting an early example of Art Nouveau. After the work was shown at an exhibition in the Grosvenor Gallery in London that year, the Glasgow Boys were invited to exhibit at the Munich Art Society, which helped to establish their international reputation.

Third Phase: Independence

By the late 1890s, many of the Glasgow Boys began to pursue more individual paths. They often still worked together, but growing reputations, new family commitments, personal developments or simply a wish to break away from their earlier styles took them in different directions. Some did not change their styles at all, some changed radically, some became successful portrait painters, while others concentrated on subjects such as animals or flowers. As they were now increasingly famous internationally, they no longer had to compete to exhibit in major venues, but were invited to do so.

In 1899, Roche, Walton, Lavery and Henry began painting mural decorations for the Banqueting Hall in Glasgow City Chambers. The opulent building, designed by William Young (1843–1900), had been finished in 1888, and the following year, some of the Glasgow Boys offered to decorate it with murals. Guthrie, Walton, Henry and Lavery had already painted large circular panels representing art, industry and science in the dome of the main building of the 1888 International Exhibition in Glasgow. By then, they were respected, and their proposal to decorate the City Chambers was endorsed by the *Scottish Art Review*, Glasgow Art Club and the Ruskin Society.

The brief was to show the 'general history of human culture from the dawn of intelligence … to the modern epoch of the development of the higher arts'. Lavery's interpretation was to paint a modern industrial city, with men working in a Clyde shipyard. By depicting the industrialized world, which conflicted with the grand architectural setting of the City Chambers, the painting caused great controversy. Yet it was part of some Glasgow Boys' evolution. Lavery and Melville had actually produced scenes of contemporary middle-class life from early in their careers, and by the last years of the nineteenth century, Guthrie, Kennedy, Dow and Roche also began to explore subjects that reflected the modern middle-class world around them. Coupled with increasing portrait commissions, these subjects became loosely perceived as the Glasgow Boys' third phase.

Locations

In emulation of artists such as Constable, Bastien-Lepage, Millet, Corot, Daubigny, Israëls and Mauve, many of the Glasgow Boys painted in rural locations. They made sketches outdoors in pencil, charcoal, watercolours or oils, returning to their studios to create finished paintings later.

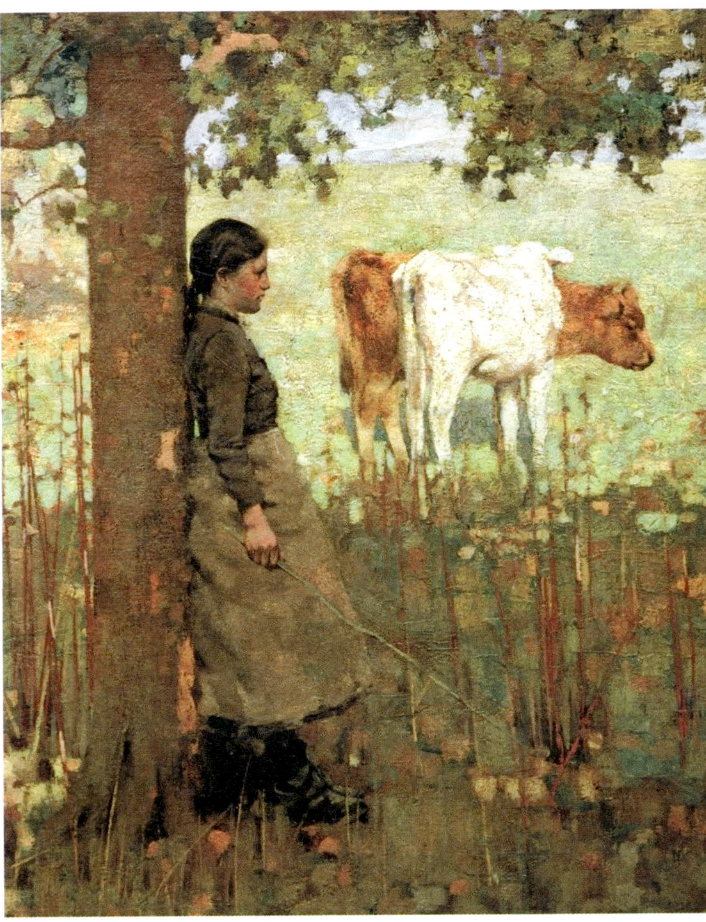

In the summer of 1881, Guthrie, Walton, Crawhall and Henry painted in Brig o' Turk, a small rural community in the Trossachs hills in Stirling, and in May 1883, they first painted in Cockburnspath, where Guthrie lived. Although predominantly a portrait painter, Guthrie emulated the *plein-air* painting methods of Bastien-Lepage in his landscapes, and his first masterpiece, *A Hind's Daughter* (*see* page 56), completed that year in Cockburnspath, helped to shape the Glasgow Boys' direction. During several subsequent summers, Henry, Melville, Morton, Hamilton and Roche also painted in Cockburnspath with Guthrie, developing their distinctive, naturalistic approach of figures in landscapes.

Some of the Boys also painted in Helensburg and Rosneath in Argyll, and some in the Dumfriesshire village of Moniaive and the small town of Kirkcudbright, where Hornel lived. From 1879 until 1897, Paterson painted in Moniaive, often joined by Macgregor and Henry. Kirkcudbright and the surrounding countryside provided a great source of inspiration for Hornel, Henry and Guthrie from the mid-1880s until the early 1890s. In 1893, financed by the art dealer Alexander Reid and the shipowner and art collector William Burrell (1861–1958), Hornel and Henry travelled to Japan, spending 19 months there, observing, painting and developing new influential styles.

Meanwhile, several of them painted in France, at Grez-sur-Loing, following the Barbizon painters. An artists' colony had been founded in the village in 1875, and initially Melville, Kennedy, Roche, Alexander Mann and Dow painted there; Lavery followed in 1883, 1884 and 1900, and Gauld in 1895. Tangier, in Morocco, also attracted some of the Boys, for its exotic light and rich colours. Crawhall painted there and in Spain between 1884 and 1893, followed by Mann and Melville in 1890 and 1891, and Lavery in the winters of 1891, 1892 and 1893, and again from 1903. When Mann first stayed there in November 1890, he remained for over a year, travelling back to Scotland through Spain with Lavery in the spring of 1892. During the 1880s, Mann, Roche, Lavery and Melville also spent time painting in Venice.

Joseph Crawhall (1861–1913)

While growing up in Northumberland, England, Joseph Crawhall was initially taught to paint from memory by his artist father. Later, he studied art at King's College London, before moving to Paris when he was 21 to work with the academically trained painter and sculptor Aimé Morot (1850–1913). While there, Crawhall studied the work of the French Realists, and became especially influenced by Bastien-Lepage.

After his sister Judith married Edward Walton's brother Richard in 1878, he and Walton became good friends, and he also formed close friendships with Guthrie and Lavery, becoming involved with the Glasgow Boys through them. He began using intense colour and tonal contrasts, and deft calligraphic lines, which reflect his interest in Japanese art. An outstanding draughtsman, he was reserved and

introspective, usually working in absolute quiet, which earned him the nickname 'The Great Silence'. Crawhall was also influenced by the Impressionists, so he focused on light, colour and composition. He specialized in animal subjects, often imbuing them with his sharp wit through a minimum of marks. Lavery once said, 'In a few lines he could sketch an animal, making it more recognizable than the most candid camera could do – and from memory.'

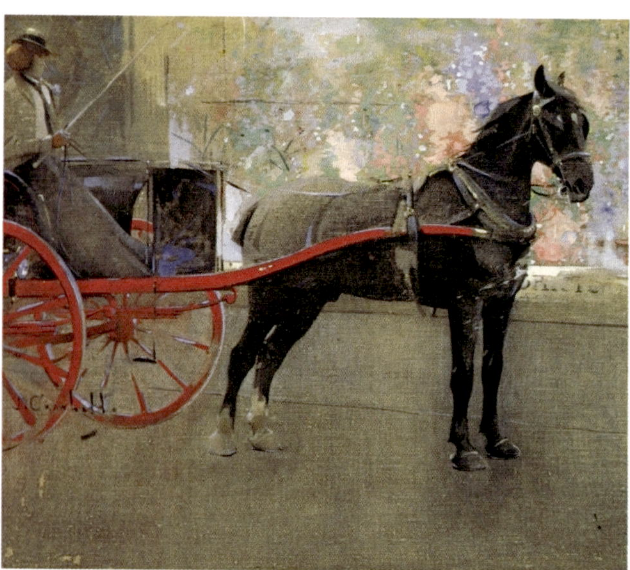

In the mid-1880s, Crawhall began using watercolours and gouache, often painting in gouache on linen supports, rather than oil on canvas. Even though he had only two major exhibitions in his lifetime, the Scottish shipbuilder William Burrell collected more works by him than any other artist. One of the first of the Boys to visit Morocco, he first went there in 1884, painting luminous and atmospheric watercolours, and spent the next nine years often travelling to paint abroad, frequently with Arthur Melville. Whistler called him 'the truest artist of the Glasgow men'.

Edward Arthur Walton (1860–1922)

Born into an artistic family in the Scottish Lowlands, Edward Walton studied for a year from the age of 16 at the Kunstakademie in Düsseldorf, while also taking private lessons with the painters Carl Wagner (1796–1867) and Fritz Ebel (1835–95). In 1877, he continued his studies at the Glasgow School of Art and joined the St Mungo Society, where he befriended other future Glasgow Boys. After his brother Richard married Crawhall's sister Judith, he and Crawhall became firm friends. From 1879, for several summers, he painted local people and landscapes in various locations, including Rosneath, Brig o' Turk, Helensburgh, Cockburnspath, Wenhaston in Surrey, Crowland in Lincolnshire and Cambuskenneth near Stirling, where he took a studio, and several other Glasgow Boys visited him.

From 1880, he exhibited at the Glasgow Institute of the Fine Arts and at the Royal Scottish Academy in Edinburgh. He was elected an associate of the RSA in 1889 and a full member in 1905. From 1879, during the winter months, he, Crawhall, Paterson, Henry and Lavery met regularly at Macgregor's studio, and with Guthrie, Henry and Lavery, he painted murals for the Glasgow International Exhibition in 1888 and for the Banqueting Hall in Glasgow City Chambers in 1899, with Roche as well. He moved to Chelsea in London near his friends Lavery and Whistler in 1894, only travelling back to Scotland occasionally, but eventually Guthrie persuaded him to return, and he moved to Edinburgh in 1904.

Throughout his career, he worked in both oils and watercolours, but from his time in London, he painted many portraits heavily influenced by Whistler's style, and he helped to persuade the Glasgow City Corporation to buy Whistler's portrait of Thomas Carlyle (1795–1881), which became the first of Whistler's works to be bought by a public body. In 1907, he accompanied Guthrie to Algiers and Spain, and in 1913 he worked in Belgium. During the First World War, he painted in Galloway, and in 1915 he served as president of the Royal Scottish Watercolour Society.

James Guthrie (1859–1930)

The son of a church minister, James Guthrie was born at Greenock, north-west of Glasgow, and as a young man began studying law at Glasgow University, but left in 1877 to pursue a career in art. He studied for a while with the Glaswegian artist James Drummond (1816–77) and applied unsuccessfully for membership of the Glasgow Art Club in 1879. Instead, he joined the St Mungo Society, where he met Walton. Through him, he also met Crawhall and other future Glasgow Boys. During that year, he moved to London to study with the London-based Scottish painter John Pettie (1839–93).

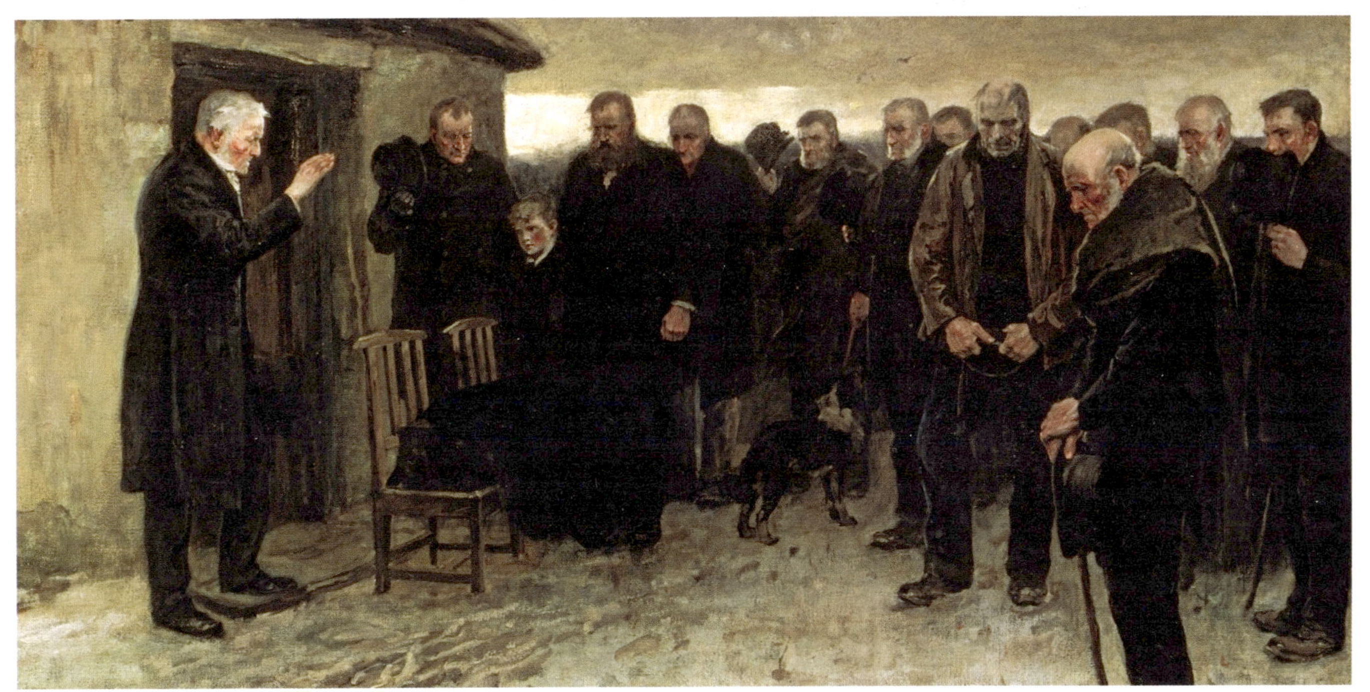

Although he stayed in London until 1881, from 1879 he returned to Scotland during the summer months to paint with Walton, Crawhall and Henry, at places such as Brig o' Turk and Cockburnspath. In 1880, he was accepted as a member of the Glasgow Art Club and in 1882 he visited Paris, where he became influenced by the work of the French Realists, in particular Bastien-Lepage. On his return to Britain, his social realist painting, *A Funeral Service in the Highlands* (1882, *see* page 54), was well received when exhibited at London's Royal Academy.

For two years from 1883, he lived in Cocksburnspath, where he painted the locals and the landscape, but from 1885 he concentrated on portraiture, and experimented with pastels in his studios in London and Glasgow. By then, he was painting prolifically, exhibiting widely and taking on several eminent positions. In 1886–87, he was vice president of the Glasgow Art Club, and in 1888 he was elected to the RSA, becoming president in 1902 until 1919. On a second trip to Paris in 1889, he visited Whistler, and in 1898, with Lavery, he was part of the committee that founded the International Society of Sculptors, Painters and Gravers, of which Whistler became president. In the 1890s, he moved first to London and then to Edinburgh. He was knighted in 1903, and made an honorary member of the Glasgow Art Club in 1904.

George Henry (1858–1943)

Born in North Ayrshire, south-west of Glasgow, George Henry first worked as a clerk while studying part-time at the Glasgow School of Art. He also briefly attended William York Macgregor's art classes.

From 1879, he began painting *en plein air* with others. For instance, in the summer of 1881, he sketched with Guthrie, Walton and Crawhall in Brig o' Turk in the Trossachs; in 1883 and 1884, they painted together in Cockburnspath, joined in 1884 by Arthur Melville. Guthrie's square-brush technique, learned from Bastien-Lepage, particularly influenced his methods.

The following year, he met and formed a strong friendship with Edward Hornel, and introduced him to the group, and in 1888 he painted murals for the Glasgow International Exhibition with Guthrie, Walton and Lavery. Hornel persuaded him to paint in Kirkcudbright and Galloway. Although he had no contact with France, his 1889 painting *A Galloway Landscape*, with its flattened perspective and bold use of colour, is strongly reminiscent of the work of Paul Gauguin (1848–1903) and the Pont-Aven School. The emphasis on colour and pattern moved away from naturalism and influenced several of the other Glasgow Boys.

In 1890, he and Hornel began sharing a studio and collaborated on paintings such as *The Druids – Bringing in the Mistletoe* (*see* page 95) and *The Star in the East* (1891). He also worked with richly coloured watercolours. From February 1893, he and Hornel painted in Japan for 19 months, but many of his oil paintings stuck together on the journey home, so his watercolours are the main record of his trip. In 1899, he, Roche, Walton and Lavery painted murals for the Banqueting Hall in Glasgow City Chambers, and his work became quite abstract, but after 1900, he abandoned experimentation and began producing fairly conventional portraits and figures in landscapes.

After standing as president of the Glasgow Art Club from 1901 to 1902, he moved to London, where he took a studio in Chelsea, although he still continued to exhibit regularly in Scotland.

E.A. Hornel (1864–1933)

Edward Atkinson Hornel was born in New South Wales, Australia, but his Scottish parents moved back to Kirkcudbright in south-west Scotland when he was two years old. He remained there for most of his life, studying for three years at the Trustees' Academy in Edinburgh, and then for two further years at the Art Academy in Antwerp, Belgium. His early work closely followed Bastien-Lepage's style, but after meeting George Henry in 1885, he began using brighter colours, thicker paint and creating more decorative compositions.

From 1890, he and Henry shared a studio, and the two collaborated on paintings in an early Art Nouveau style, painting with rich colours and gold. He used various methods to achieve textural effects, such as applying impasto paint, then scraping, smoothing or dragging it, or staining areas with thin, translucent washes. He travelled with Henry to Japan, where, from 1893 to 1894, he produced about 30 paintings in an even more decorative, tapestry-like style, which he exhibited in Glasgow in 1895.

The proceeds from the sale of these works enabled him to buy Broughton House, an eighteenth-century townhouse in Kirkcudbright, in 1901. He lived there with his sister Elizabeth ('Tizzy') for the rest of his life, adding a studio and gallery, and creating a Japanese-style garden. By then, he had become a member of the Glasgow Art Club and exhibited in the annual exhibitions, but he rejected his election to the Royal Scottish Academy in Edinburgh. In 1907, he and Tizzy travelled t o Ceylon (now Sri Lanka) to visit their cousin, and in 1920 he travelled with Tizzy to Burma (now Myanmar), Japan, Canada and America.

John Lavery (1856–1941)

After John Lavery's parents died when he was three, he left Northern Ireland to live with relatives in North Ayrshire, in Scotland. At 17, he was apprenticed to a photographer and painter, and three years later, he attended the Haldane Academy in Glasgow, then Heatherley's

School of Art in London. He exhibited at the Glasgow Institute of the Fine Arts in 1880, and in 1881 he studied in Paris at the Académie Julian, under William-Adolphe Bouguereau (1825–1905), and in the evenings at the Académie Colarossi. While in France, like many of the Boys, he became enthralled by Bastien-Lepage's painting style.

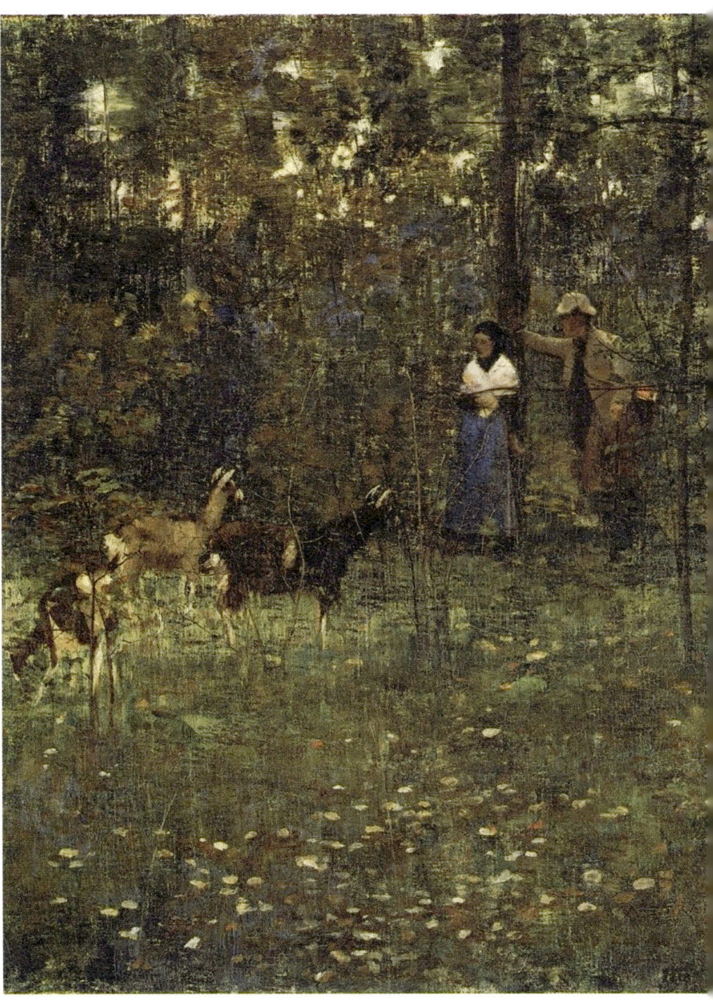

From 1879 and throughout the 1880s, he painted with other Glasgow Boys in France, Morocco, Venice and Spain, and between 1885 and 1896 he lived mainly in Glasgow. He then settled in London, although he often wintered in Morocco, and later bought a property near Tangier. In London, he became vice president of the International Society, friends with Whistler, and friend and tutor to Winston Churchill.

In 1888, the Glasgow Corporation commissioned him to paint *The State Visit of Her Majesty, Queen Victoria to the Glasgow International Exhibition.* The work took him two years and established him as a society portraitist.

With Guthrie, he was part of the group that founded the International Society of Sculptors, Painters and Gravers. He painted portraits of both the Moroccan and British royal families, and was appointed official war artist for the Royal Navy during the First World War. However, ill health and a car accident prevented him from travelling to the front. He was knighted in 1918, and he became a member of the Royal Scottish Academy, the Royal Academy and academies in Rome, Antwerp, Brussels and Stockholm. In 1940, he published his autobiography, *The Life of a Painter.*

Arthur Melville (1855–1904)

Born in Angus and raised near Edinburgh, Arthur Melville painted with intense colours, vivid light effects and dramatic compositions. In his teens, he became a grocer's apprentice and took evening drawing classes in Edinburgh. He entered the Edinburgh Trustees' Academy in 1875, and went to France in 1878 to study the work of the French Impressionists. There, he began to experiment with watercolour. Inspired by the Barbizon School painters, especially Corot and Millet, he entered the Académie Julian, and the following year he painted at Grez-sur-Loing.

Between 1880 and 1882, he travelled to Persia (now Iran), the Middle East and Turkey, where he developed a powerful use of colour. To portray the Middle Eastern light, he developed a technique of using watercolour on wet paper with gouache. He was also influenced by the impasto paintings of Adolphe Monticelli, developing his own textural, mosaic-like surfaces in vivid colours. In 1883, he returned to Edinburgh to paint the first of a series of portrait commissions, and at the Glasgow Institute exhibition, he met Guthrie, and through him, Crawhall and Walton. During the following winter, all four painted at Cockburnspath. He and Guthrie visited Lavery and then travelled to Orkney.

In 1889, he took a studio in Kensington and travelled to Paris to the Exposition Universelle. Over the next few years, he spent time in Spain, North Africa and Venice. He became renowned for his outstanding and unique watercolour technique. In 1899, he moved to Surrey, where he began painting more religious subjects. Five years later, on a visit to Spain, he caught typhoid and died.

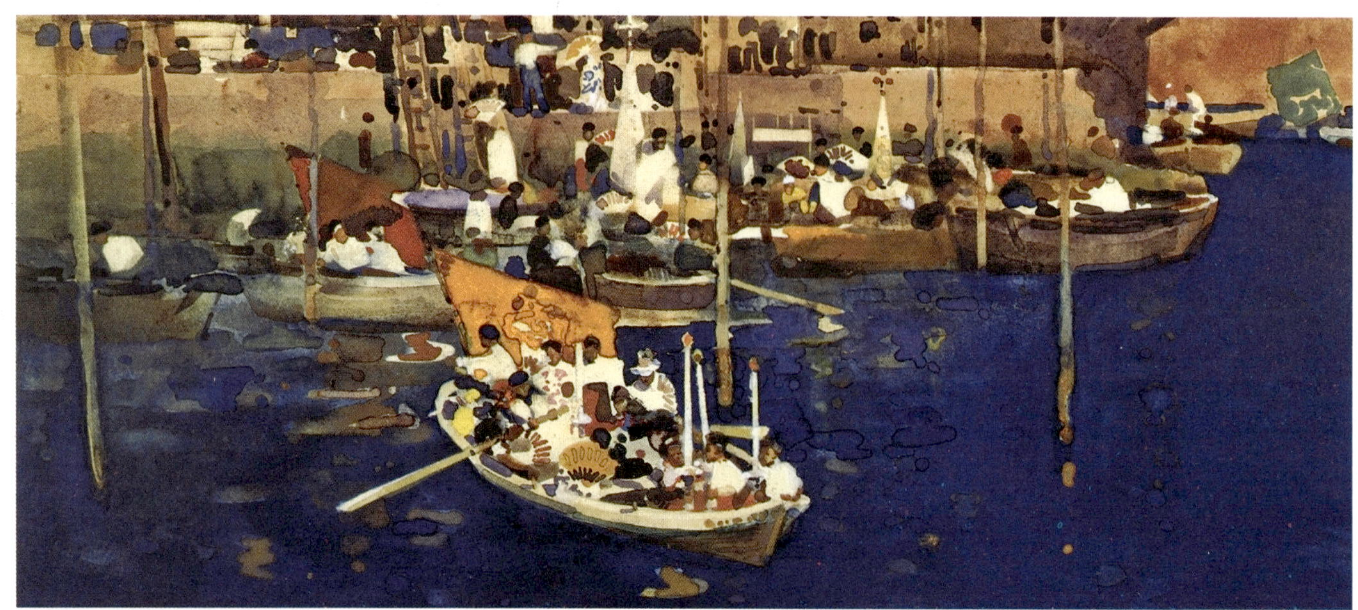

William York Macgregor (1855–1923)

When William York Macgregor was two years old, his shipbuilder father died and his family moved from the Scottish Lowlands to Glasgow. He met James Paterson while studying at the Glasgow School of Art. In 1877, they painted together at St Andrews, Stonehaven and Nairn. In the same year, they applied to join the Glasgow Art Club, but after being rejected, they left Glasgow for London, where Macgregor studied under Alphonse Legros at the Slade School of Fine Art. From 1879, especially during the winter months, he invited fellow artists and art students to his studio at Bath Street in Glasgow, where he ran informal art classes. It became a regular meeting place for many of the Boys, and he became known as the 'Father of the Glasgow Boys'. His 1884 painting, *The Vegetable Stall* (*see* page 108), shows a direct influence of Bastien-Lepage.

From 1885, severe asthma forced him to move away from the polluted atmosphere of Glasgow. He travelled north-west and settled in Stirlingshire, and also spent two winters in southern England. From 1888 to 1890, he lived in South Africa. During that time, Guthrie became seen as the Glasgow Boys' leader. By 1890, however, with greatly improved health, Macgregor returned to Scotland, moving to the Bridge of Allan in Stirlingshire, and resumed painting *en plein air,* but his later paintings were more austere than his earlier works. Although he had been rejected in 1877, he had by that time become a member of the Glasgow Art Club, and he exhibited at the Royal Scottish Academy from 1875 and twice at London's Royal Academy. He became a member of the Royal Scottish Watercolour Society in 1885 and of the New English Art Club (NEAC) in 1892.

Thomas Millie Dow (1848–1919)

Born in Fife, Thomas Millie Dow initially trained for a career in law, but on deciding he would rather be an artist, studied art in Edinburgh. From 1877, for two years, he took classes at the prestigious École des Beaux-Arts in Paris, under Jean-Léon Gérôme (1824–1904), then entered the studios of Rudolphe Julien (1839–1907) and Carolus-Duran (1837–1917). While in Paris, he met and became influenced by the English artist William Stott (1857–1900) and the American Abbott

Handerson Thayer (1849–1921). He also made friends with fellow Scottish painters studying there, including Lavery, Roche, Paterson and Alexander Mann, and occasionally sketched with them in the villages of Barbizon and Grez-sur-Loing.

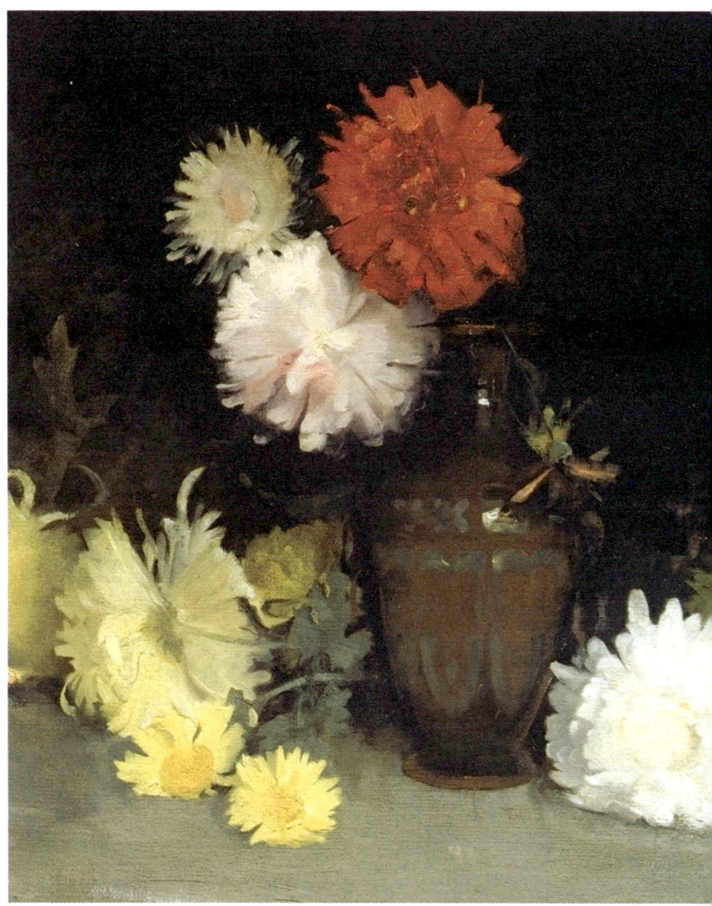

Back in Scotland, Dow painted along the east coast, and south-west in Moniaive, with other Glasgow Boys. From 1878, he exhibited at the Royal Scottish Academy in Edinburgh and, from the following year, also at the Glasgow Institute of the Fine Arts. In 1883, he travelled to New York and up the Hudson River to visit Abbott Thayer and his wife, staying with them until the following summer. He also travelled to Italy and Tangier, and lived for a while in St Ives in Cornwall. Working in oils, watercolours and pastels, he produced flower studies, landscapes and portraits, but from 1893 he focused more on decorative, allegorical works.

David Gauld (1865–1936)

Glasgow-born David Gauld was apprenticed to a lithographer and first attracted attention with his Japanese-inspired pen-and-ink illustrations, published in the *Glasgow Weekly Citizen* in the late 1880s. From 1882 to 1885, and again in 1889, he studied part-time at the Glasgow School of Art. For a short time in 1889, he studied in Paris and painted in Brittany. Along with other Glasgow Boys, he painted *en plein air* in Grez-sur-Loing, and although, like them, he was inspired by French Realism, his style evolved with more diverse influences, including Art Nouveau, the Pre-Raphaelites, Japanese *ukiyo-e* art, Symbolism, medieval mythology and Early Renaissance painting. In turn, his ideas influenced other Glasgow Boys, especially during their second phase.

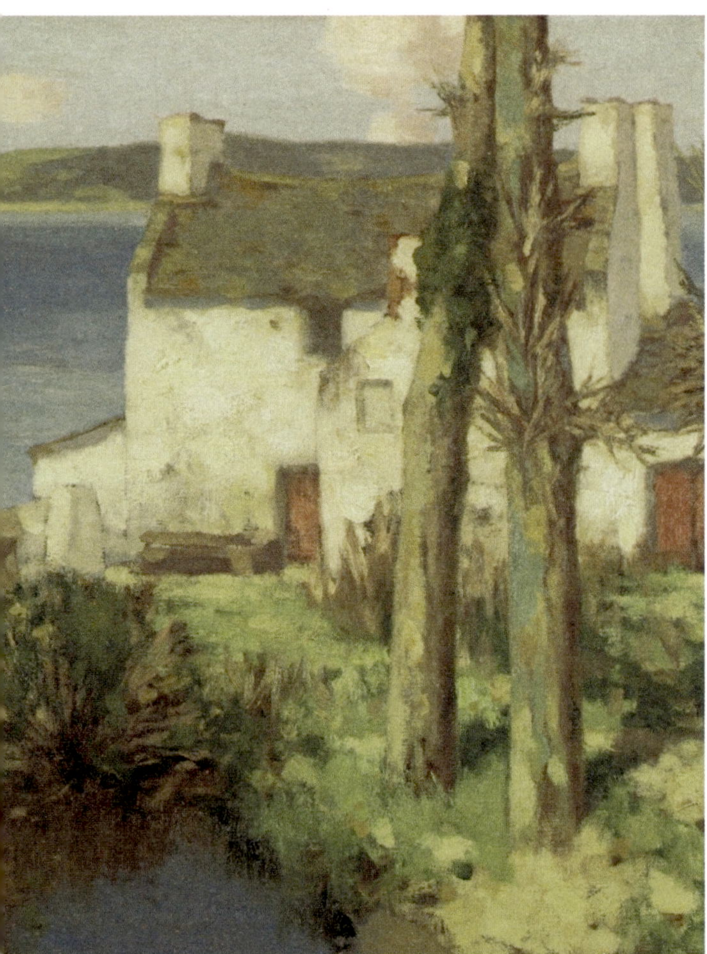

His sense of colour and decorative aspects of his compositions transferred well to stained glass design, and from the early 1890s he designed stained glass for the Glasgow-based firm J. & W. Guthrie, as well as for several churches, including St Andrew's in Buenos Aires. For a short time, he shared a studio in Kirkcudbright with another Scottish artist, William Stewart MacGeorge (1861–1931), and from 1891–94 he and Harrington Mann shared a studio in Glasgow.

From the mid-1890s, he began producing the work he became known for – studies of cattle and rural scenes, painted loosely from direct observation in the Ayrshire countryside. He was a good friend of Charles Rennie Mackintosh, elected an associate member of the Royal Scottish Academy in 1918, became a full member in 1924, and in 1935 he was appointed director of Design Studies at the Glasgow School of Art.

William Kennedy (1859–1918)

After being orphaned, William Kennedy was brought up in Paisley by his older brother. He studied at Paisley School of Art and began exhibiting at the Paisley Art Institute from 1879. In 1880, he went to Paris to study at the Académie Julian, where he met fellow art students John Lavery, Alexander Roche and Thomas Millie Dow. He was taught by several esteemed artists, including Bouguereau, Raphaël Collin (1850–1916) and Tony Robert-Fleury (1837–1911), as well as the Glasgow Boys' hero, Jules Bastien-Lepage. In direct response, Kennedy's early work displays a powerful influence of Bastien-Lepage, but he later reduced his tonal contrasts and created compositions that show a greater influence of Whistler and Japanese *ukiyo-e* prints.

In 1885, he returned to Scotland, settled in Stirling and painted rural landscapes and colourful figures. Highly respected by all the Glasgow Boys, he painted *en plein air* with Guthrie, Walton and Henry in the nearby village of Cambuskenneth. In 1887, for a short time, the group formed an actual 'Glasgow Boys Society', and elected Kennedy their president. In his forties, he moved to Berkshire in England, where he painted idealized, atmospheric images of the local countryside, using smooth brushwork and building up meticulous details to convey the effects of sunlight. In 1912, for health reasons, he moved to Tangier.

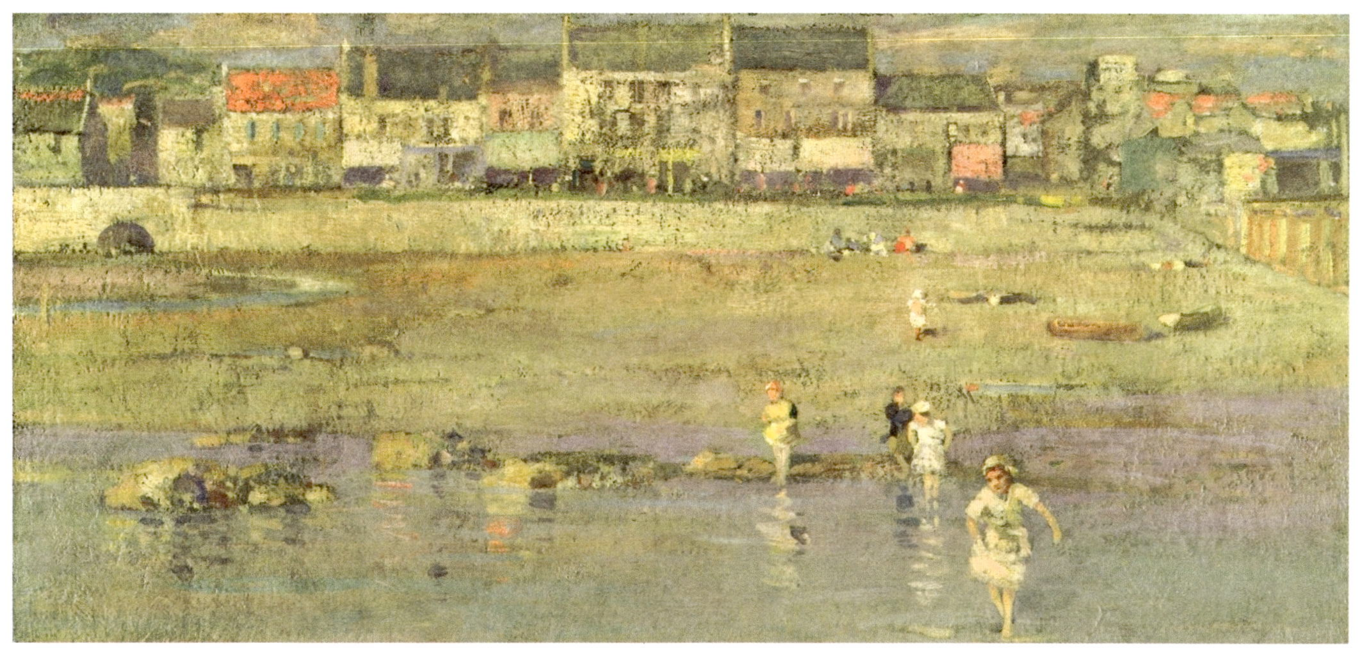

James Whitelaw Hamilton (1860–1932)

Showing great artistic aptitude from an early age, James Whitelaw
Hamilton began his working life as a businessman, though he
also painted for pleasure with Guthrie, Walton and Crawhall at
Cockburnspath. He soon determined to become a professional artist
and studied for a short time at the Glasgow School of Art, then moved to
Paris to train in the studios of the artists Pascal-Adolphe-Jean Dagnan-
Bouveret (1852–1929) and Aimé Morot, with his friend Crawhall.

On his return to Scotland in 1884, using oils, pastels and watercolours,
he painted figures in landscapes, often featuring water, and nocturnal
scenes reminiscent of Whistler's work. His home in Helensburgh became
a favourite meeting place for the Glasgow Boys, and he exhibited regularly.
He became a member of numerous societies, including the New English
Art Club (NEAC), the Royal Scottish Society of Painters in Watercolours
(RSW), the Munich Secession and the Glasgow Institute of the Fine Arts.
For many years, he was the Institute's honorary secretary.

In 1897, he won a gold medal at the Munich International Exhibition,
and in 1901 he was awarded a Cavaliere of the Order of the Crown
of Italy. His work was shown in the British Pavilion at all eight Venice
Biennales between 1897 and 1910, and he became an associate of
the RSA in 1911, and a full academician there in 1922.

Alexander Mann (1853–1908)

From the age of 10, Glasgow-born Alexander Mann took drawing lessons
with Robert Greenlees (1820–94), then went to evening classes at the
Glasgow School of Art, where Greenlees was headmaster, from 1863–81.
In 1877, he moved to Paris to study at the Académie Julian, then with
the Realist painter Mihály Munkácsy (1844–1900), and from 1881–85
with Carolus-Duran. He remained in Paris for the next 15 years,
travelling back to Scotland often, and exhibiting in Paris at the annual
Salon, and in Britain at the Royal Academy, the Royal Institute of Oil
Painters, the Fine Art Society, the New English Art Club and the Society
of British Artists, where Whistler was appointed president in 1886.

During this intense exhibiting period, his paintings show a clear
influence of the Barbizon and Hague Schools of painting. He was
the first Scottish member of the NEAC, followed soon after by friends
including Lavery and Dow. His 1885 painting *A Bead Stringer, Venice*

received an honourable mention at the Salon. His sense of light and subtle colour, as well as his close friendships with Dow and Lavery, mark him as a member of the Glasgow Boys, but he was more detached from the group than many of the others. Over his career, he travelled to various countries in Europe, to Morocco and the Americas, and in later life, he settled in Berkshire, England.

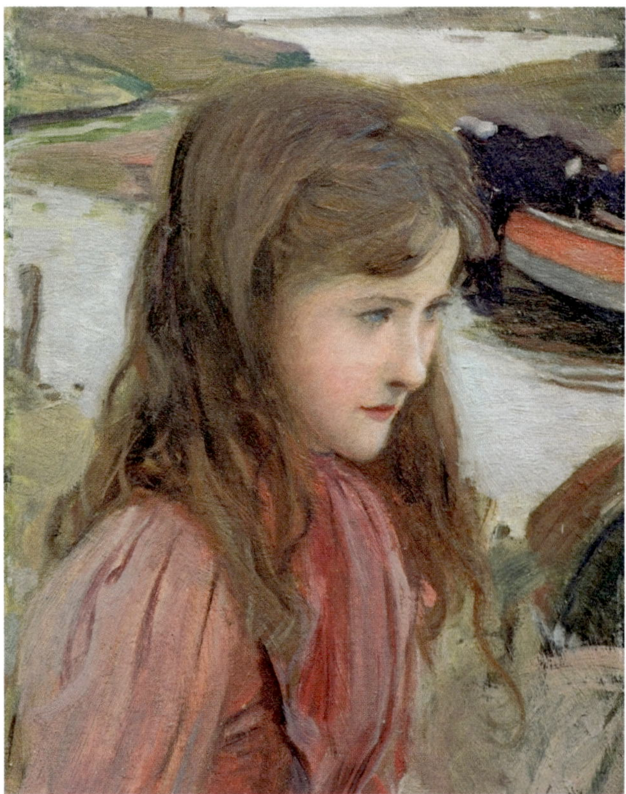

Harrington Mann (1864–1937)

Harrington Mann grew up in Glasgow and studied at the Glasgow School of Art and the Slade School of Fine Art in London, with William York Macgregor, under Alphonse Legros. While at the Slade, he won a 'Travelling Scholarship', enabling him to spend time in Italy from 1887. From there, he travelled to Algiers, Tangier and Spain, before continuing his studies in Paris at the Académie Julian, taught by the figure painters Gustave Boulanger (1824–88) and Jules-Joseph Lefebvre (1836–1911). During that decade, he often painted images

of Yorkshire fishing communities, but by the 1890s, he had become recognized more for his portraits. Like many of the Glasgow Boys, he also became known for his naturalistic landscape and figure paintings, which were marked by his strong sense of colour and design.

During the 1890s, with David Gauld, he designed stained glass for the firm J. & W. Guthrie and numerous churches. He was also commissioned to paint several eminent portraits, including members of the British royal family and some American patrons. So, in 1900, he moved to London and also opened a studio in New York, from then on dividing his time between the two cities. In colour and brushwork, his later work was influenced by Whistler and John Singer Sargent (1856–1925). As well as paintings and stained glass, he also drew illustrations for the *Daily Graphic* and the *Scottish Art Review*. In 1933, his book, *The Technique of Portrait Painting*, was published.

James Stuart Park (1862–1933)

As a young child, James Stuart Park and his Scottish parents moved from Worcestershire in England to the west of Scotland. In the mid-1880s, he attended evening classes at the Glasgow School of Art, then studied in Paris under Lefebvre, Boulanger and Fernand Cormon (1845–1924) at the same time as Harrington Mann. Although he also painted portraits, nearly all his paintings are of flowers, set against dark backgrounds.

He took a studio in Glasgow, first exhibited at the Glasgow Institute of the Fine Arts in 1883, then began exhibiting more broadly. In line with the Glasgow Boys' second and more decorative phase of painting, he developed a more stylized approach, which improved his reputation among the Glasgow Boys and attracted more attention in wider artistic circles. From 1889, for three years, he painted delicate flower paintings and girls' heads surrounded by flowers against dark backgrounds, using flat brushmarks, emphasizing pattern and decoration. Reflecting newly fashionable Art Nouveau styles, these became extremely popular. In the late 1890s, Park moved to Kilmarnock in East Ayrshire, where he continued painting flowers, making direct studies from plants grown in local greenhouses, continuing in the style that made his work so successful.

William Page Atkinson Wells (1872–1923)

Because he was younger, didn't mix with the others and spent most of his career away from Glasgow, William Page Atkinson Wells was one of the most loosely connected of the Glasgow Boys. Nonetheless, he was born in Glasgow, and painted in a similar naturalistic style. He followed in the footsteps of Harrington Mann and William York Macgregor by studying at the Slade School of Fine Art in London under Alphonse Legros. After finishing there, however, he moved to Sydney, Australia, where he continued painting landscapes. He returned to Europe five years later, to Paris, to study under Bouguereau and Gabriel Ferrier (1847–1914), and also to paint in rural France, where he emulated the approaches of the Barbizon and Hague Schools, working outdoors, using clear colours and painterly brushwork.

After a brief return to Glasgow at the turn of the twentieth century, he lived in Lancashire, in north-west England, until about 1910, then on the Isle of Man. In both places, he painted light-filled atmospheric landscapes and village scenes. He never returned to live in Glasgow, but spent the last years of his life in Appledore, Devon, where he continued to paint rural scenes in his original style, using a light palette, amalgamating influences of Constable, Millet and Bastien-Lepage.

David Young Cameron (1865–1945)

Despite not being an 'official' Glasgow Boy, David Young Cameron was born in Glasgow, and from 1881 studied at the Glasgow School of Art. Then in 1885, he went to the Edinburgh School of Art, where he was encouraged to take up etching, because he was so skilled with pen and ink. Over his career, he produced hundreds of etchings of calm, atmospheric scenes. The influence of the etchers Charles Méryon (1821–68) and Francis Seymour Haden (1818–1910) is apparent in these. From 1883, he also painted landscapes and buildings in oils and watercolours.

Although his work was influenced by the Glasgow Boys and the Hague School, and he knew most of the Glasgow Boys and often exhibited with them, he did not paint with them, and his approach to painting was different. In 1889, he was elected an associate of the Royal Society

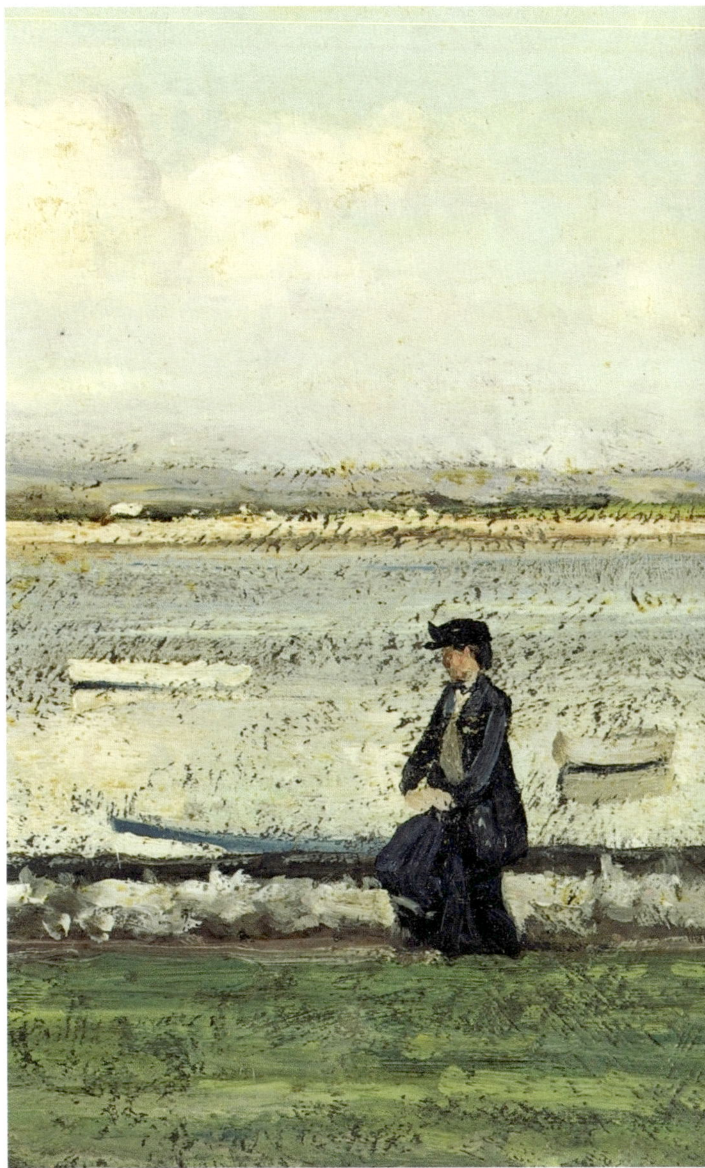

of Painter-Etchers, and a fellow in 1895. At that time, the demand for Scottish prints was high on both sides of the Atlantic, and by the 1890s he had become internationally sought after. He visited and worked in the Netherlands and Italy, but his Scottish views were the most popular. He received various medals and awards for his etchings, was knighted in 1924, and later given the prestigious appointment of King's Painter and Limner in Scotland.

Alexander Ignatius Roche (1861–1921)

After initially training as an architect, Glasgow-born Alexander Roche enrolled in painting classes at the Glasgow School of Art. In 1881, he studied under Gustave Boulanger and Jean-Leon Gérôme, at L'École des Beaux-Arts, in Paris, where he met William Kennedy, John Lavery and Thomas Millie Dow. He joined them on painting trips to Grez-sur-Loing, and on his return to Scotland in 1885, he went painting with the Glasgow Boys regularly, attending Macgregor's studio meetings and joining the St Mungo Society.

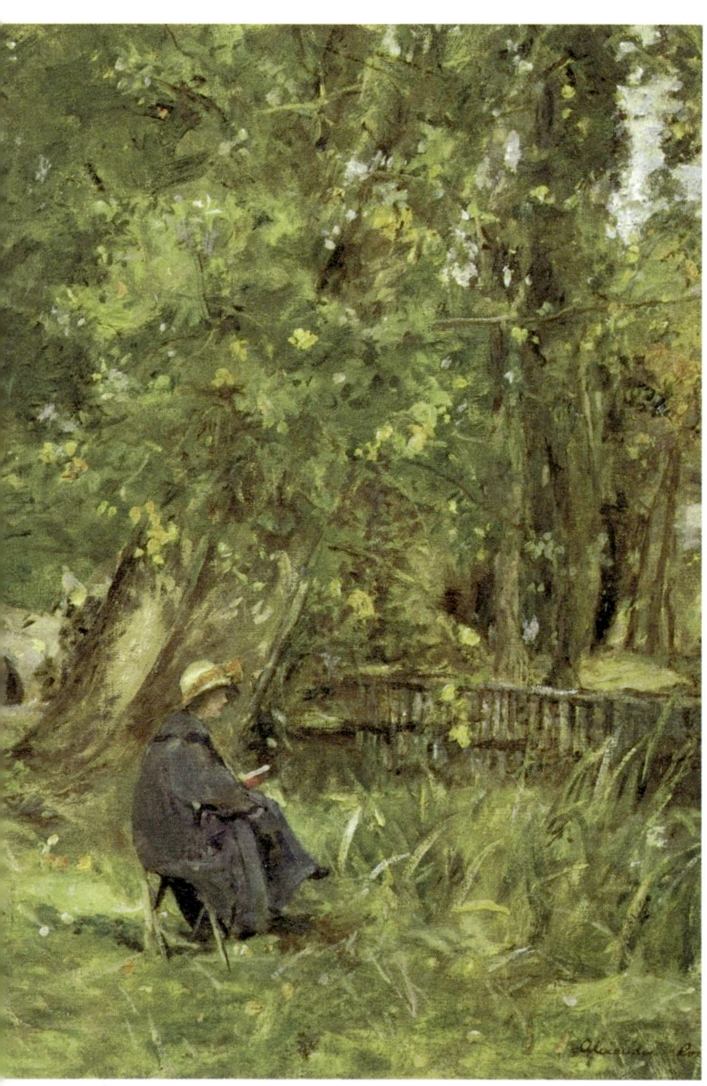

In 1888, alongside Guthrie, Walton, Lavery, Henry and Hornel, he painted murals for Glasgow's International Exhibition. That year, he travelled to Capri, and over the following few years, he also visited and painted in Florence and Venice. In 1896, he moved to Edinburgh, where he concentrated on portraiture, occasionally travelling to America to carry out commissions. Three years later, he was commissioned to paint murals for the Banqueting Hall of Glasgow City Chambers, and asked Henry, Walton and Lavery to join him. He, Guthrie, Kennedy and Dow were among the first of the group to paint subjects that reflected the modern industrial world. At the age of 49, he suffered a cerebral haemorrhage, which left his right hand paralyzed, so he taught himself to paint with his left.

Thomas Corsan Morton (1859–1928)

Thomas Corsan Morton was born in Glasgow and worked briefly in a lawyer's office before attending the Glasgow School of Art. He then went to the Slade School in London and to L'École des Beaux Arts in Paris, at around the same time as Harrington Mann, Roche and Park, where he studied under Boulanger and Lefebvre. With other Glasgow Boys, during the 1880s, he painted landscapes in Kirkcudbright and in Cockburnspath, often staying with James Guthrie. He worked in oils and pastels, and exhibited widely – again, frequently with other Glasgow Boys – including at the Grosvenor Gallery, the New English Art Club, the Society of British Artists, the Royal Scottish Academy, the Royal Scottish Society of Painters in Watercolours, the Glasgow Institute of the Fine Arts, the Walker Art Gallery in Liverpool, Manchester City Art Gallery, and at Secessionist exhibitions in Munich.

He taught landscape painting at the Glasgow School of Art and assisted Francis Newbery with life-drawing classes. In May 1908, he was appointed keeper of the Scottish National Gallery in Edinburgh, and after retiring from that post in 1925, he became curator of the newly established Art Gallery in Kirkcaldy, on the east coast of Scotland. For years, he lived near Newton Mearns, south-west of Glasgow, where he painted the surrounding countryside using his technique of layering patchy brushwork in clear colours and strong contrasts, portraying natural effects of light.

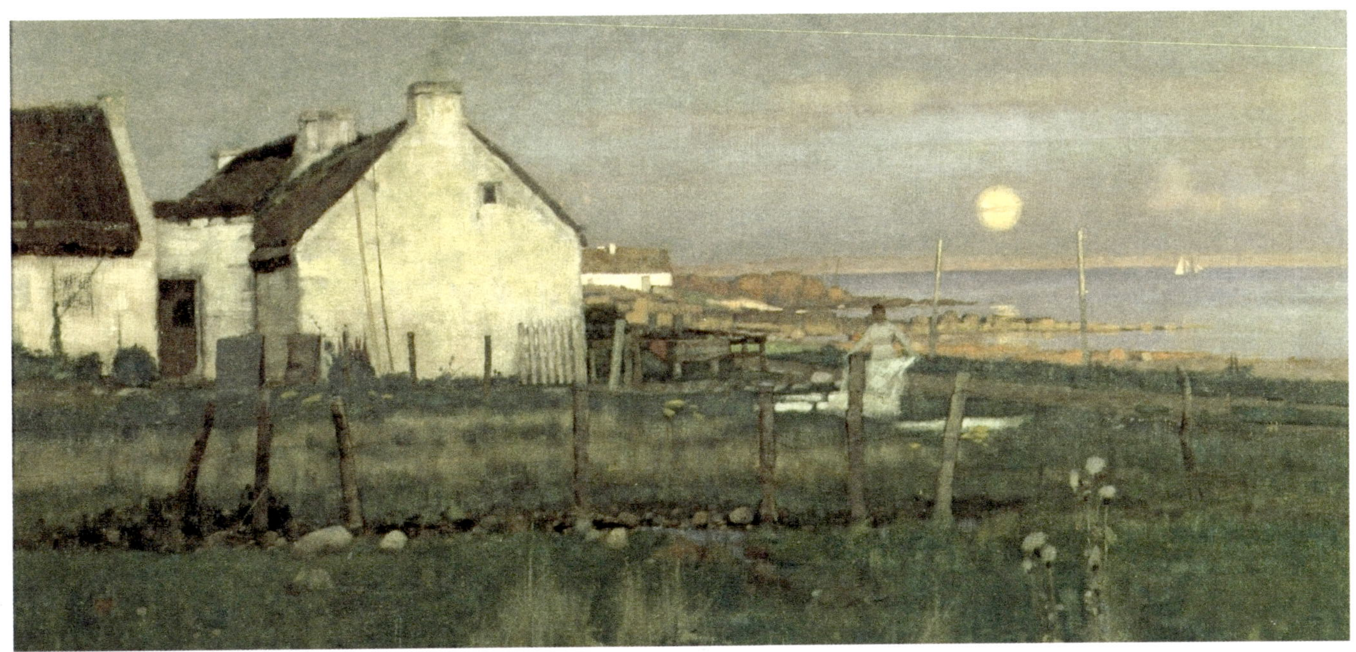

James Nairn (1859–1904)

After five years working at an architect's office in Glasgow, James McLachlan (or MacLauchlan) Nairn entered the Glasgow School of Art to study painting in 1879. Four years later, he enrolled at the Académie Julian in Paris, and later, during the 1880s, back in Scotland, he exhibited at the Glasgow Institute of the Fine Arts and the Royal Scottish Academy. Like other Glasgow Boys, he painted *en plein air,* depicting atmospheric, light-filled images of landscapes and fishing scenes, inspired by the Barbizon and Hague Schools and Impressionism.

Due to ill health, in 1890, he emigrated to New Zealand, where he taught practical art and lectured at the Wellington Technical School. Teaching and demonstrating his naturalistic style and encouraging *plein-air* painting, he introduced ideas of Realism, Impressionism and Post-Impressionism to New Zealand. He continued working in the style he had developed in Scotland and Paris, painting outdoors, using visible brushmarks, strong tonal contrasts and impasto paint, capturing the effects of sunlight on the sea or land. In 1892, to give local artists an alternative to the formal New Zealand Academy of Fine Arts, he established the Wellington Art Club.

George Pirie (1863–1946)

Although George Pirie was associated with the Glasgow Boys in the 1880s, most of his ideas about painting differed from theirs. He was born in Argyllshire, but moved to Glasgow as a child. After graduating from Glasgow University, he studied painting at the Glasgow School of Art, then at the Slade School of Art in London, and finally at the Académie Julian in Paris, under Boulanger and Lefebvre, and the sculptor Emmanuel Frémiet (1824–1910). In France, he crossed paths with Harrington Mann, Roche, Park and Nairn, and through them, became linked with the Glasgow Boys.

As well as landscapes, he frequently painted animals and birds. In the early 1890s, he travelled to Texan ranches, where he drew horses using his fluid style, smooth brushmarks and subdued palette. Another technique he used was adding watercolour to pencil drawings, and he worked extensively in pastel. He exhibited widely at the Royal Academy in London, as well as in Scottish galleries, and during his later years, he lived away from Glasgow, in Torrance in East Dunbartonshire. From 1933 to 1944, he served as president of the Royal Scottish Academy, and was knighted in 1937.

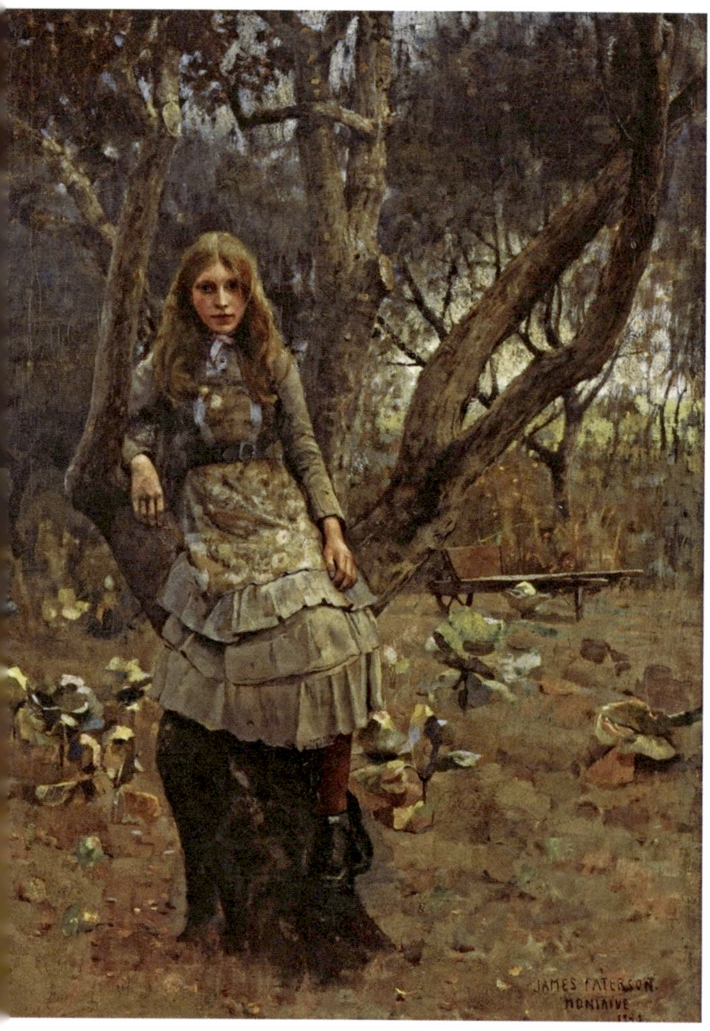

John Quinton Pringle (1864–1925)

Glasgow-born John Quinton Pringle left school in 1876 and became apprenticed to an optician while painting as a hobby. Using a bursary awarded by the Tureen Street School, where he learnt to draw, he attended evening and Saturday morning classes at the Glasgow School of Art from 1883–85. In 1891, he won the South Kensington National Competition for life drawing; the prize was a week at South Kensington School, in London. In 1896, he opened a shop in Glasgow, offering optical and electrical repairs, and began exhibiting his miniature paintings.

He continued painting, exhibiting and mixing with the Glasgow Boys while running his shop, and like so many of them, his painting style was influenced by Bastien-Lepage. Many of his paintings are small-scale oils, including portraits and scenes of his local environment. His work with optics made him focus on the illusions he could create with colour, and his small, square brushmarks recall both Bastien-Lepage and the early divisionism of Georges Seurat (1859–91). Using a restricted palette, he painted in Normandy and on the island of Whalsay, in Shetland. In 1902, he participated in the Vienna Secessionist Exhibition, and in 1914, was included in the exhibition Twentieth Century Art: A Review of Modern Movements at the Whitechapel Art Gallery in London, and in a retrospective at the Glasgow School of Art in 1922.

James Paterson (1854–1932)

The eldest son of a successful cotton manufacturer, James Paterson studied at the Western Academy in Glasgow with Macgregor. After leaving school, he worked in the family business, studying at the Glasgow School of Art in the evenings, again with Macgregor, and from 1877, he and Macgregor painted together outdoors. In 1878, he persuaded his parents to allow him to leave his job and give him an allowance to develop his art. For the next five years, he spent winters studying in Paris and summers travelling and painting in Scotland and elsewhere in Europe.

In Paris, he studied with Jacquesson de la Chevreuse (1839–1903) and Jean Paul Laurens (1838–1921). Over five years in Paris, he became acquainted with the work of Corot and Bastien-Lepage. On his return to Glasgow, he painted with Macgregor, Guthrie, Walton and Hornel, emulating the broad brushstrokes of the French Realists. In 1879, he discovered the Dumfriesshire village of Moniaive, and in 1884, as a wedding present, his parents gave him a cottage there. He remained in Moniaive until 1905, producing atmospheric views of the area, incorporating closely observed details and the effects of changing light. In 1885, he was elected to the Royal Scottish Society of Painters in Watercolour. The following year, he became an associate member of the Royal Scottish Academy, was awarded full membership in 1910, served as president in 1922, and as librarian and secretary from 1924.

Lasting Influence

Despite initially encountering resistance from Edinburgh and London's Royal Academies of Art, the Glasgow Boys eventually eroded artistic barriers, drawing positive attention to Glasgow, and creating a precedent for other Scottish artists to be taken seriously.

From the mid-1880s, they began to be invited to exhibit at significant exhibitions and galleries, including those they had either aspired to join or shunned early on in their careers, specifically the Royal Scottish Academy in Edinburgh and the Royal Glasgow Institute. Although many of their techniques were a synthesis of several influences, their innovations were often in advance of others. For instance, Henry and Hornel's use of gold paint prefigures Gustav Klimt, their emphasis on pattern and inclusion in many paintings of single female figures anticipated elements of Mackintosh's work and Art Nouveau styles, and Melville, Crawhall, Walton and Paterson's use of watercolours and pastels was unique.

The Boys' individual successes and the publicity attracted by the huge international exhibition in 1888 drew attention to Glasgow, and many of them became part of the Glasgow Institute of the Fine Arts' Hanging Committee and served on its Council, from where they guided Glasgow towards appreciating and showing more experimental art. Although it took longer to be accepted elsewhere, they became acknowledged far beyond Scotland as masters of naturalism, attracting diverse and significant buyers. For instance, the creator of the Ballets Russes, Sergei Diaghilev (1872–1929) took their work to Saint Petersburg in 1897, while one of their main supporters was Alexander Reid, a friend of Van Gogh, and one of the most progressive dealers in European art. By the end of the nineteenth century, the Glasgow Boys had achieved what few other Scottish artists had done – they had provided an alternative to their country's traditional art, offered fresh ideas that fused styles and motifs from other cultures with innovative experimentation, gained the respect of art officialdom, and added 'avant-garde art centre' to the list of Glasgow's accolades.

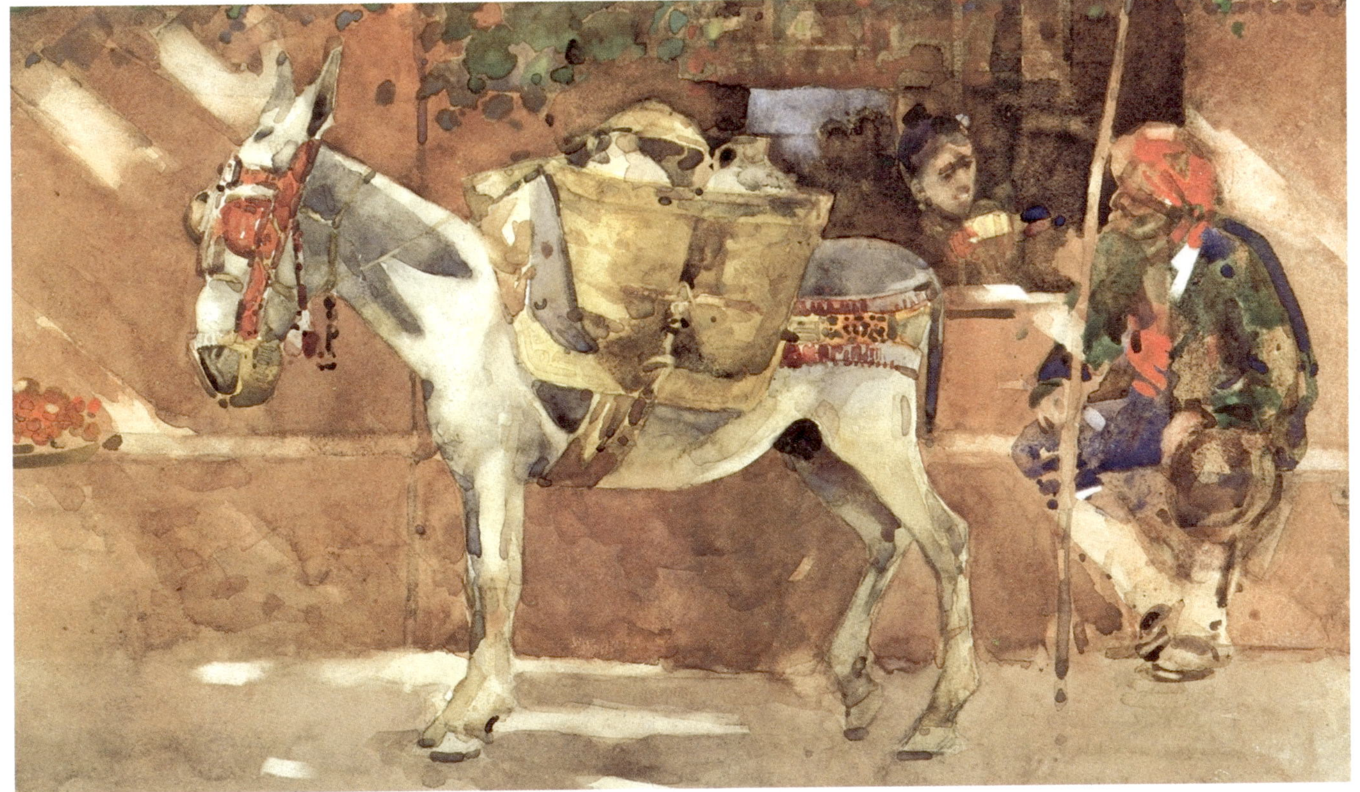

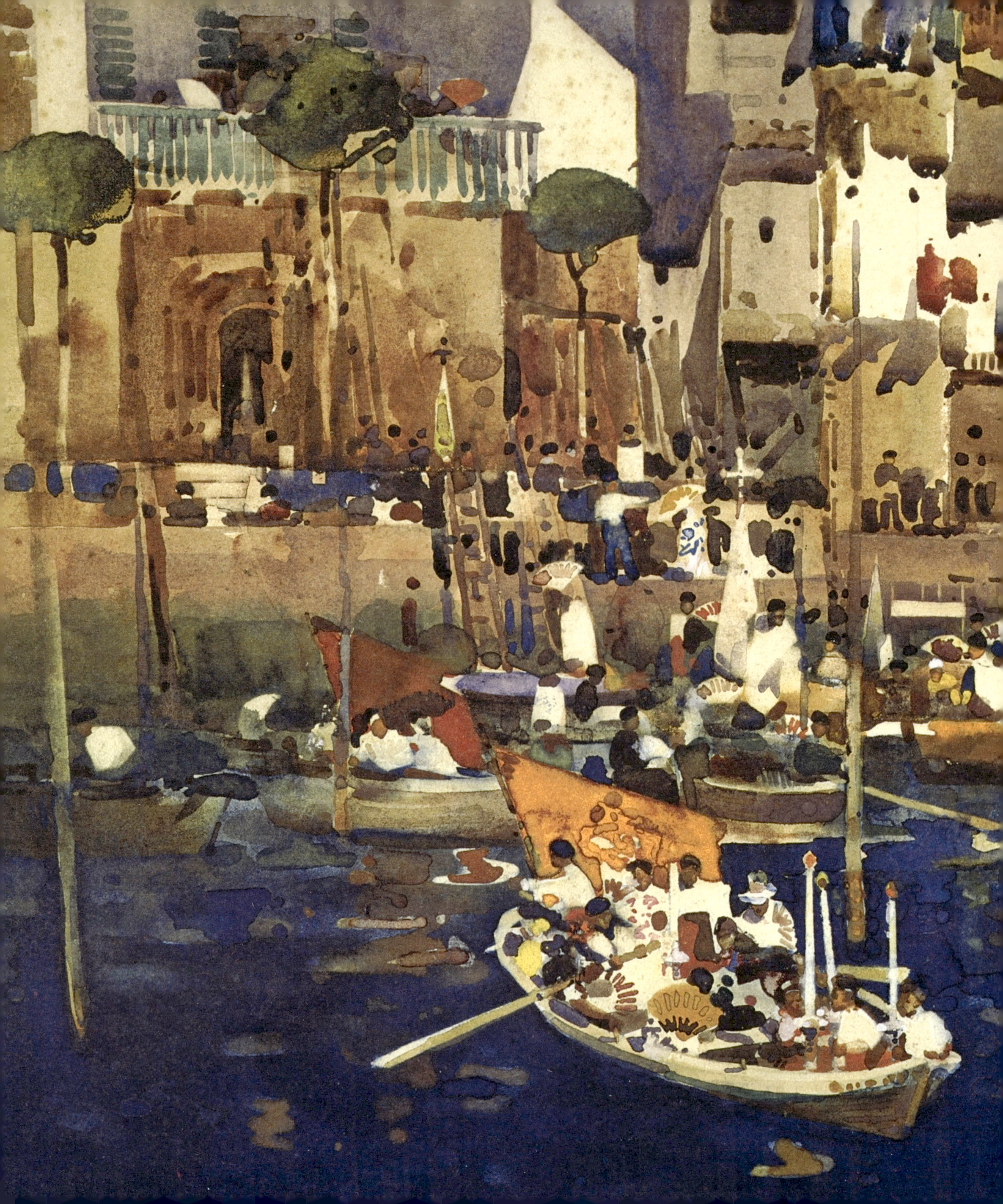

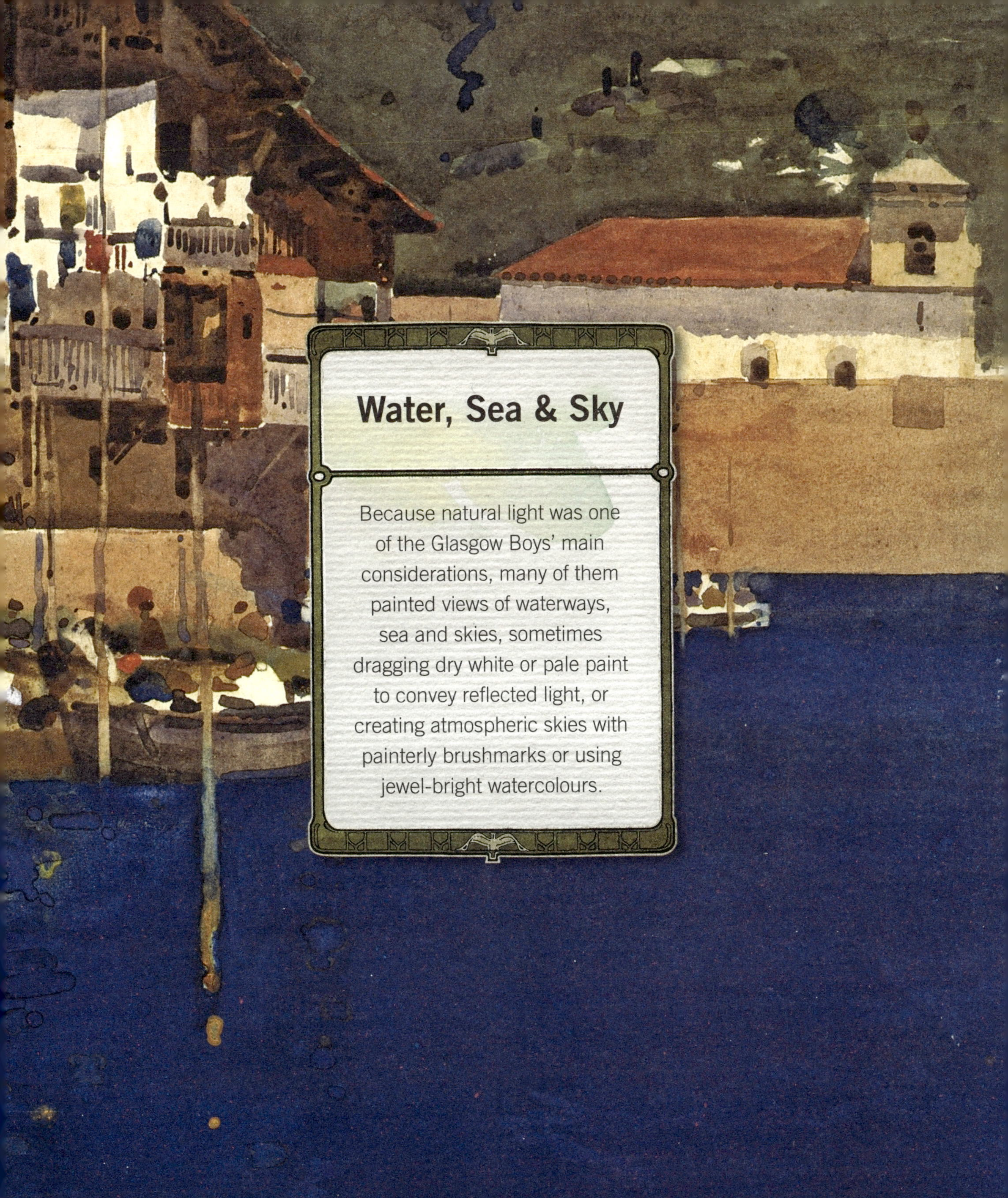

Water, Sea & Sky

Because natural light was one of the Glasgow Boys' main considerations, many of them painted views of waterways, sea and skies, sometimes dragging dry white or pale paint to convey reflected light, or creating atmospheric skies with painterly brushmarks or using jewel-bright watercolours.

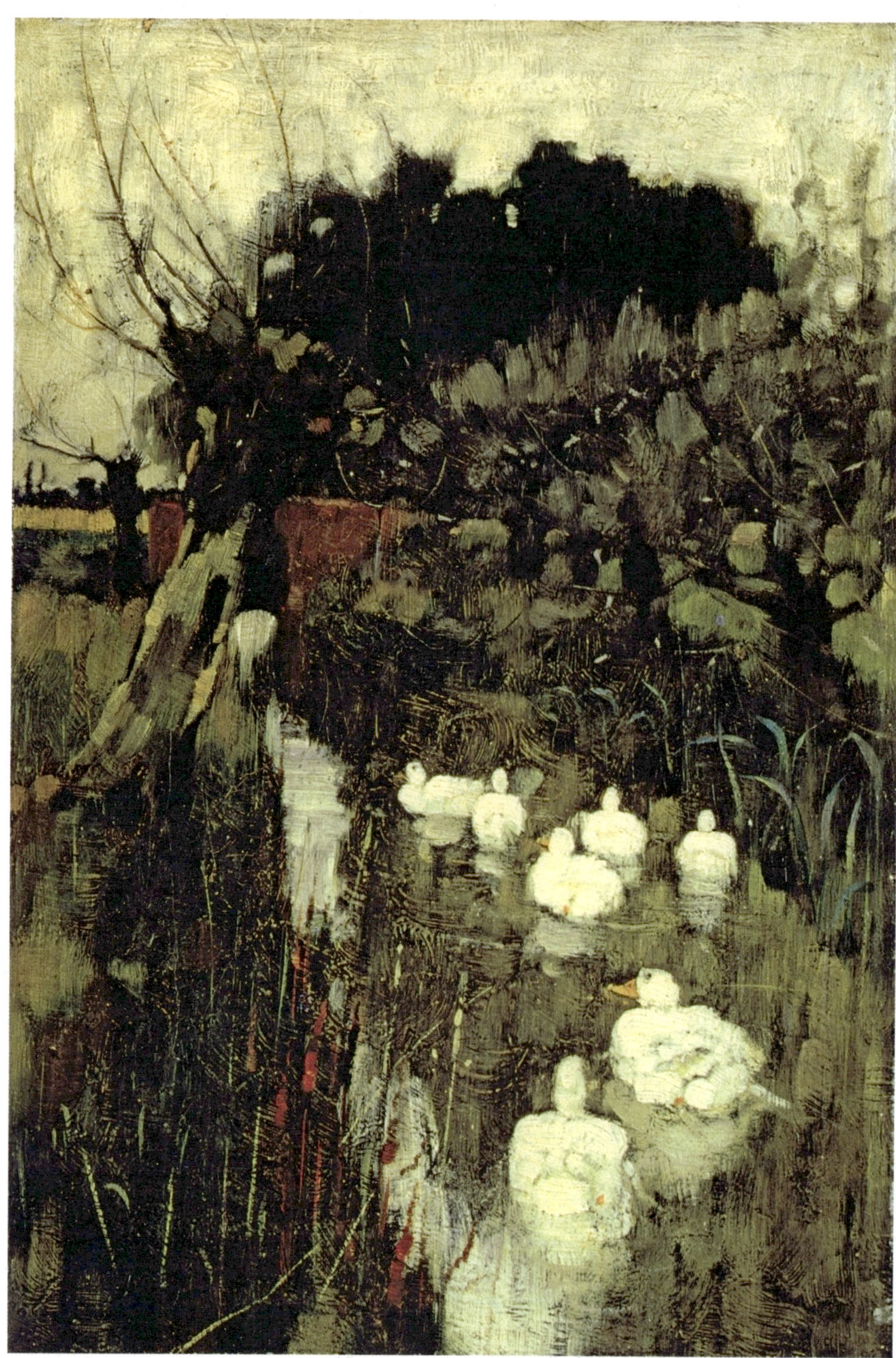

Joseph Crawhall (1861–1913)
Oil on canvas, 32.2 x 22.3 cm (12⅔ x 8¾ in)
• The Higgins Art Gallery, Bedford

A Lincolnshire Stream, 1882 Before he abandoned oil paints in favour of watercolours and gouache, Crawhall sketched in oils outdoors, then returned to his studio to complete his paintings. His portrait format scene of ducks demonstrates his original thinking for the time.

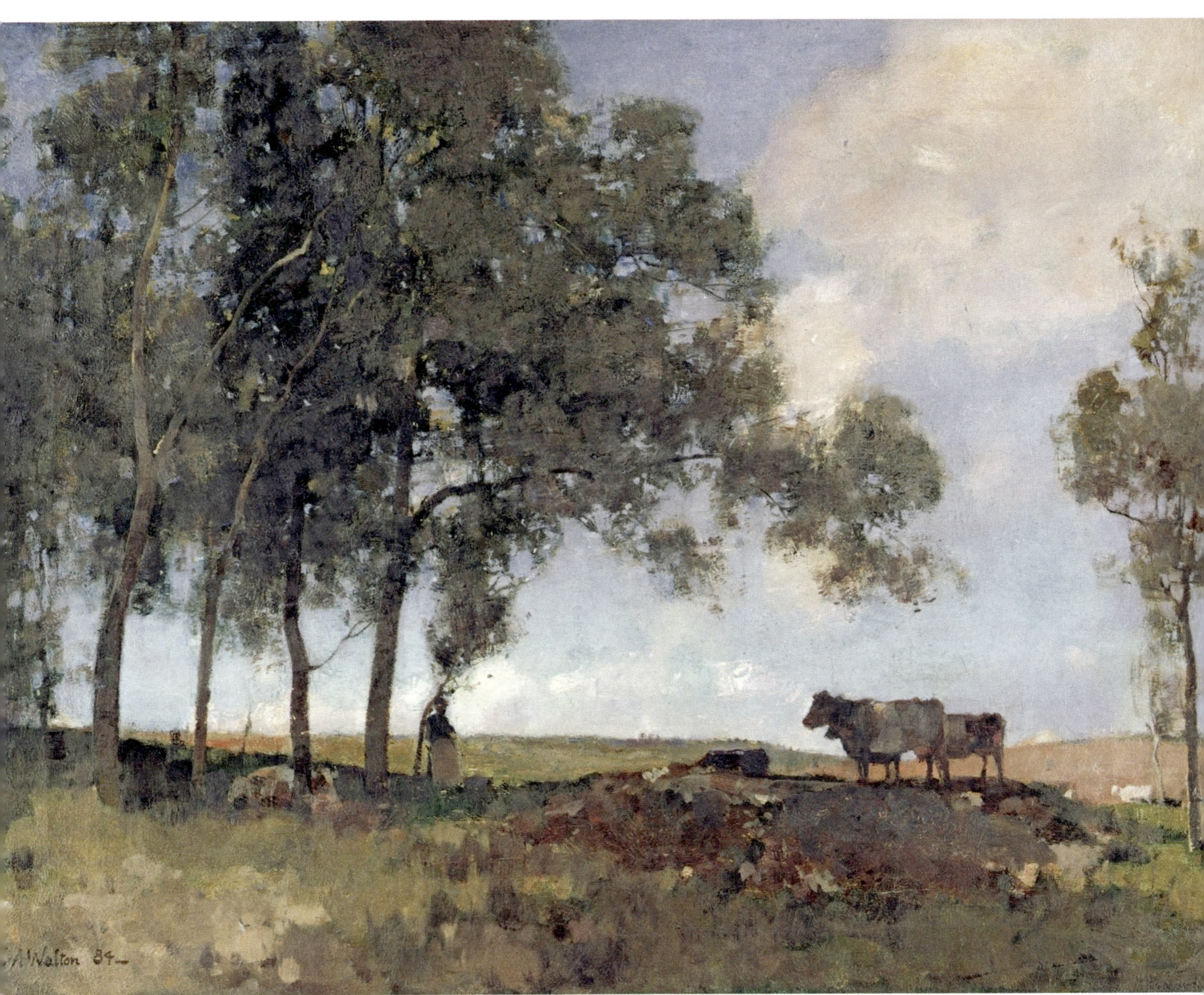

Edward Arthur Walton (1860–1922)
Oil on canvas, 53.4 x 71 cm (21 x 28 in)
• The Hunterian Museum and Art Gallery, Glasgow

Autumn Sunshine, 1883–84 Many of Walton's Cockburnspath paintings were executed in full sunlight, and here this serves to throw the trees and cows into silhouette. The sketchy paint application contrasts with the more accepted smooth academic finish of the time.

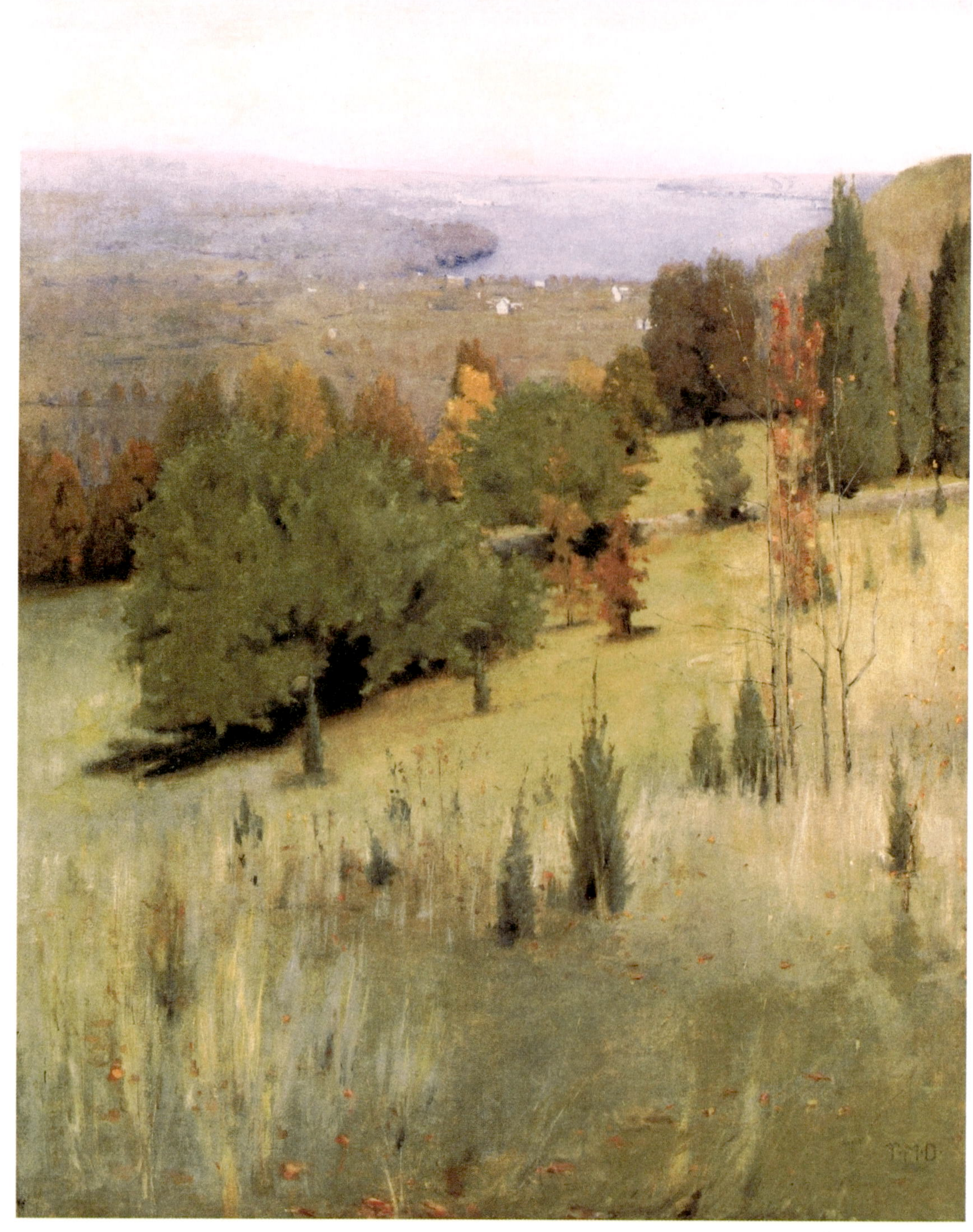

Thomas Millie Dow (1848–1919)
Oil on canvas, 123.2 x 97.8 cm (48½ x 38½ in)
• Kelvingrove Art Gallery and Museum, Glasgow

The Hudson River, 1884 In September 1883, Dow sailed to New York from Glasgow, to visit his friend Abbott Thayer and his wife at Cornwall-on-Hudson. He painted several views from Thayer's house, including this autumnal scene across the landscape to the Hudson River.

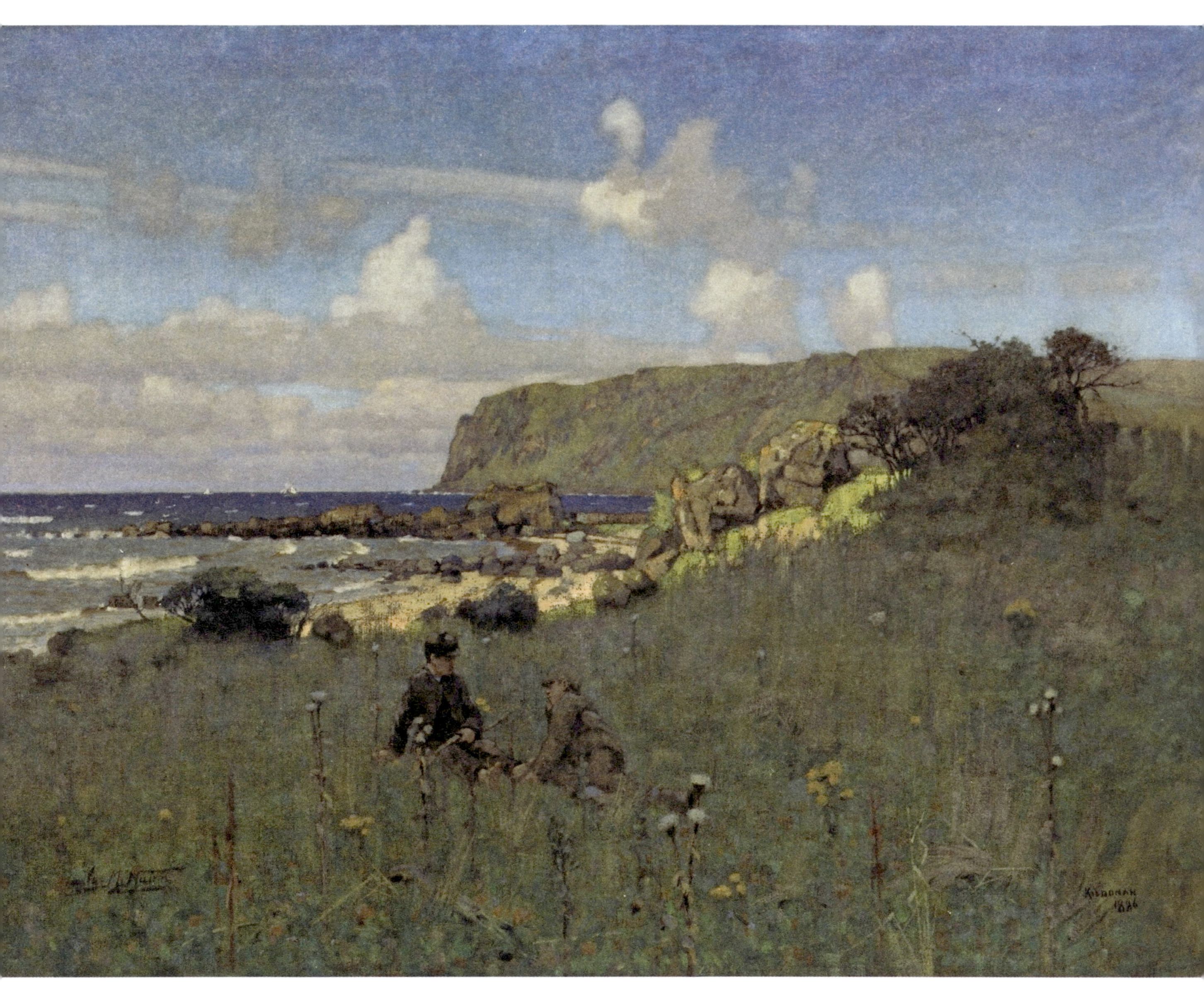

James Nairn (1859–1904)
Oil on canvas, 120.4 x 149.7 cm (47⅔ x 59 in)
• Kelvingrove Art Gallery and Museum, Glasgow

Kildonan, 1886 Before moving to New Zealand, Nairn spent his summers away from
Glasgow, producing many sketches that he could work up in his studio during the winter.
In 1886, he painted this view in Kildonan, a village on the south coast of the Isle of Arran.

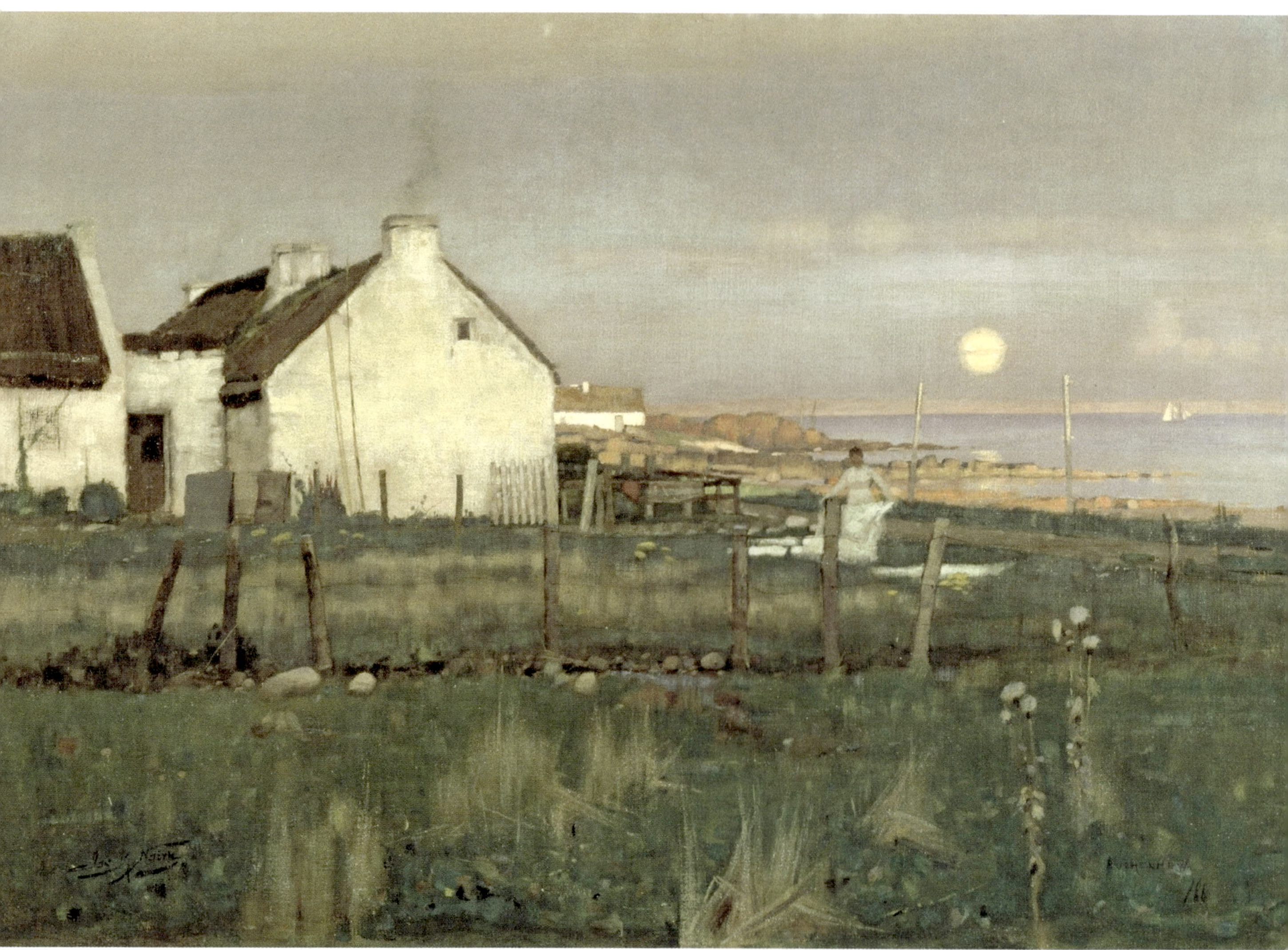

James Nairn (1859–1904)
Oil on canvas, 61 x 91.5 cm (24 x 36 in) • Private collection

Auchenhew, Arran, 1886 In the summer of 1886, Nairn painted this view with a lowering sun and a girl in white. Fascinated by the effects of light, Nairn used some Impressionist ideas, including a bright palette and visible brushmarks, and tonal elements of the Barbizon and Hague Schools.

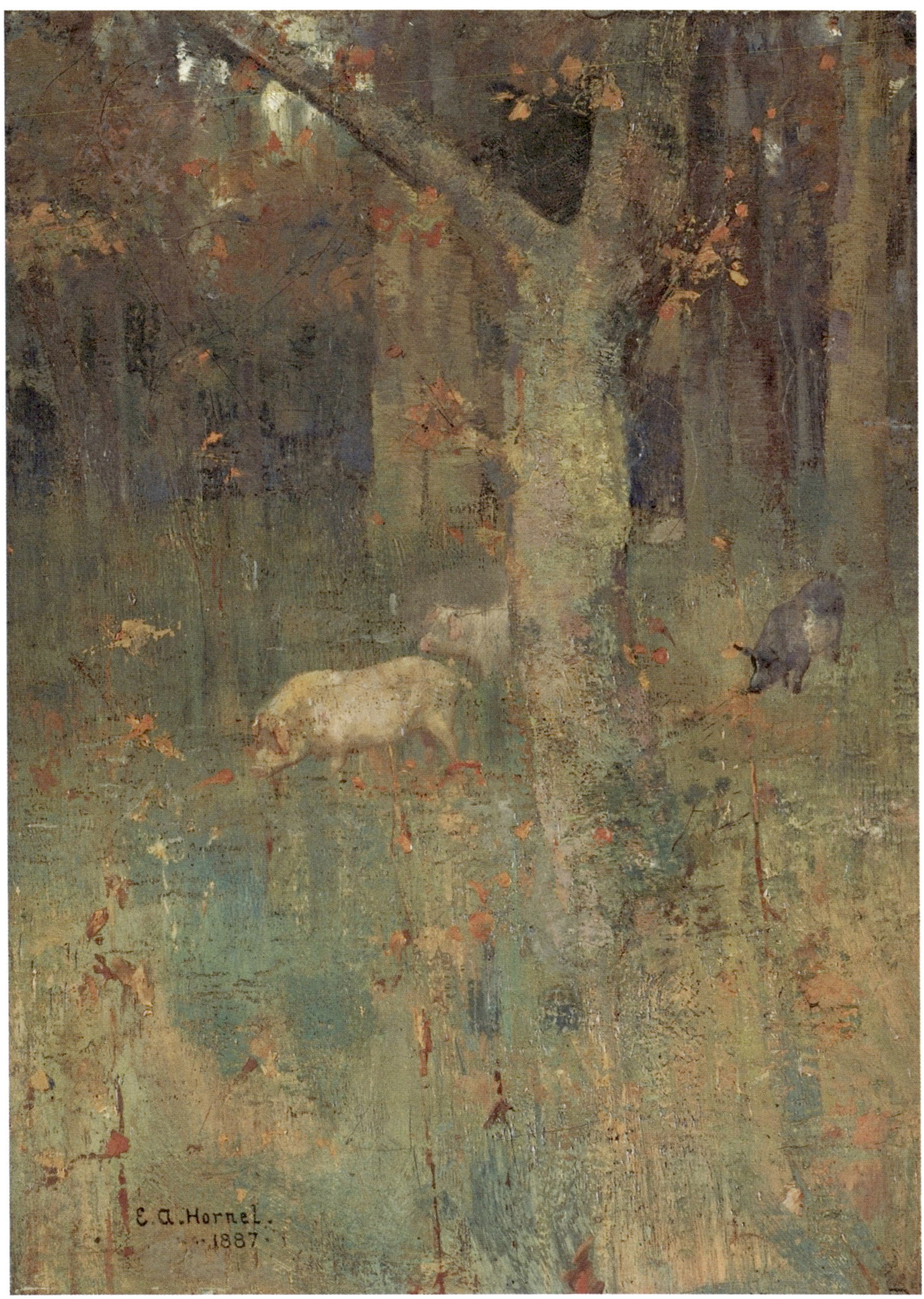

E.A. Hornel (1864–1933)
Oil on canvas, 40.6 x 30.5 cm (16 x 12 in) • Private collection

Pigs in a Wood, 1887 Colourful impasto paint and broken brushwork applied vertically create a misty impression. Although this was still the early phase of the Glasgow Boys, Hornel veered towards the decorative, showing his fascination for Whistler and Japanese art, and anticipating Art Nouveau.

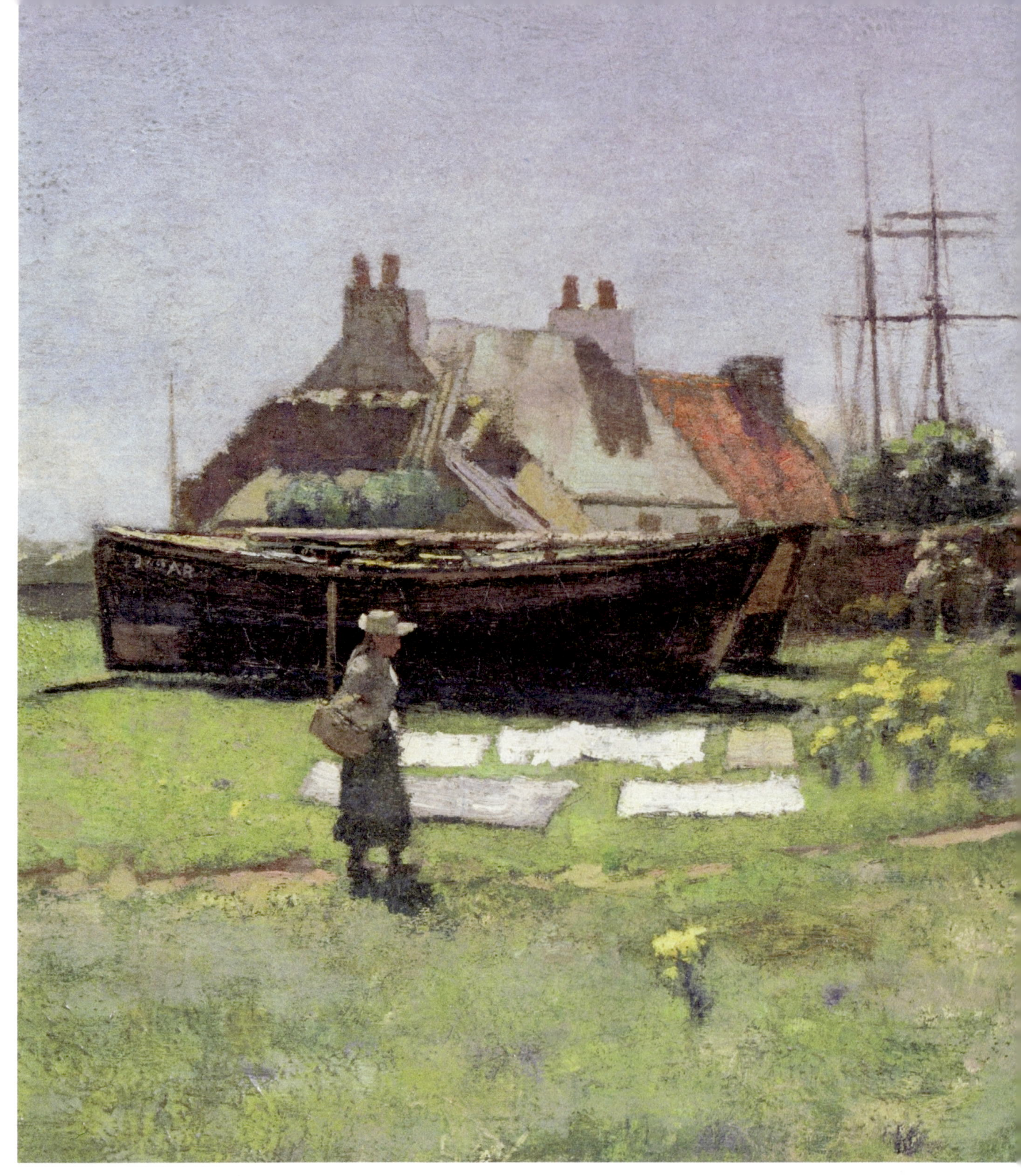

James Nairn (1859–1904)
Oil on canvas, 30.5 x 45.7 cm (12 x 18 in)
• The Fleming-Wyfold Art Foundation, London

View of Corrie on Arran, 1887 A common element of Nairn's work is the inclusion of single female figures in landscapes. Effects of shimmering sunlight are created with broken brushmarks and clear, bright colours layered on top of each other, which reflect his admiration of Impressionism.

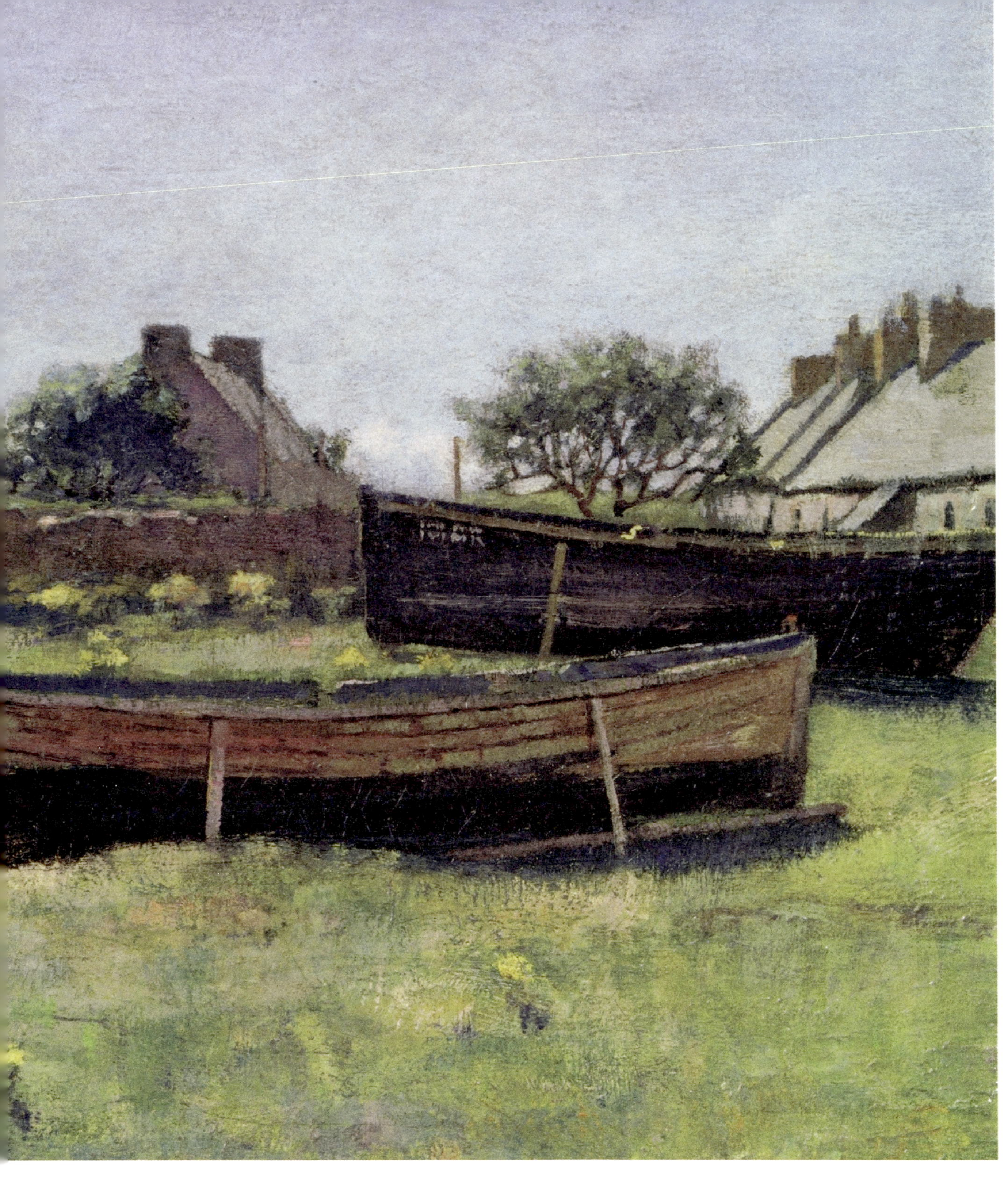

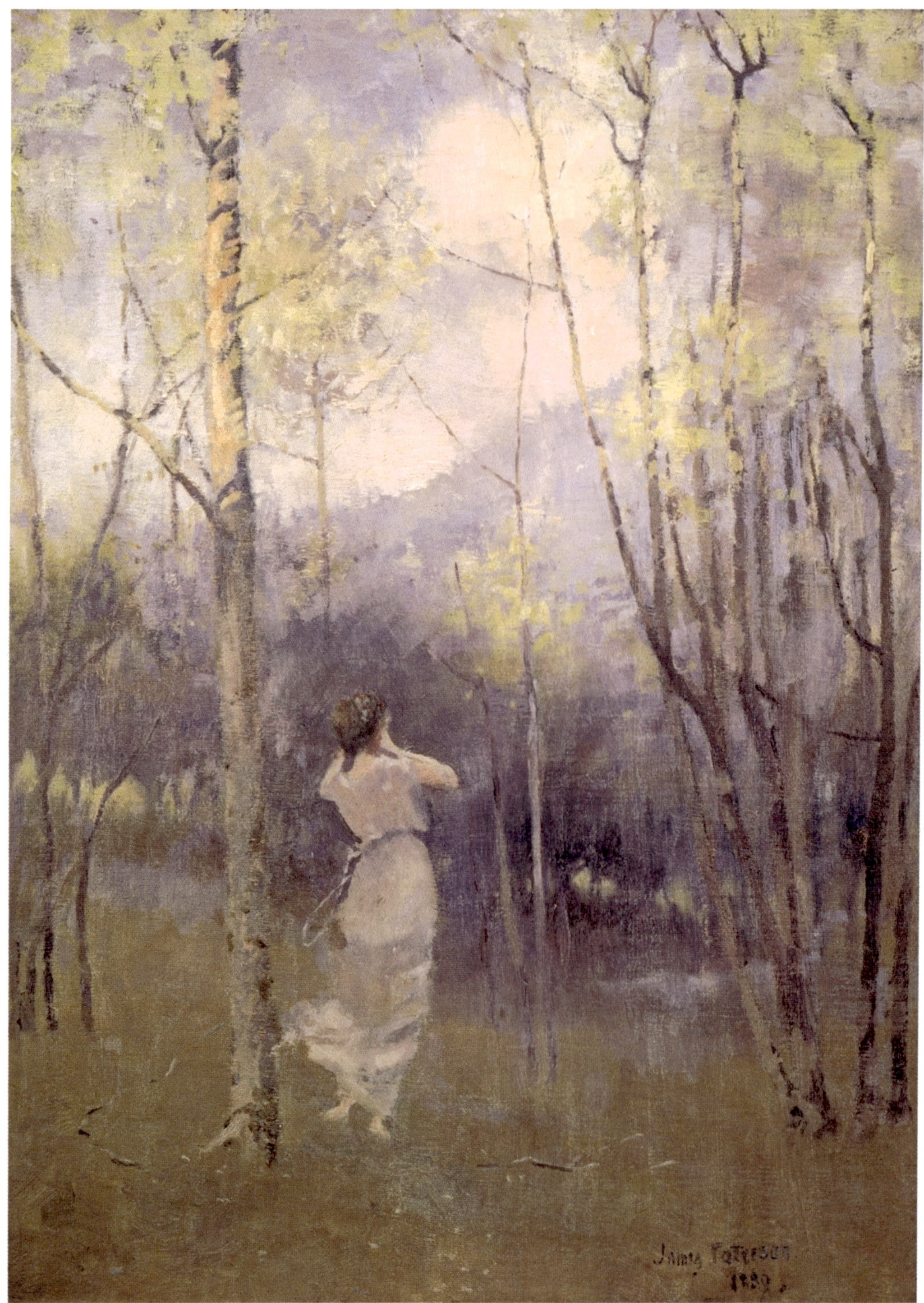

James Paterson (1854–1932)
Oil on canvas, 39.3 x 29.2 cm (15⅔ x 11⅔ in) • Private collection

Spring in Moniaive, 1889 A great admirer of the work of Corot and Bastien-Lepage, Paterson painted with similar flat brushstrokes. When he first moved to Moniaive, he painted mostly portraits, but while living there, he began painting more landscapes, including this atmospheric view.

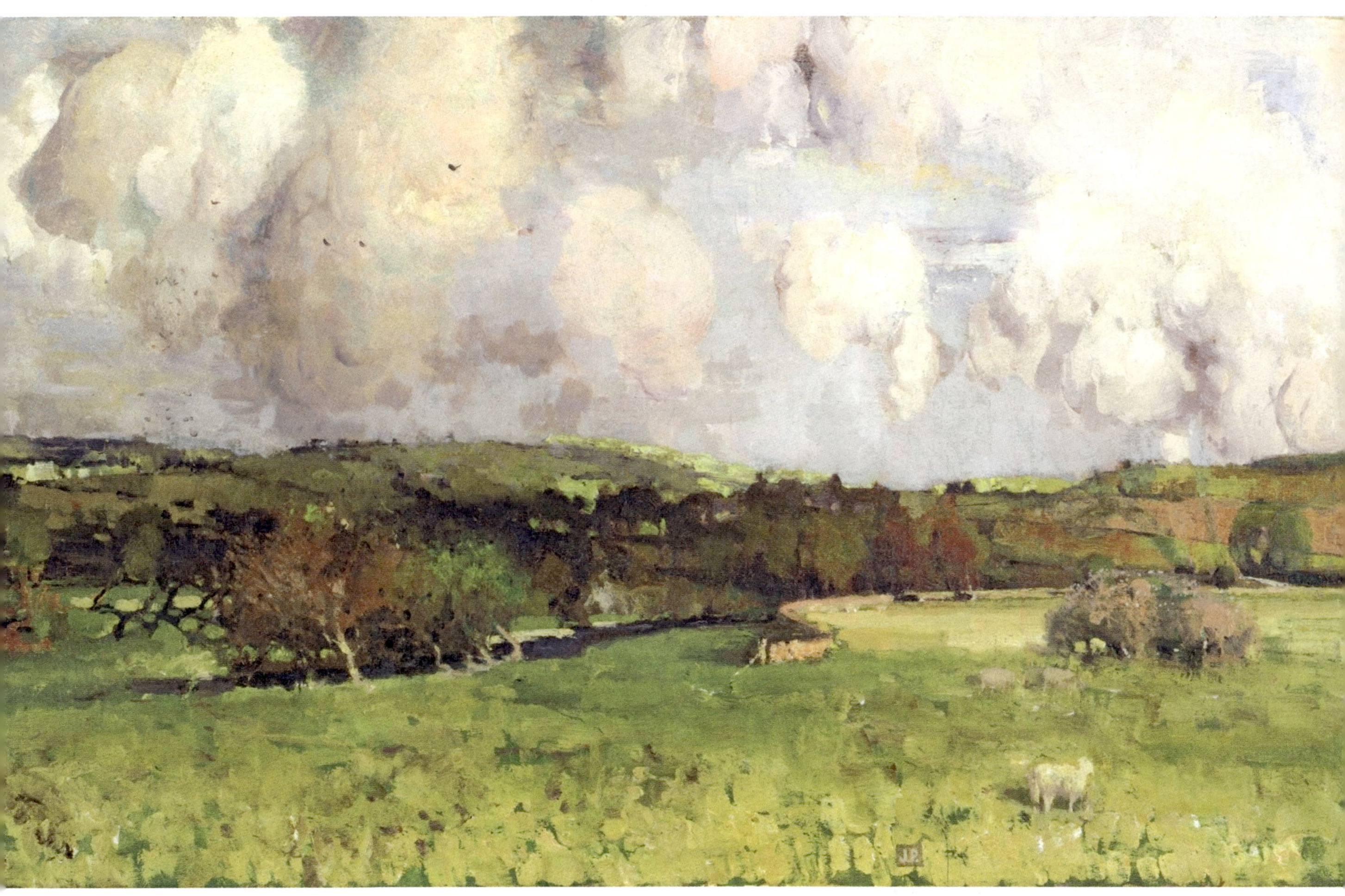

James Paterson (1854–1932)
Oil on canvas, 45.1 x 76.3 cm (17¾ x 30 in)
• Yale Center for British Art, Connecticut, USA

Castlefern, *c.* 1890–95 After Paterson studied the work of the Realists and Impressionists in Paris, he focused on similar methods of capturing tonal values. Here, he builds a luminous atmosphere with both bold and light, and solid and feathery brushwork, and an overall silvery tonality.

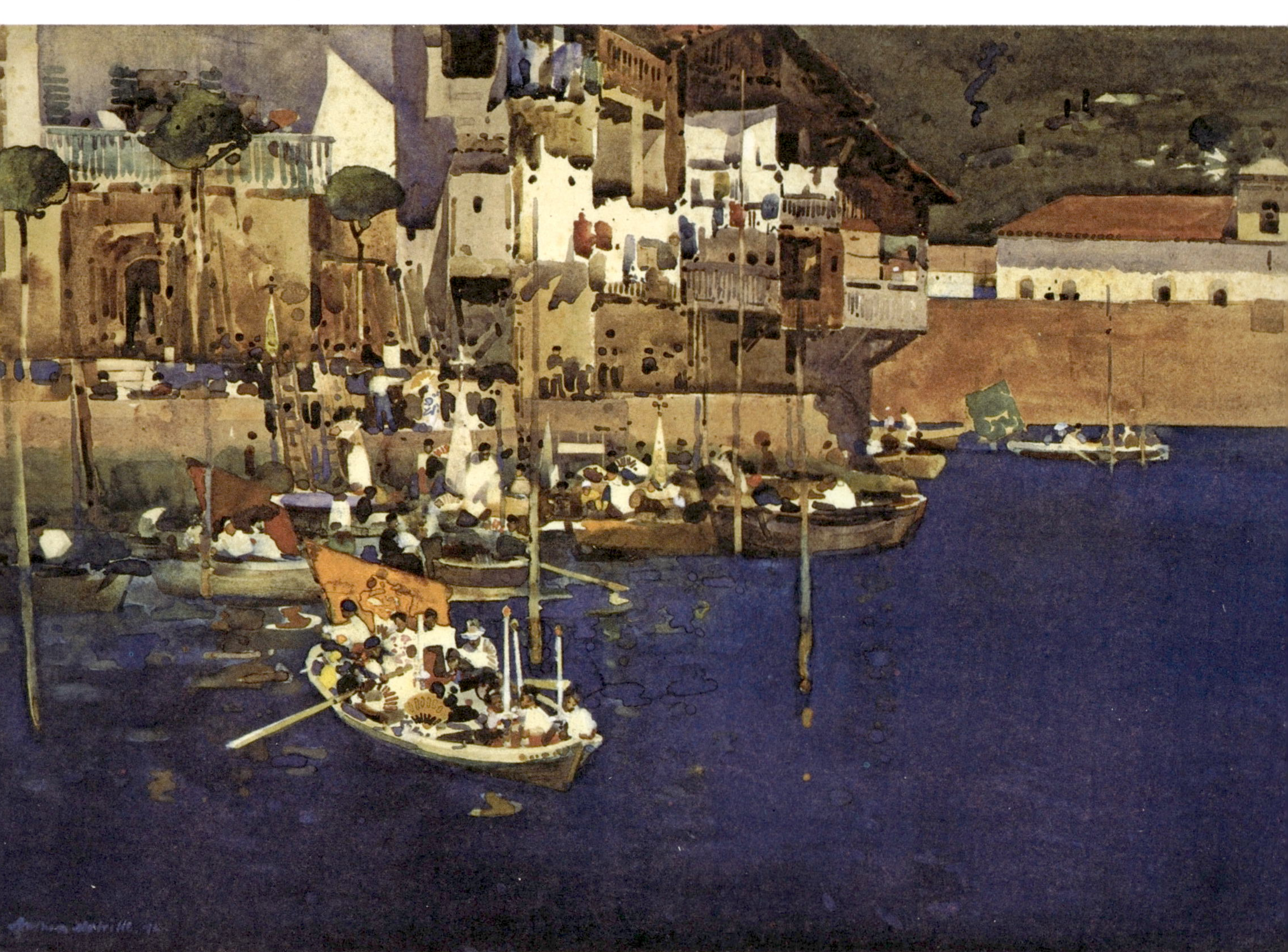

Arthur Melville (1855–1904)
Watercolour on paper, 51.3 x 78.7 cm (20¼ x 31 in)
• Kelvingrove Art Gallery and Museum, Glasgow

A Mediterranean Port, 1892 Between 1890 and 1899, Melville visited Spain six times. The trips inspired some of his brightest watercolours. Another of his paintings, *The Sapphire Sea* (1892), used the same intense, rich ultramarine that contrasts with the white and terracotta buildings.

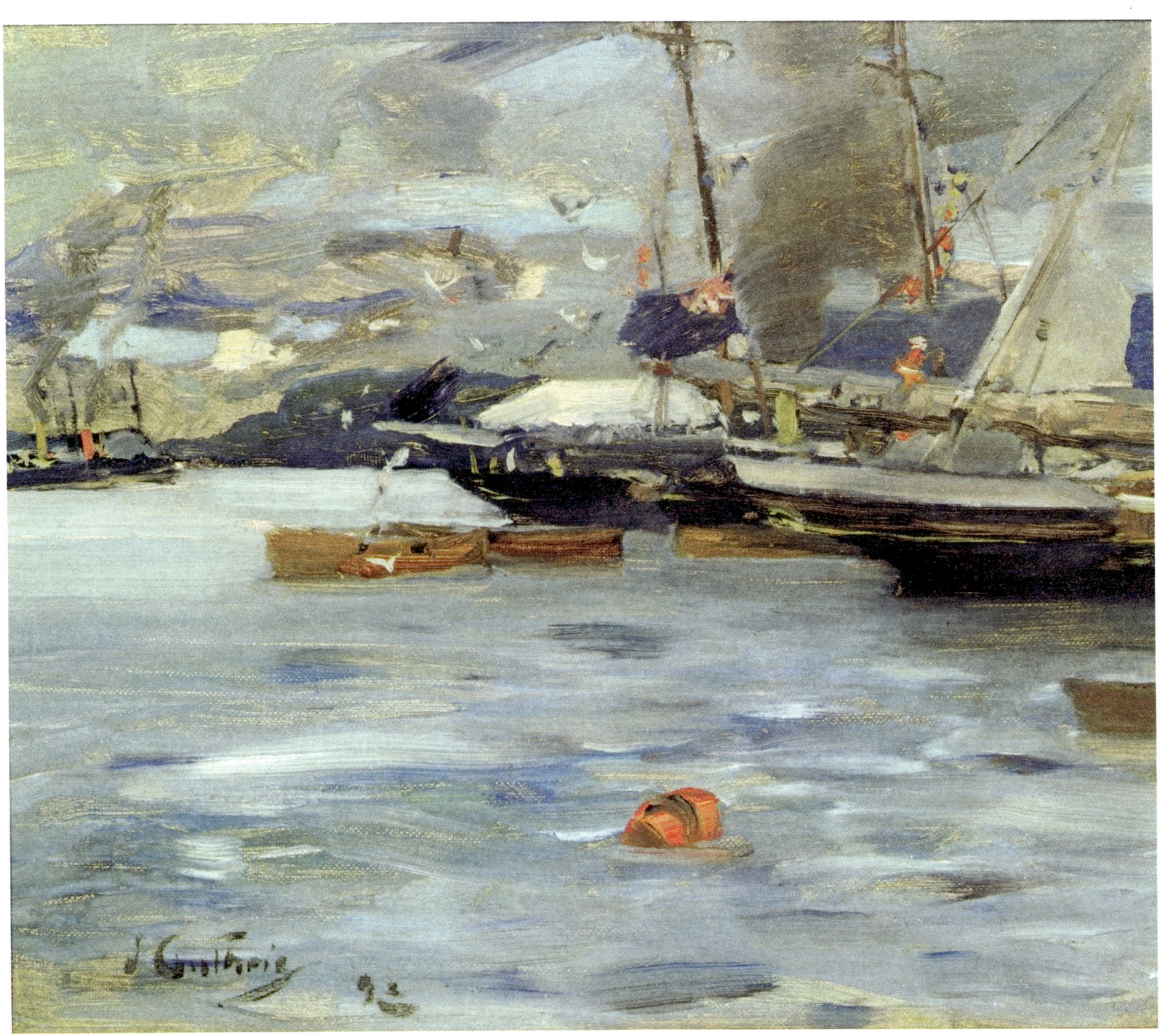

James Guthrie (1859–1930)
Oil on canvas, 25.4 x 30.5 cm (10 x 12 in) • Private collection

Moored Yachts, Oban, 1893 The Glasgow Boys first received international recognition largely through Guthrie's paintings. By the time he painted this, Oban was a bustling town, with a new railway, and was seen as an example of modernity.

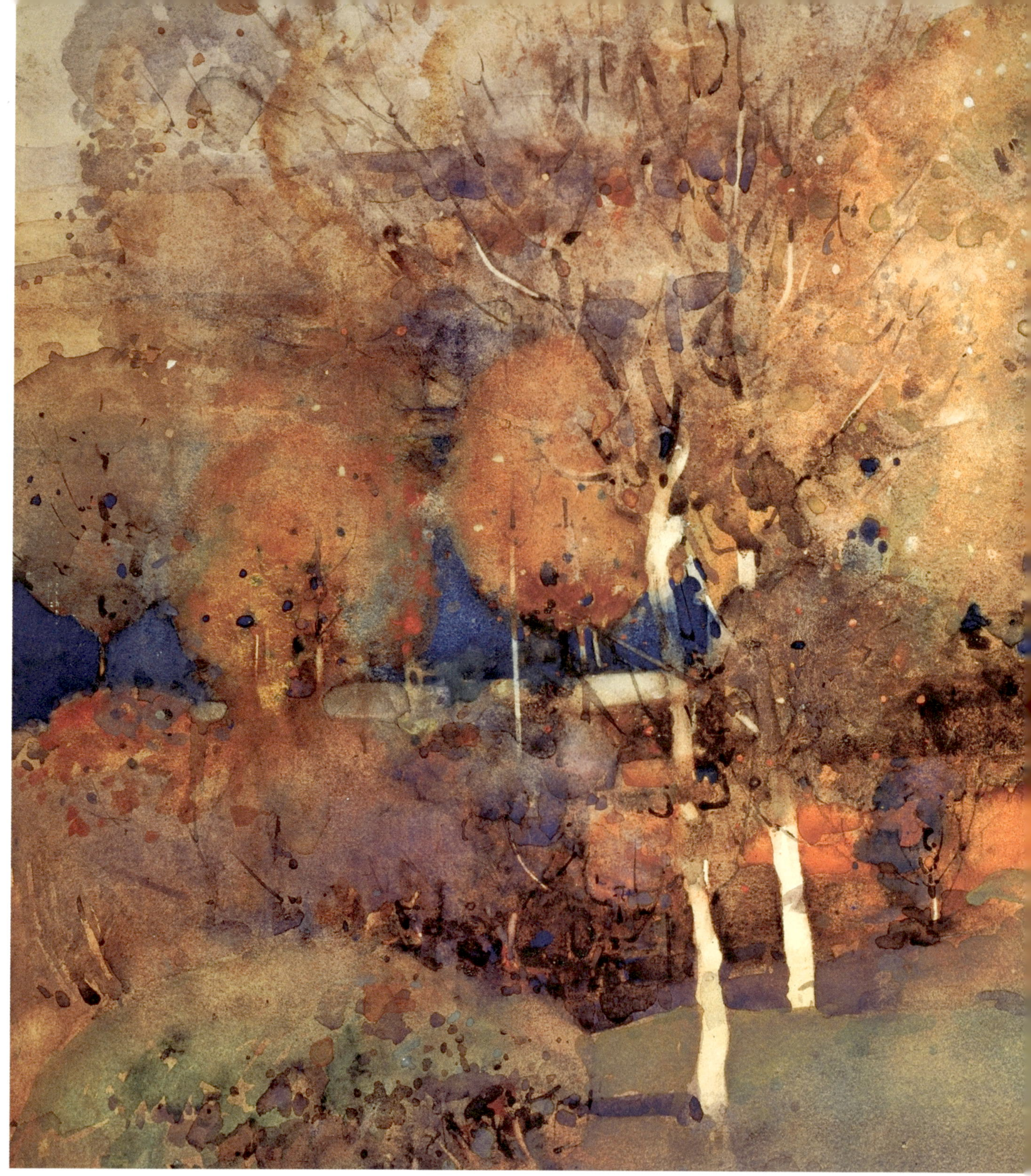

Arthur Melville (1855–1904)
Watercolour on paper, 59 x 85 cm (23¼ x 33⅗ in)
• Kelvingrove Art Gallery and Museum, Glasgow

Autumn, Loch Lomond, 1893 Until he died at just 49, Melville was one of the few painters to constantly experiment, especially exploiting the potential of watercolour and gouache. Bordering on abstraction, this depicts the brilliant blue water of the loch, glimpsed through autumnal trees.

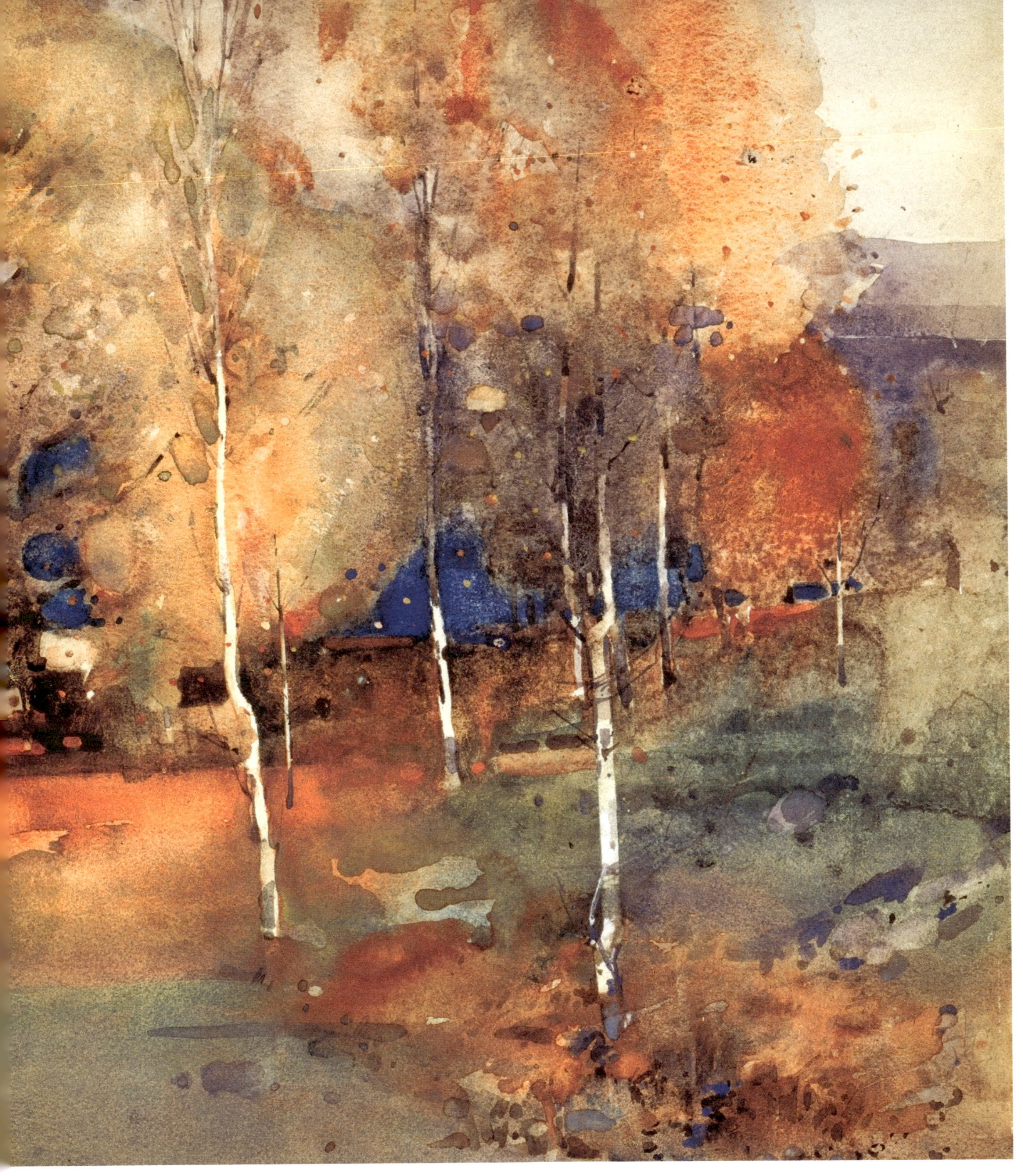

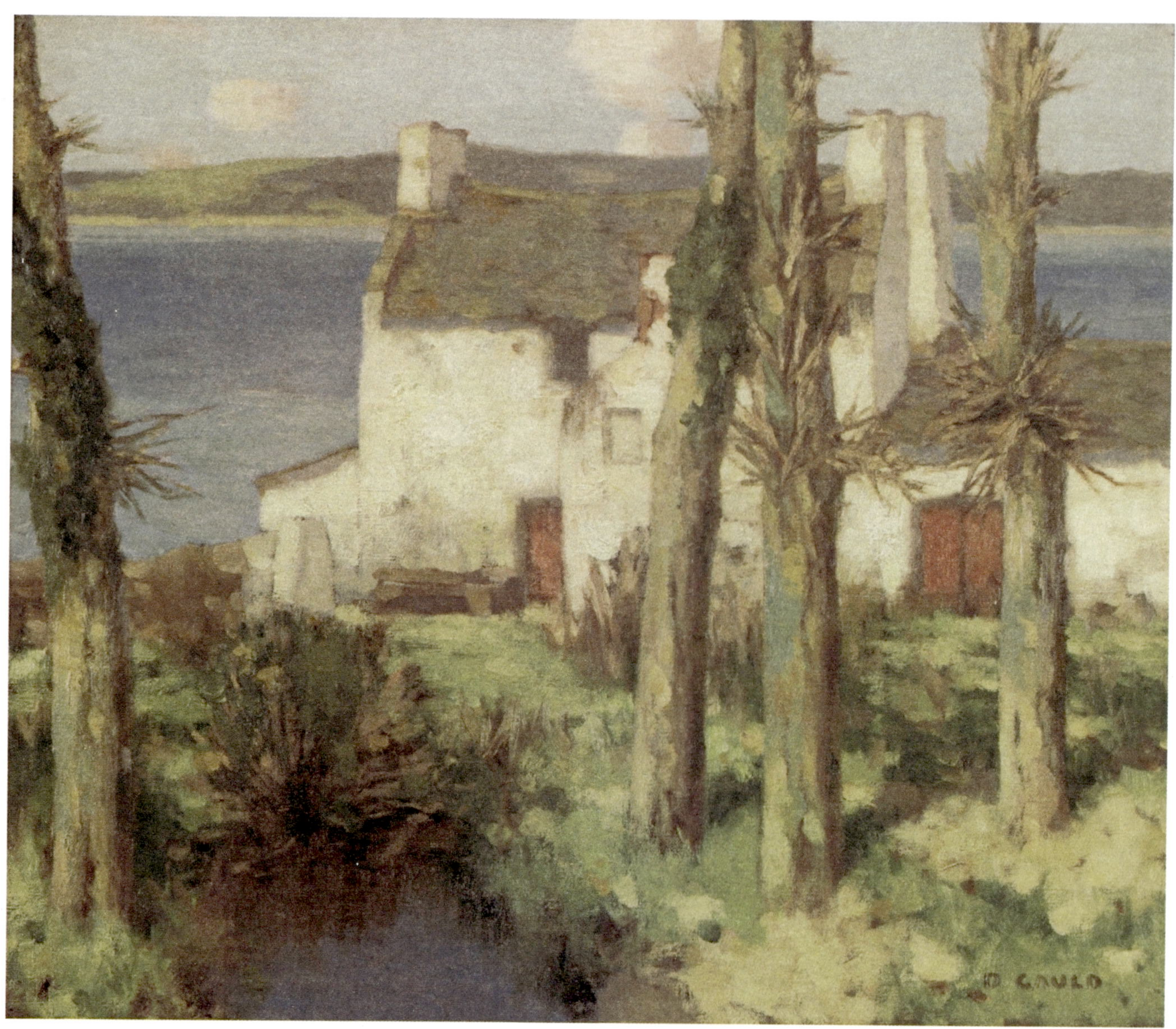

David Gauld (1865–1936)
Oil on canvas, 50.2 x 60.3 cm (19¾ x 23¾ in)
• The Fleming-Wyfold Art Foundation, London

A Breton Village, *c.* **1895** Bathed in bright summer light, this view of the sea and a small house in Brittany demonstrates Gauld's *plein-air* techniques. Painted in France, he built up bright-coloured patches, creating subtle tonal contrasts.

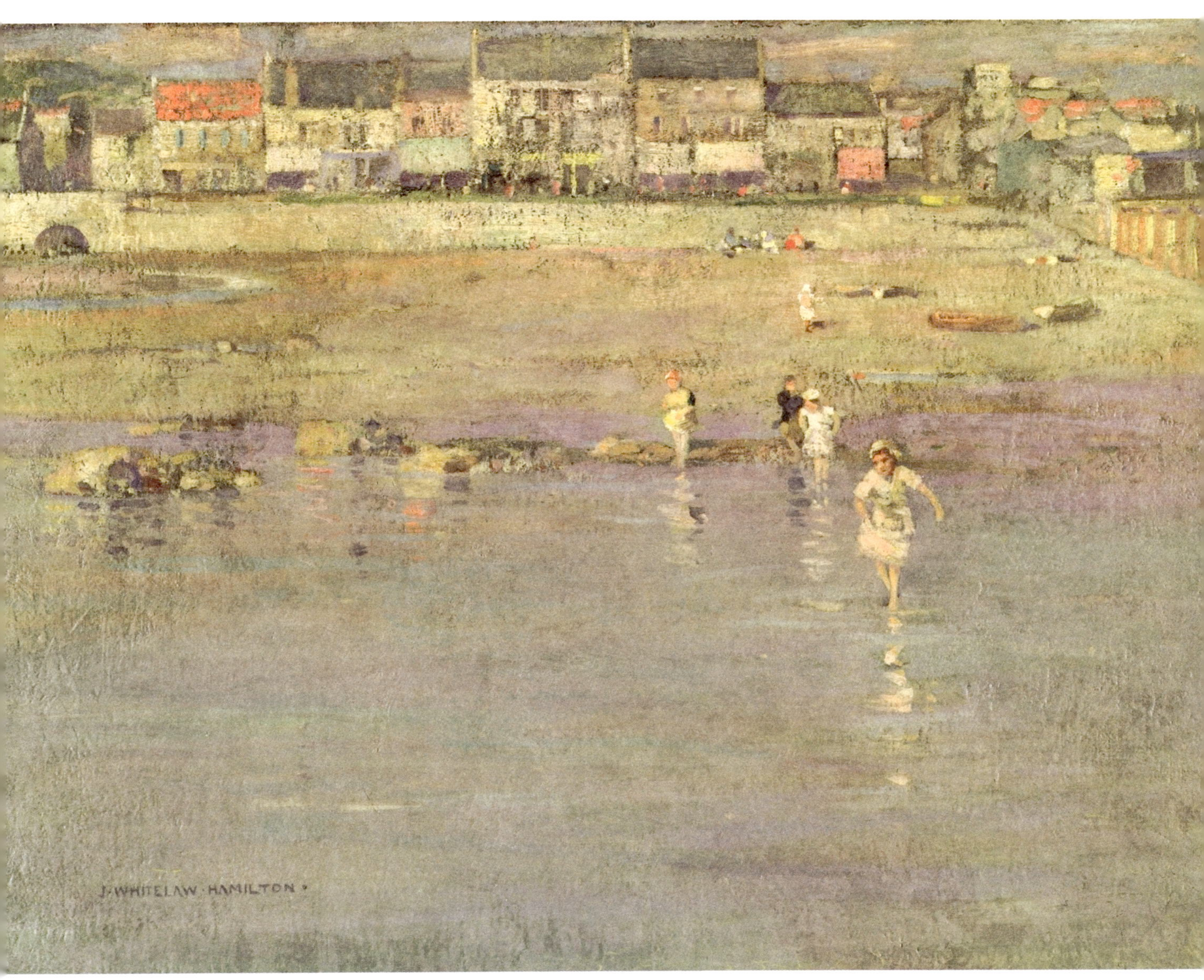

James Whitelaw Hamilton (1860–1932)
Oil on canvas, 45.7 x 61 cm (18 x 24 in)
• Yale Center for British Art, Connecticut

Ebbing Tide, *c.* **1896** Calm views of quays, harbours and beaches with a few figures in subtle, rich colours and vigorous paint marks made Hamilton famous. Although friends with the other Glasgow Boys, he was less involved, and on the edge of the group.

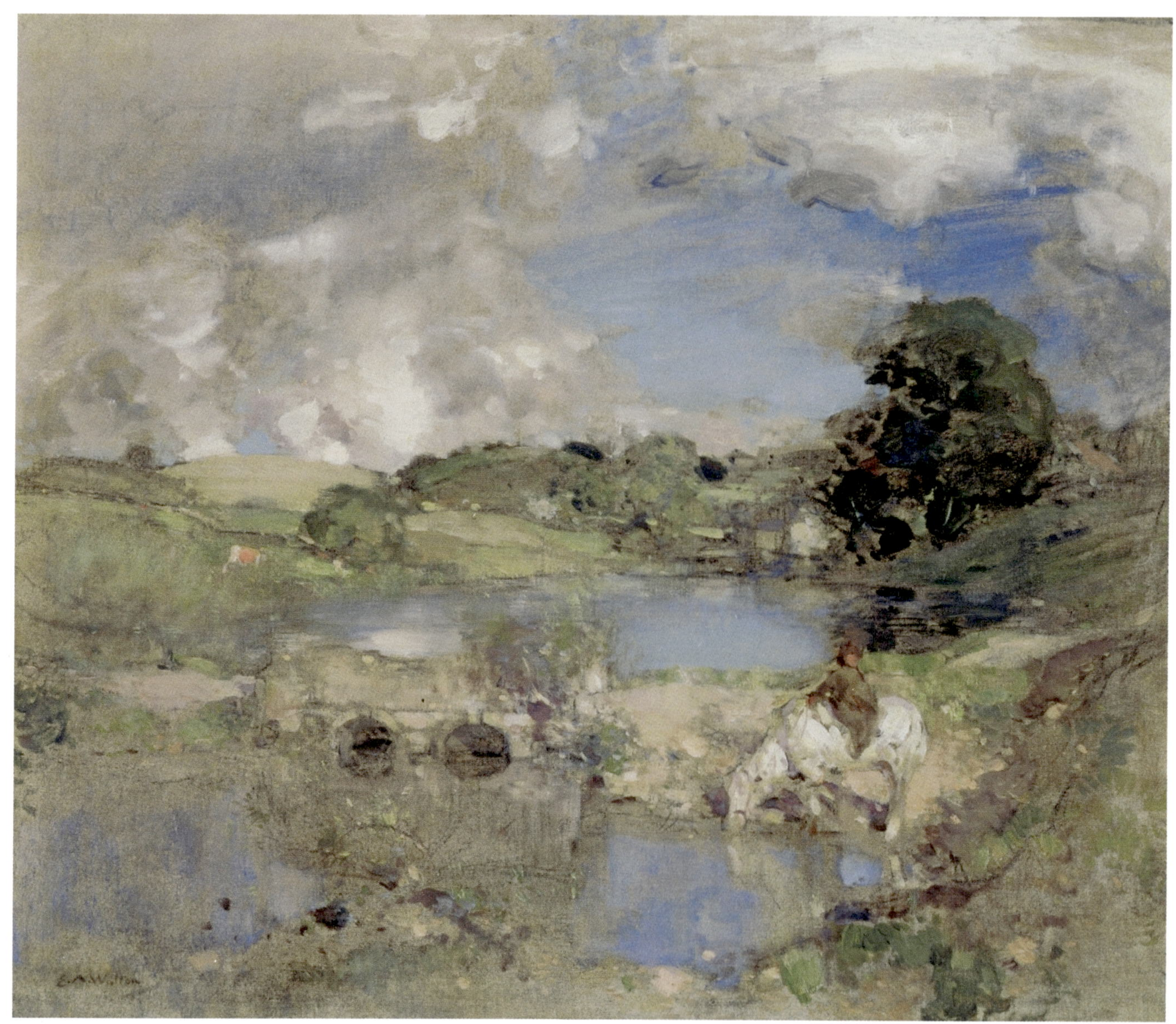

Edward Arthur Walton (1860–1922)
Oil on canvas, 70 x 82.5 cm (27½ x 32⅔ in)
• The Fleming-Wyfold Art Foundation, London

The White Horse, _c._ 1898 By 1898, Walton had been an associate of the RSA for nine years, and his earlier rejection had been forgotten. Using some of the Symbolists' ideas, this also shows Whistler's influence in the restricted palette, and the expression of light and a breeze.

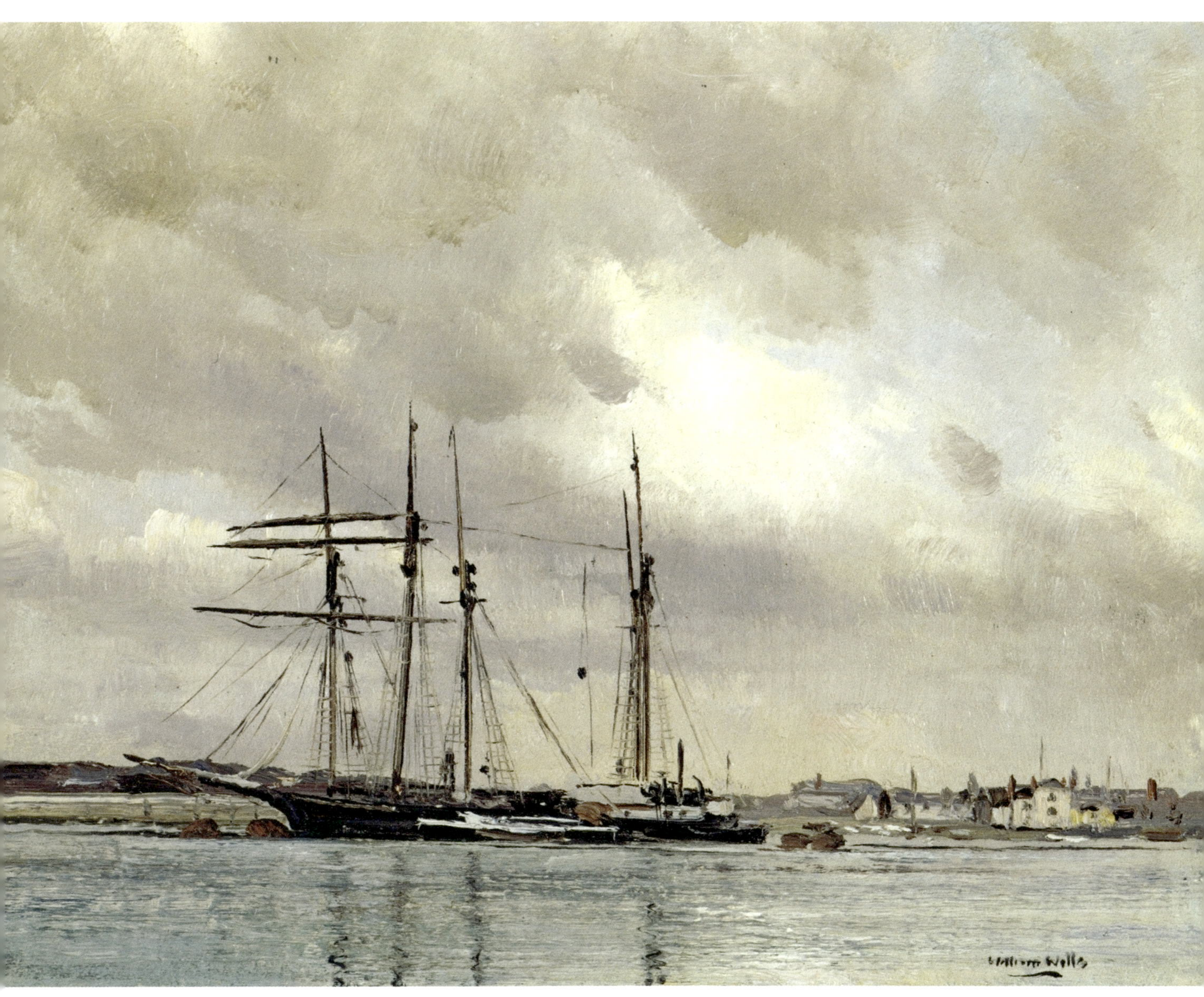

William Page Atkinson Wells (1872–1923)
Oil on board, 30.5 x 40.5 cm (12 x 16 in) • Private collection

Boats in Harbour, Loading China Clay, *c.* **1900** While Wells often used thick paint and visible brushmarks, he also worked, as here, with smooth paint and a restricted, subdued palette that captured close details. The theme of modernity made it stand out against accepted subjects.

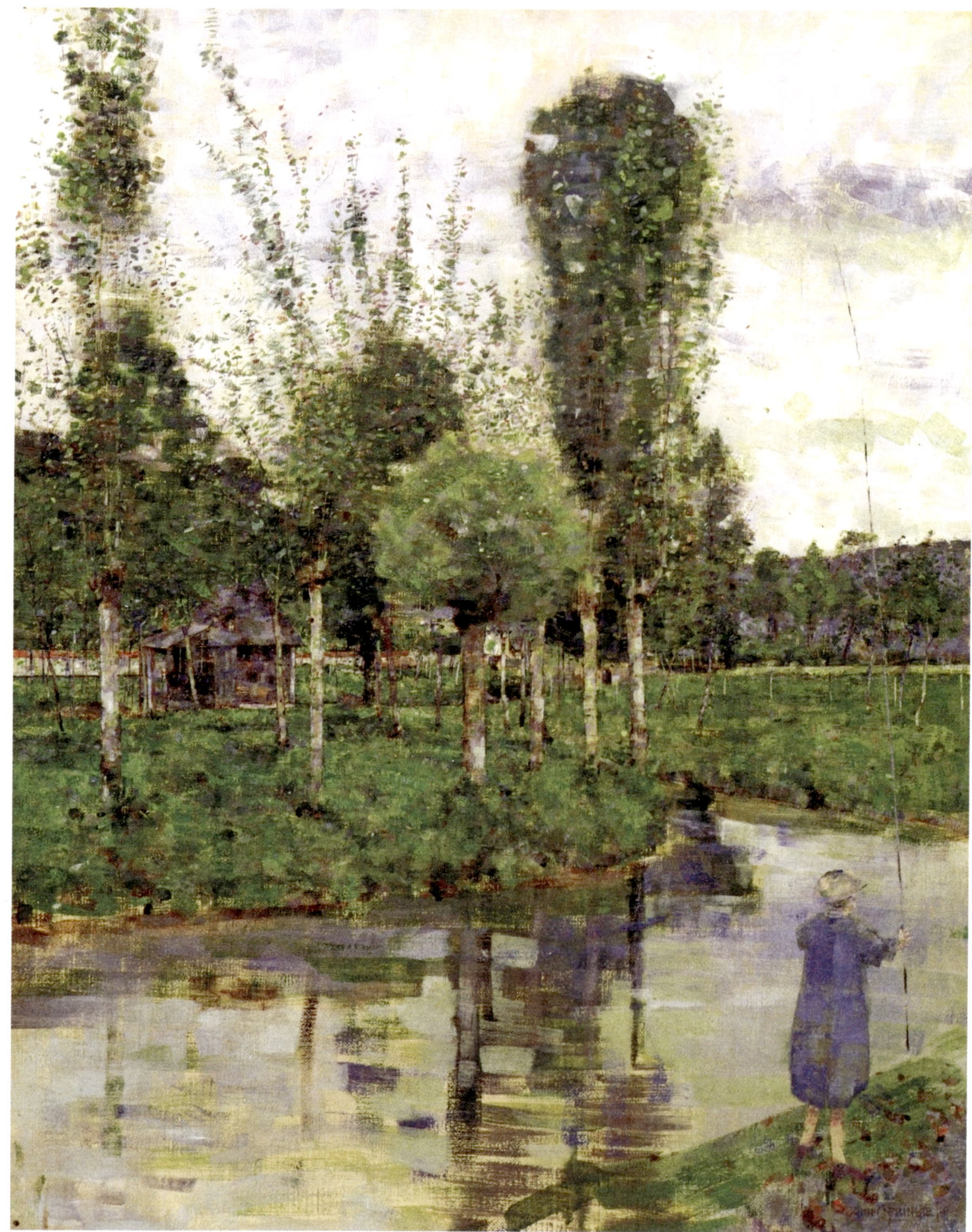

John Quinton Pringle (1864–1925)
Oil on canvas, 53.5 x 43 cm (21 x 17 in)
• Kelvingrove Art Gallery and Museum, Glasgow

On The River, Sainte-Gertrude, Caudebec, Normandy, 1910 Following the Barbizon and Hague School approaches, Pringle painted this on his only foreign trip – to Normandy, in 1910, using both wet- and dry-brush techniques.

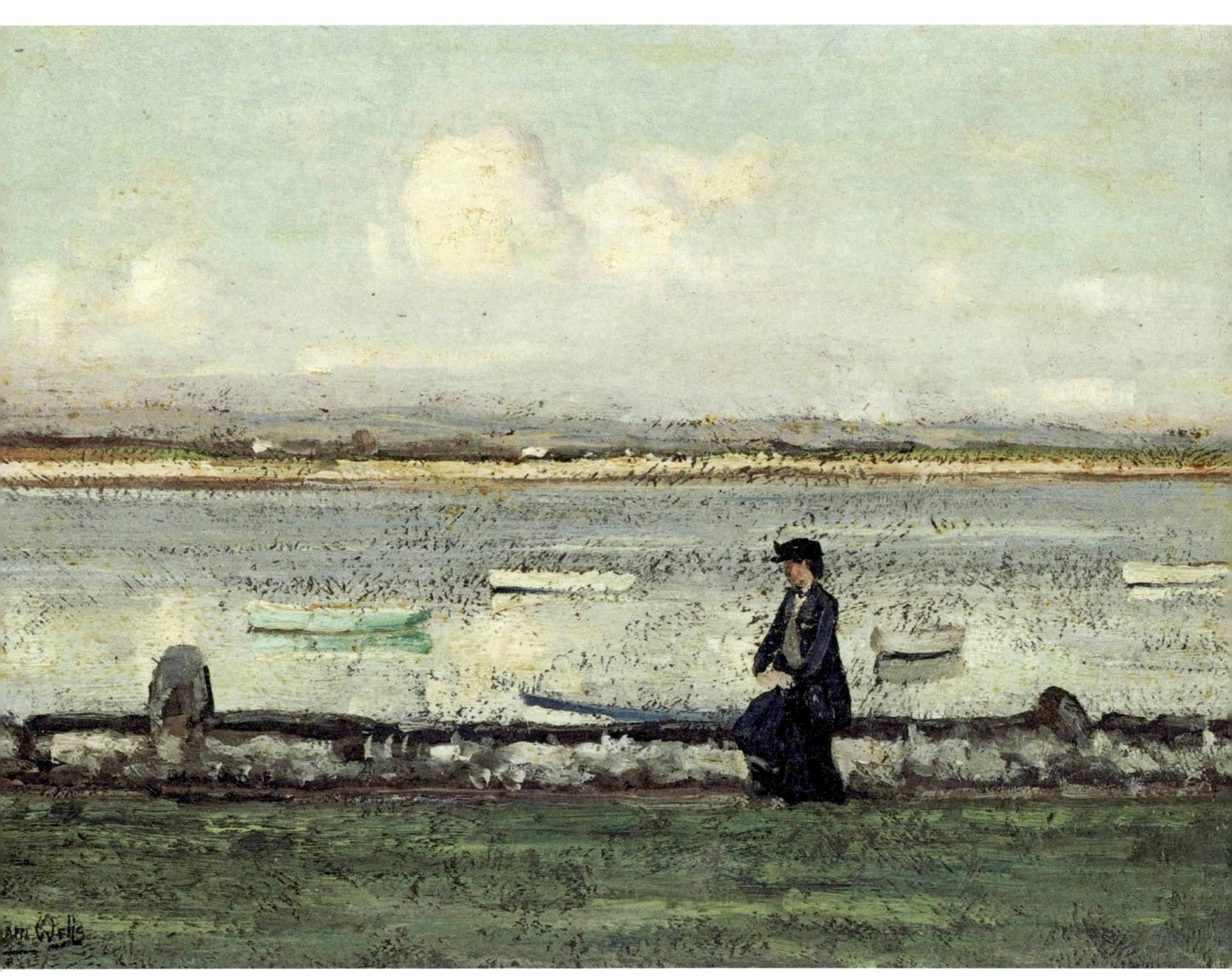

William Page Atkinson Wells (1872–1923)
Oil on canvas, 25.5 x 35.5 cm (10 x 14 in)
• Harris Museum and Art Gallery, Preston, Lancashire

The Lune at Sunderland Point, *c.* 1910 Despite not painting with the other Glasgow Boys, Wells
employed similar methods and themes. His artistic education echoed theirs, and he painted this after
returning to the UK from Australia, using his characteristic impasto paint and loose brushmarks.

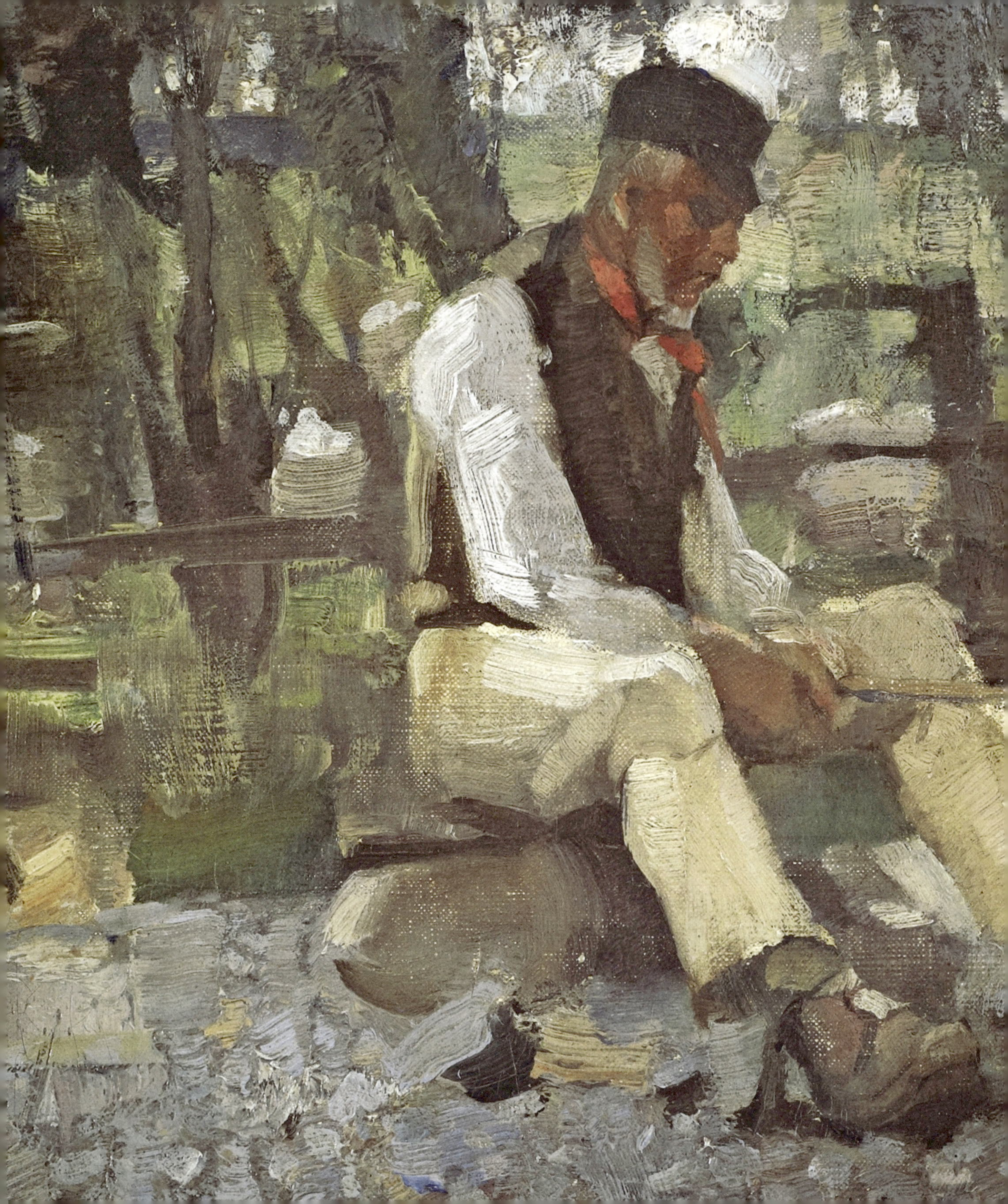

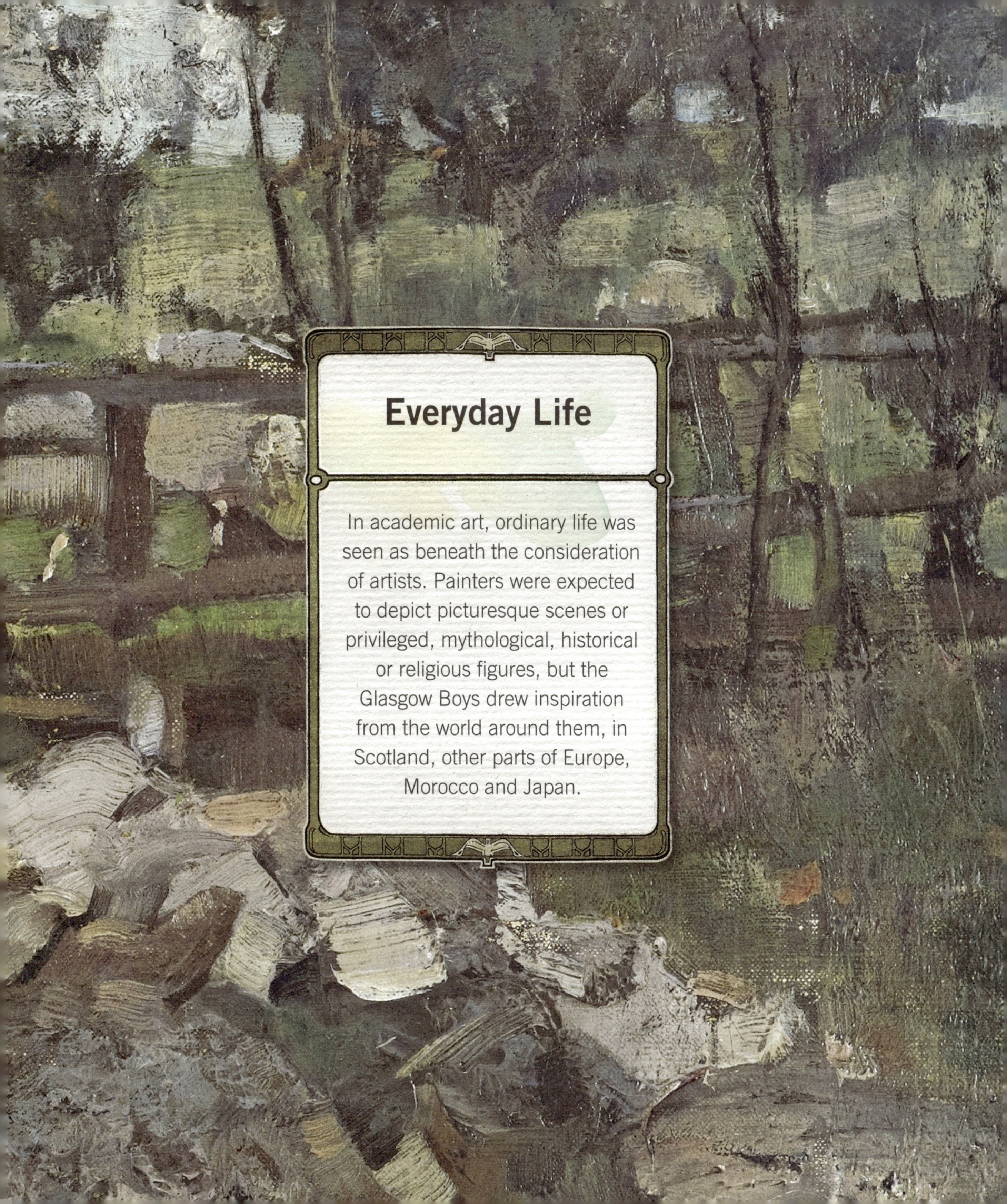

Everyday Life

In academic art, ordinary life was seen as beneath the consideration of artists. Painters were expected to depict picturesque scenes or privileged, mythological, historical or religious figures, but the Glasgow Boys drew inspiration from the world around them, in Scotland, other parts of Europe, Morocco and Japan.

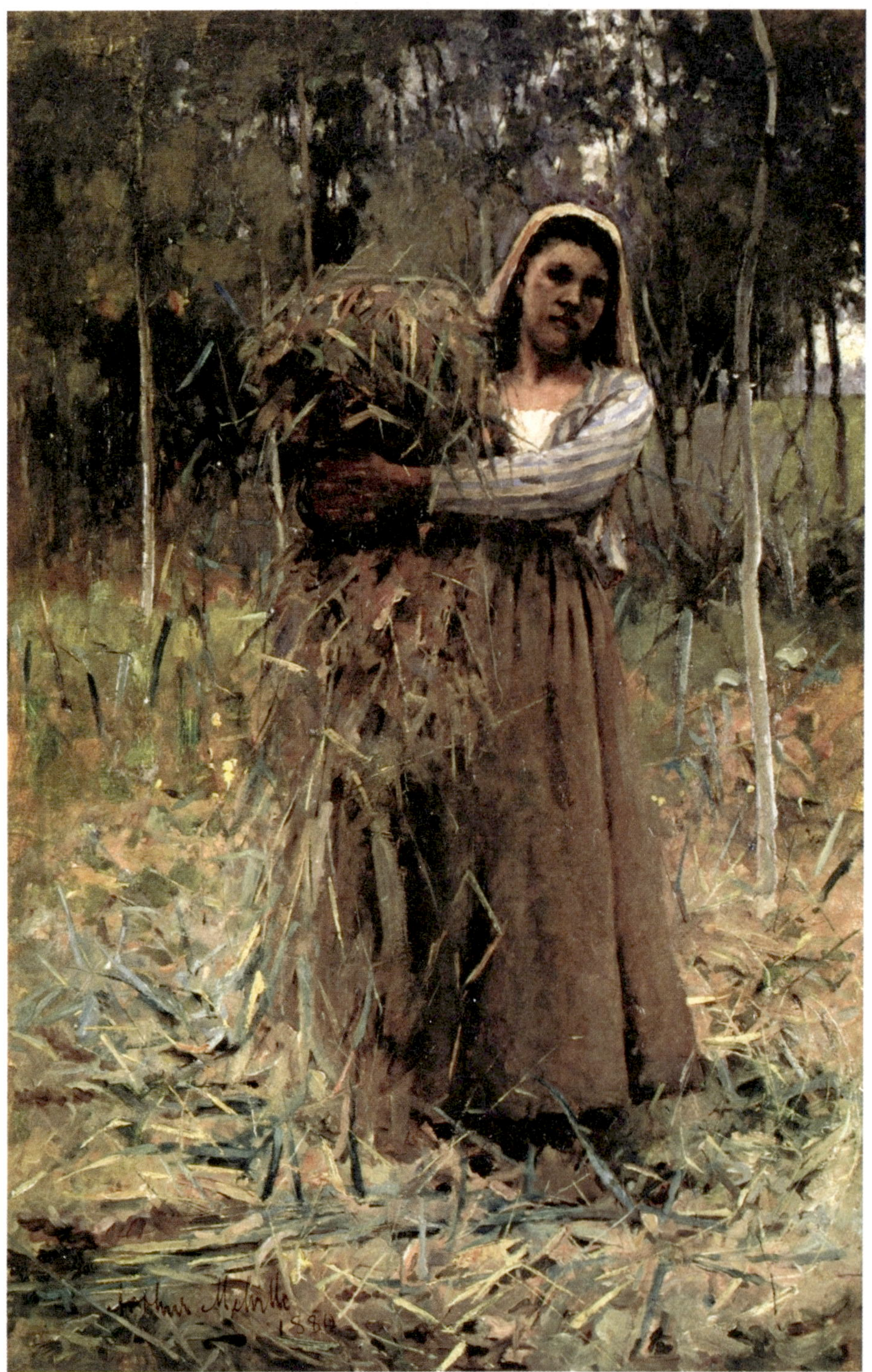

Arthur Melville (1855–1904)
Oil on canvas, 103 x 69 cm (40½ x 27 in)
• Falmouth Art Gallery, Cornwall

The Peasant Girl (The Faggot Collector), 1880 While he was at the artists' colony in Grez-sur-Loing, Melville frequently painted single peasant women at their daily tasks. This evolved mainly from the tuition he received from James Campbell Noble (1846–1913) at the RSA schools.

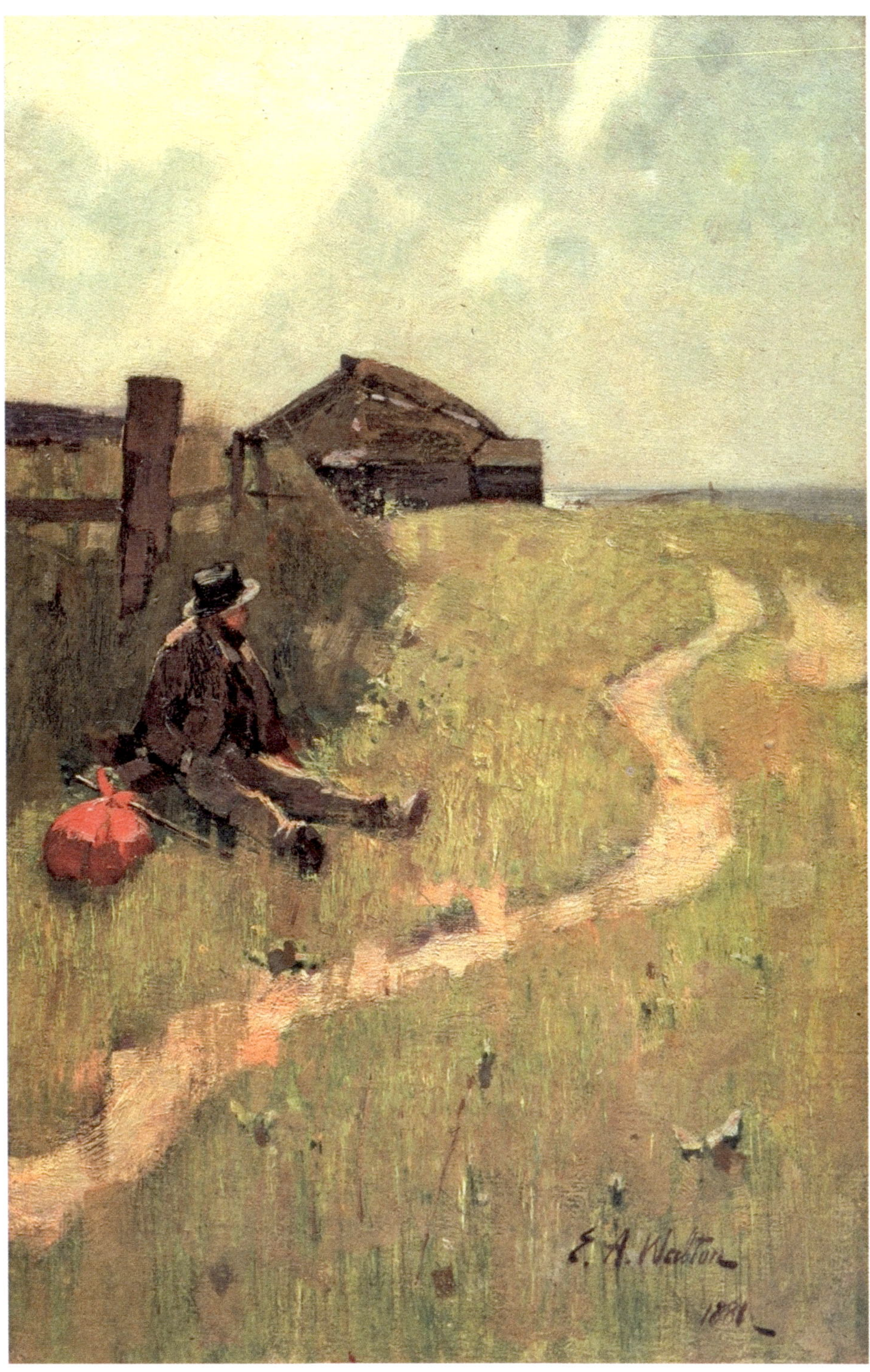

Edward Arthur Walton (1860–1922)
Oil on canvas, 46 x 30.5 cm (18 x 12 in) • Private collection

The Wayfarer, 1881 Painted during the summer of 1881, when Walton was staying in Brig o' Turk with Guthrie, Henry and Crawhall, this vivid composition is the result of their discussions about painting real life and the sighting of a wayfarer taking a rest in a field.

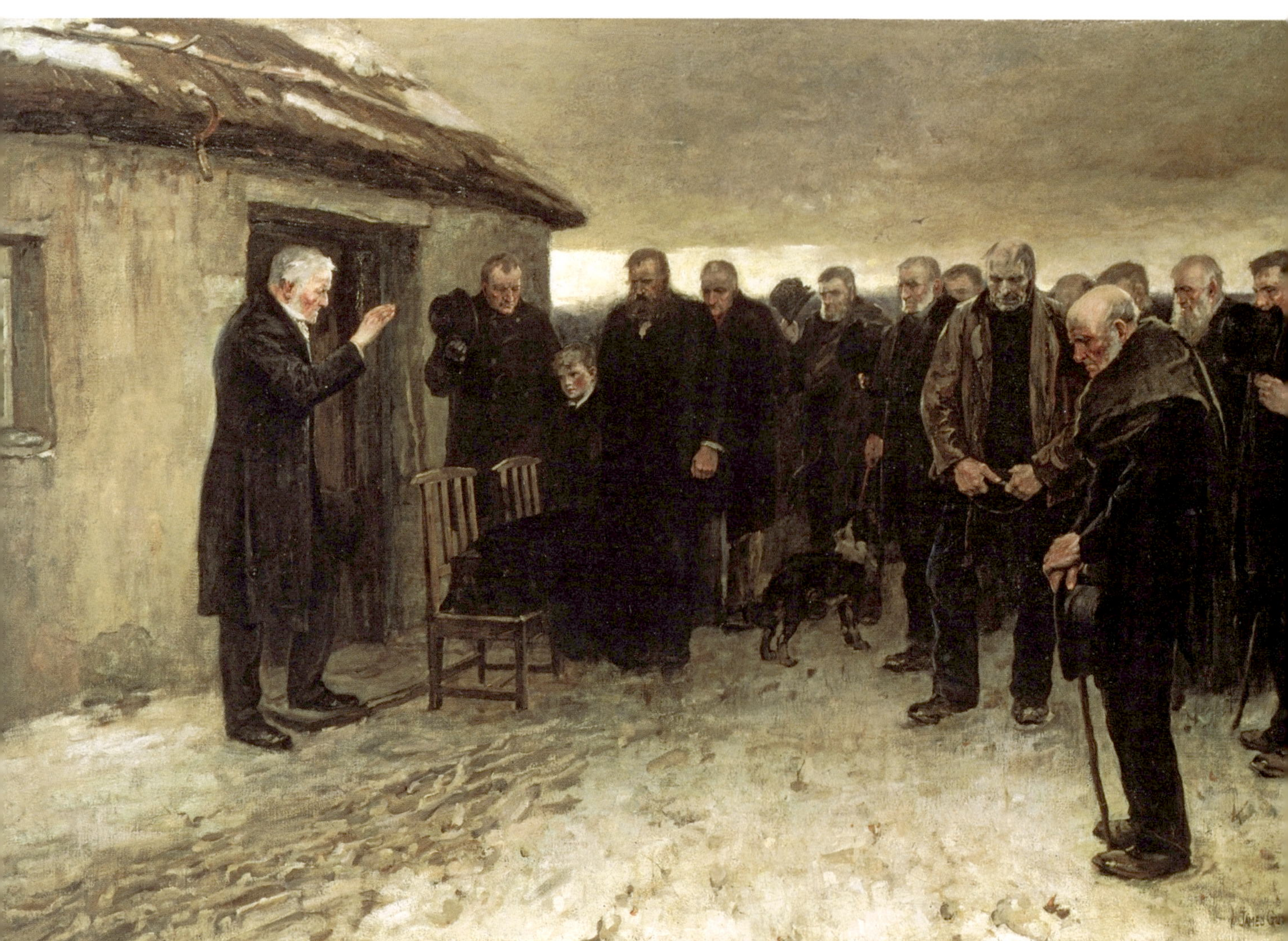

James Guthrie (1859–1930)
Oil on canvas, 129.5 x 193 cm (60 x 76 in)
• Kelvingrove Art Gallery and Museum, Glasgow

A Funeral Service in the Highlands, 1882 This complex and melancholy work depicts a child's funeral that Guthrie attended while staying at Brig o' Turk. The child had drowned and Guthrie made some drawings and sketches on the spot, then painted the work quickly, using local residents as models.

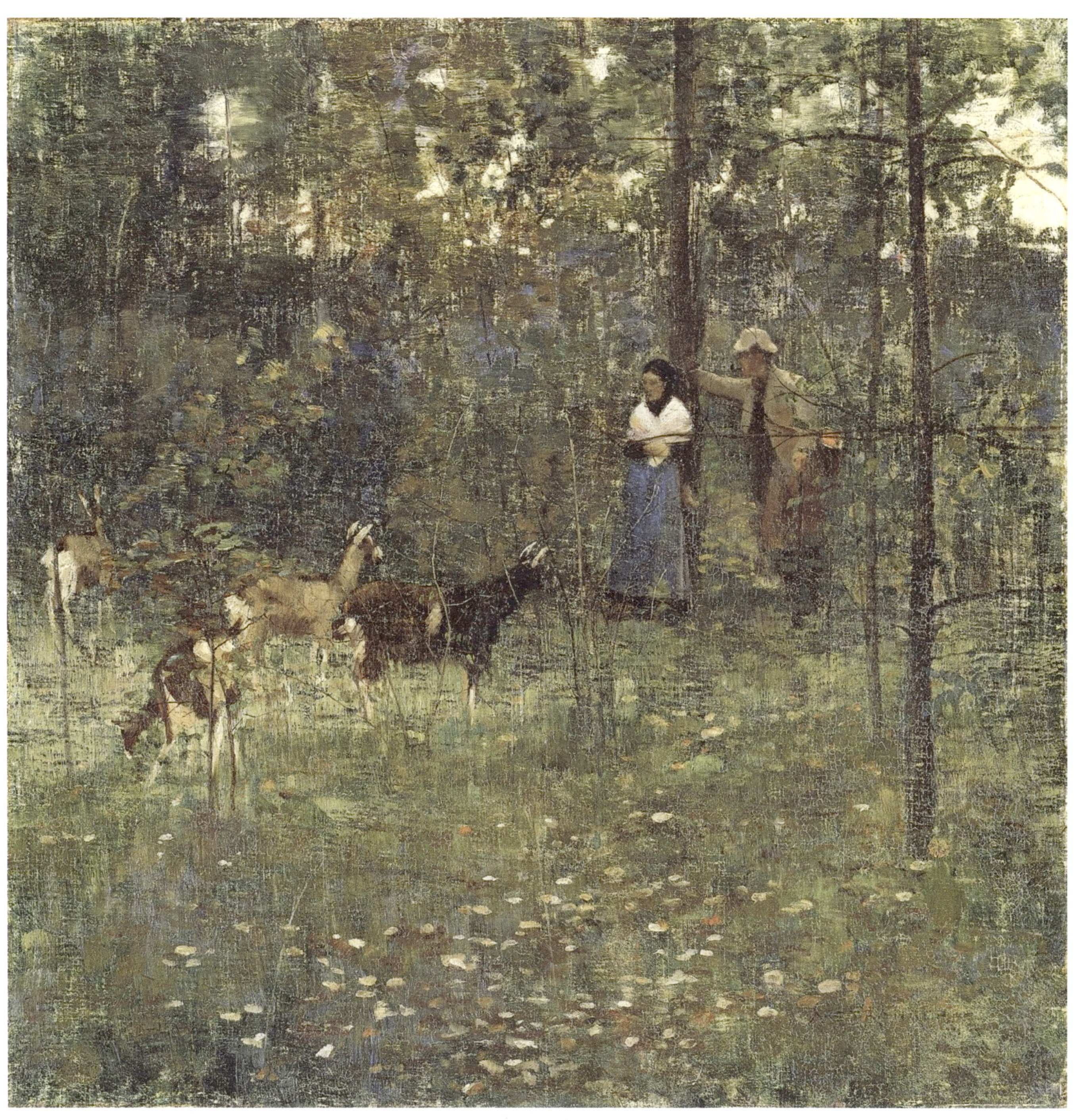

John Lavery (1856–1941)
Oil on canvas, 50 x 50 cm (19⅔ x 19⅔ in) • Private collection

A Stranger, 1883 Executed at Nogent-sur-Marne in the spring of 1883, this is the result of Lavery's study of the figure and his assimilation of the work of artists he admired, including Robert-Fleury, Bouguereau, Pierre Puvis de Chavannes (1824-98) and Bastien-Lepage.

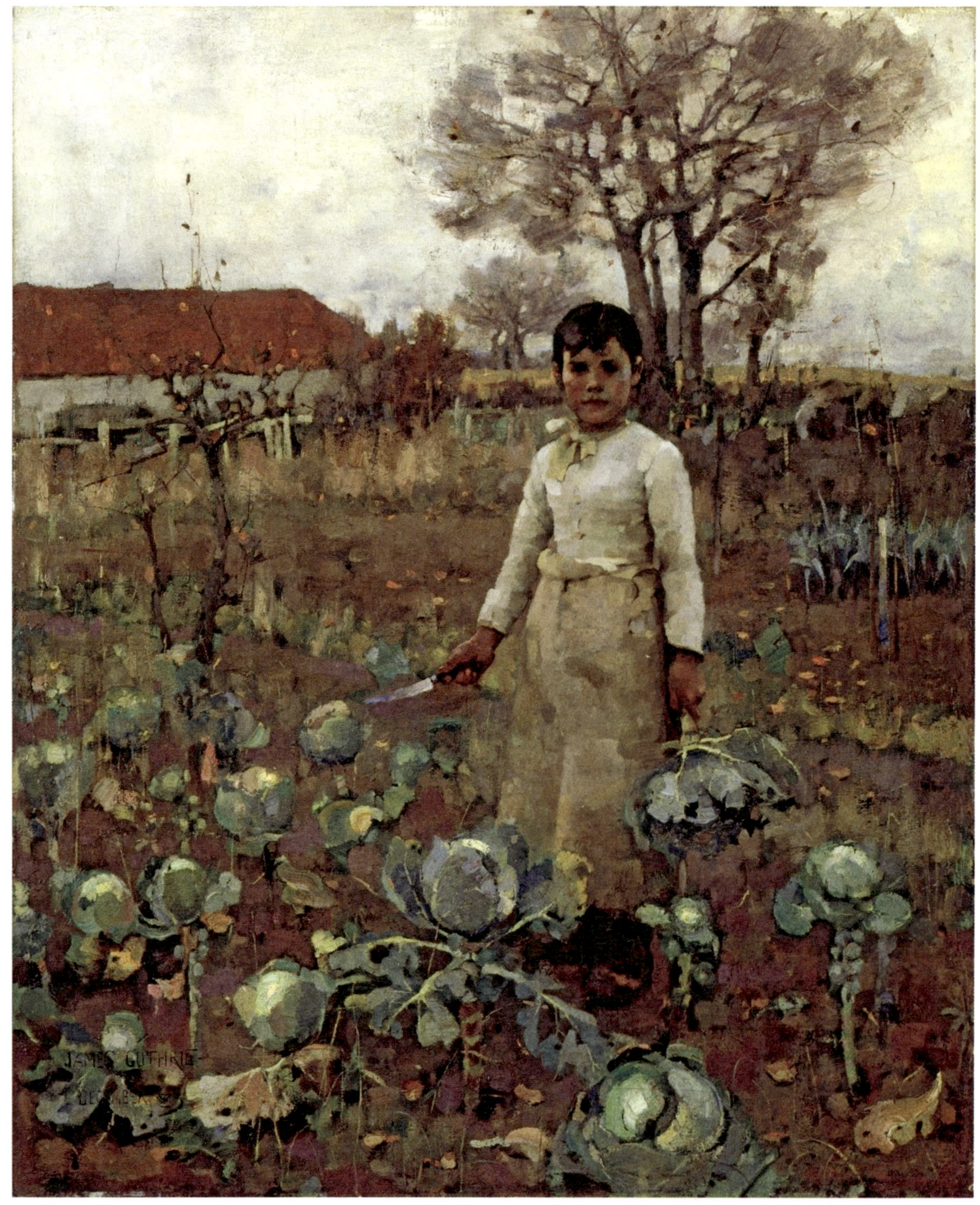

James Guthrie (1859–1930)
Oil on canvas, 91.5 x 76.2 cm (36 x 30 in)
• National Galleries of Scotland, Edinburgh

A Hind's Daughter, 1883 This was Guthrie's first major painting after moving to Cockburnspath.
A 'hind' was a skilled farmworker. This hind's daughter has just stood up after cutting cabbage.
Earth colours and square brushstrokes evolved from Guthrie's admiration of Bastien-Lepage.

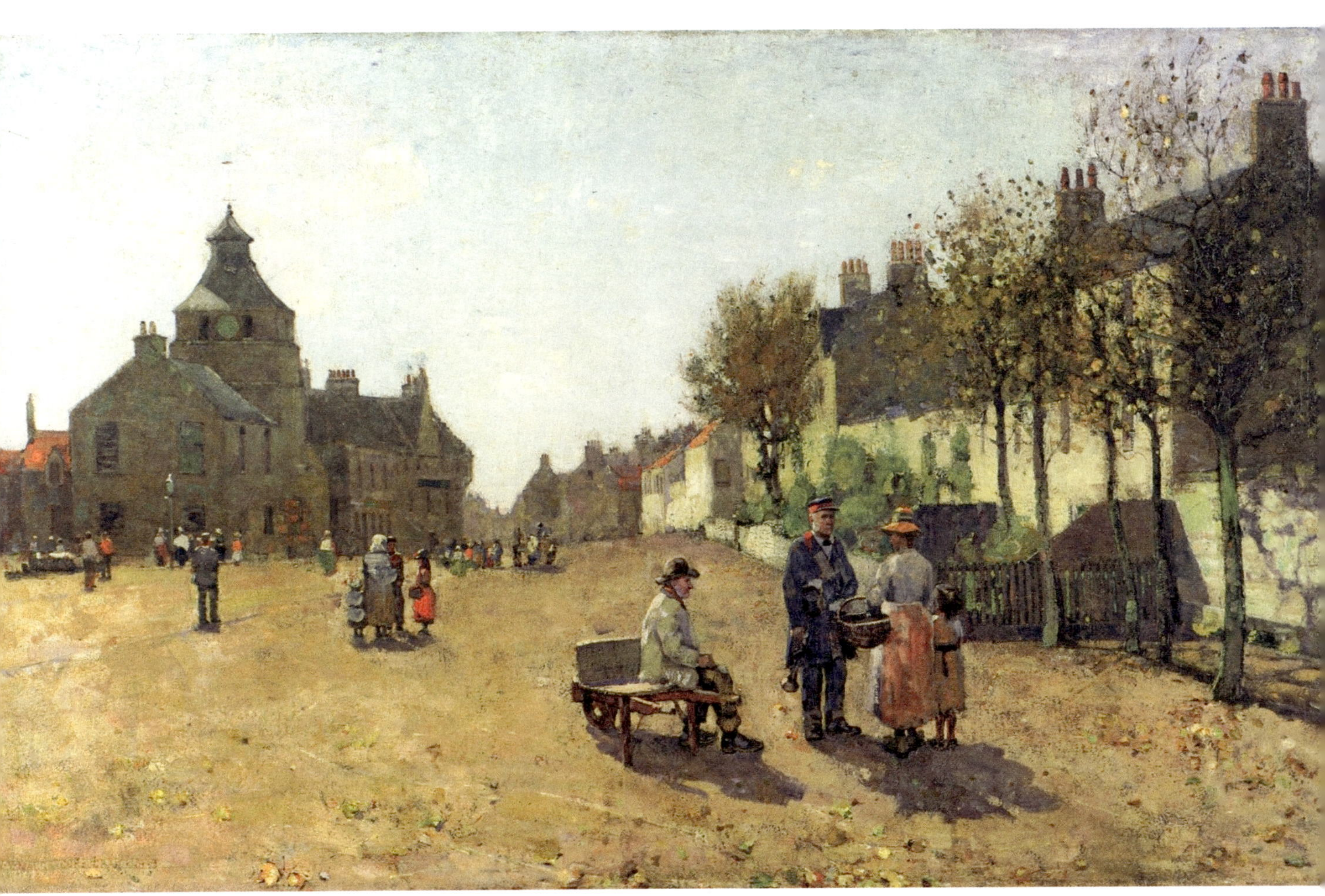

William York Macgregor (1855–1923)
Oil on canvas, 91 x 150 cm (35⅘ x 59 in)
• The Stirling Smith Art Gallery and Museum, Stirling

Crail, Fife, 1883 Produced while Macgregor was living in Crail, this shows how he used ideas from others, but made them his own. As well as being inspired by Bastien-Lepage, he blended other ideas and often painted images, as here, in direct sunlight.

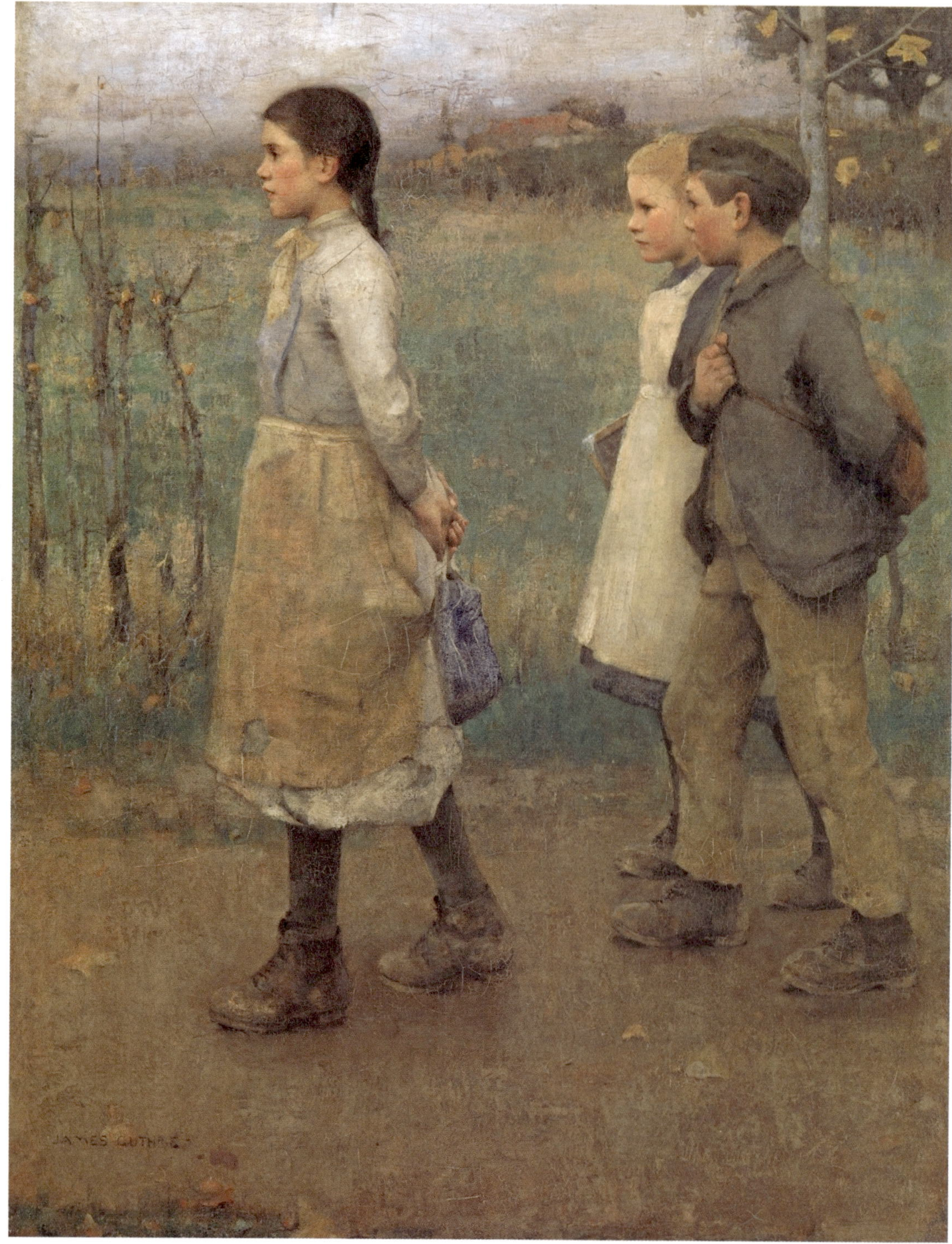

James Guthrie (1859–1930)
Tempera on canvas, 118.2 x 91.6 cm (46½ x 30 in)
• Museum voor Schone Kunsten, Ghent

Schoolmates, 1884–85 Guthrie made numerous oil sketches and drawings in preparation for this painting of children in Cockburnspath, which he intended to enter for the Glasgow Institute's 1885 annual exhibition, but he did not complete it in time.

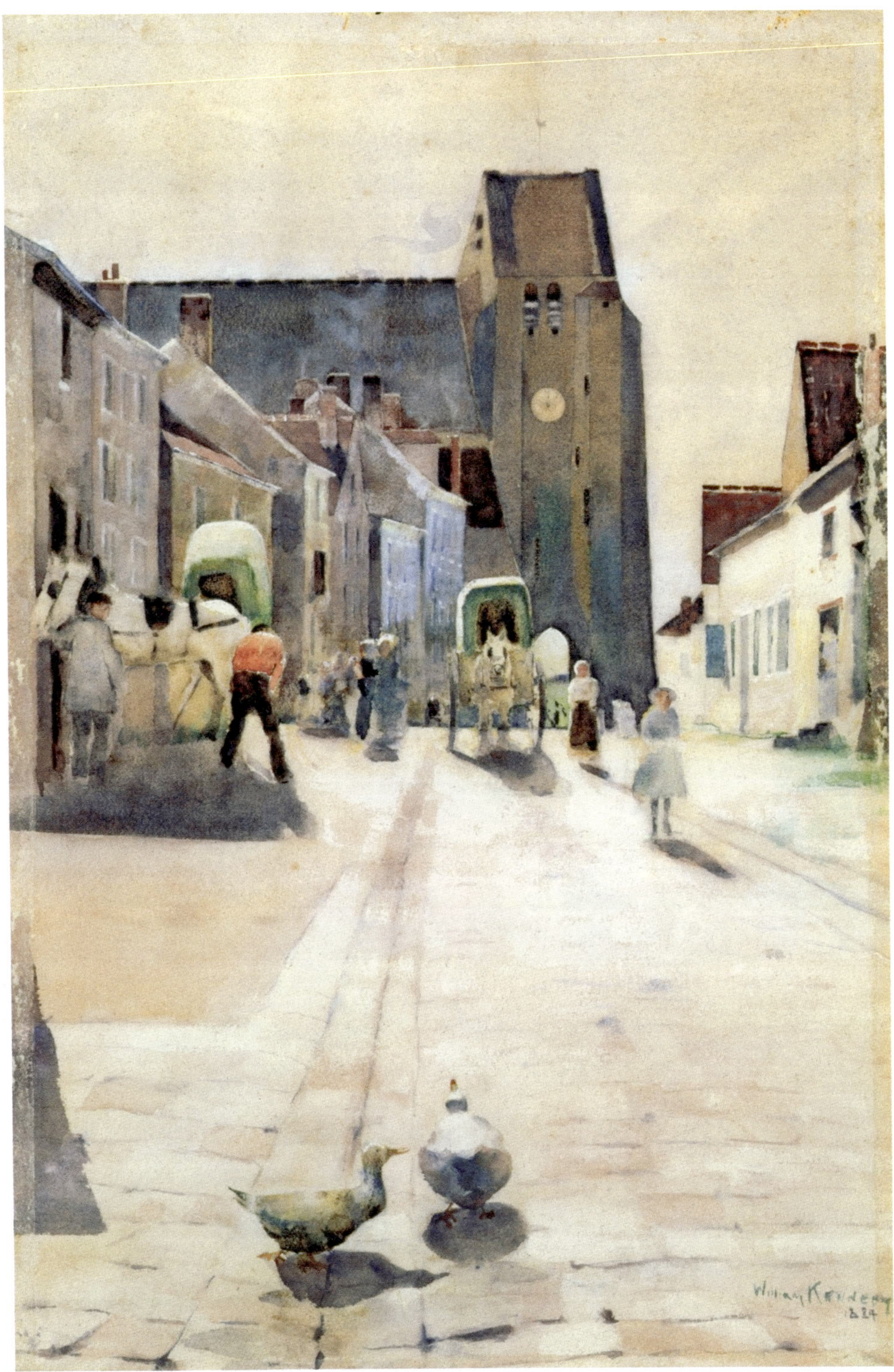

William Kennedy (1859–1918)
Watercolour on paper, dimensions unknown
• Private collection

The Main Street, Grez-sur-Loing, 1884 With no soft focus in the background, as in Realist paintings, Kennedy painted this with sharp attention to every part of the scene. The image of a street, built up with blocks of colour, appears almost abstract.

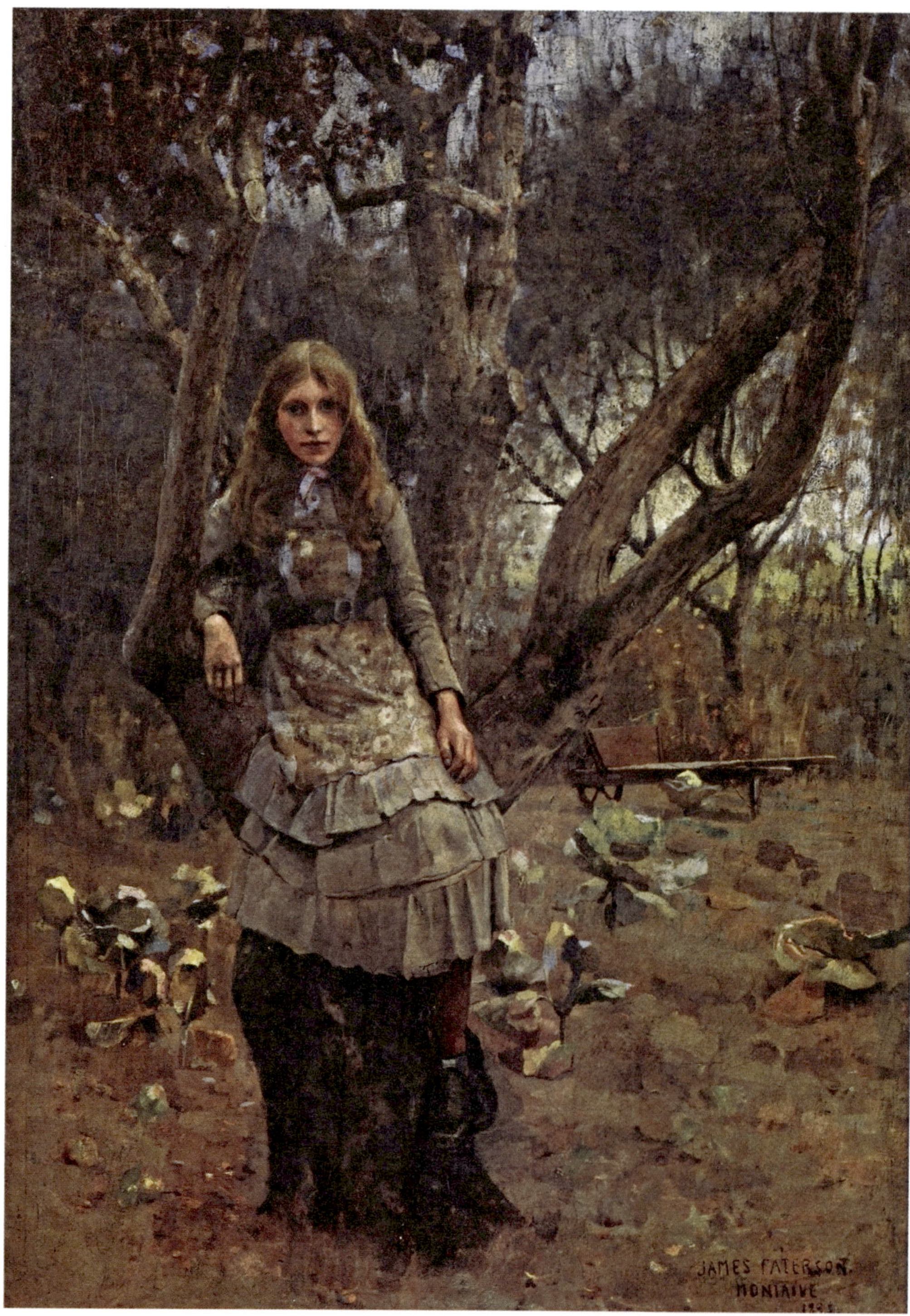

Jarnes Paterson (1854–1932)
Oil on canvas, 107 x 84.5 cm (42 x 33¼ in)
• The Ellis Campbell Collection

The Old Apple Tree, Moniaive, 1884–85 A girl leans on a tree, looking directly at viewers. Using techniques learned in France, Paterson based this picture on a classical composition and applied varied brushmarks and extra details in the foreground.

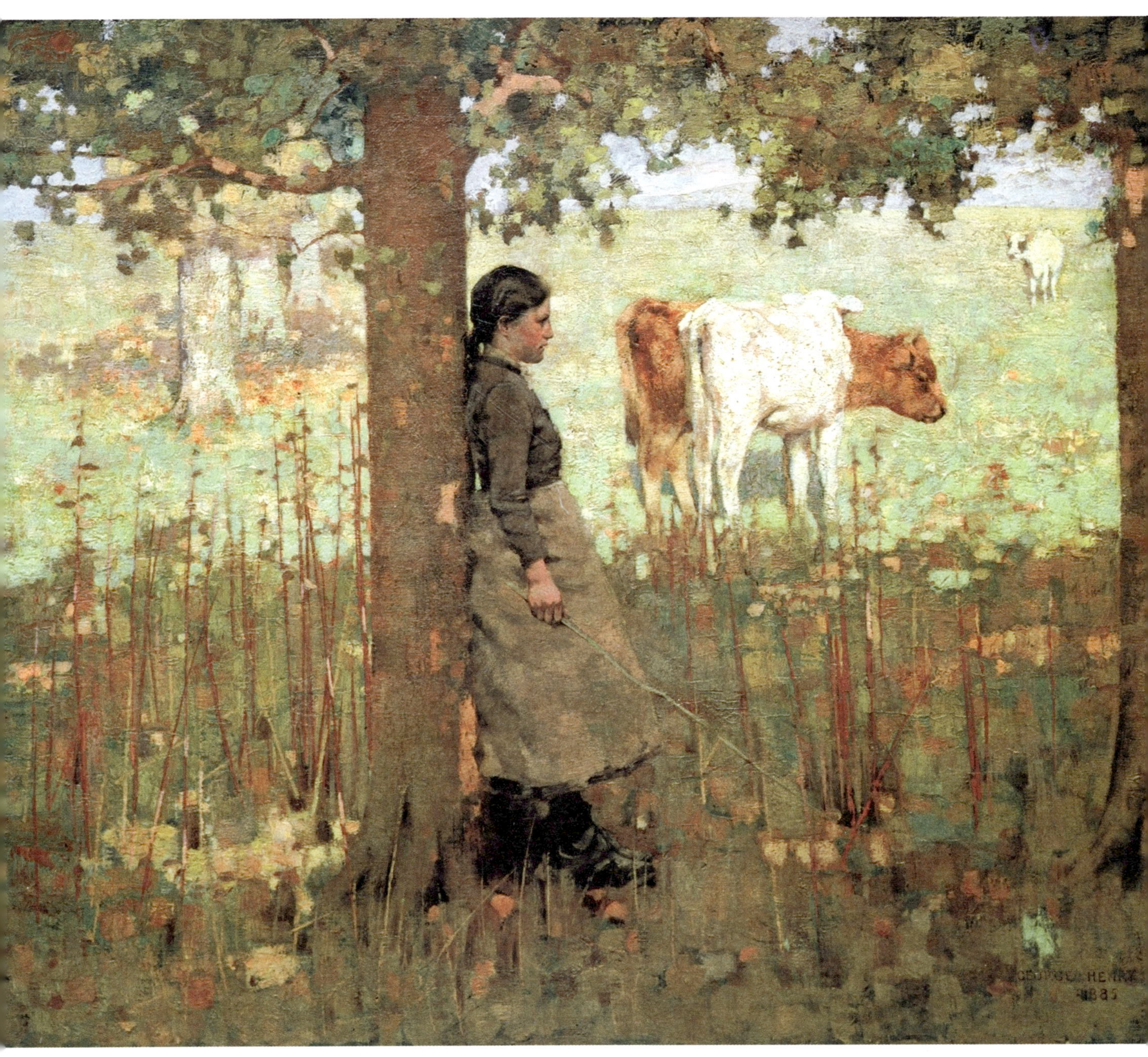

George Henry (1858–1943)
Oil on canvas, 107 x 84.5 cm (42 x 33¼ in) • Private collection

Noon, 1885 Created with slabs of colour, sometimes applied with brushes and sometimes
with palette knives, this image of a girl taking shade under a tree in a shimmering field shows
Henry's keen interest in pattern and the texture of paint.

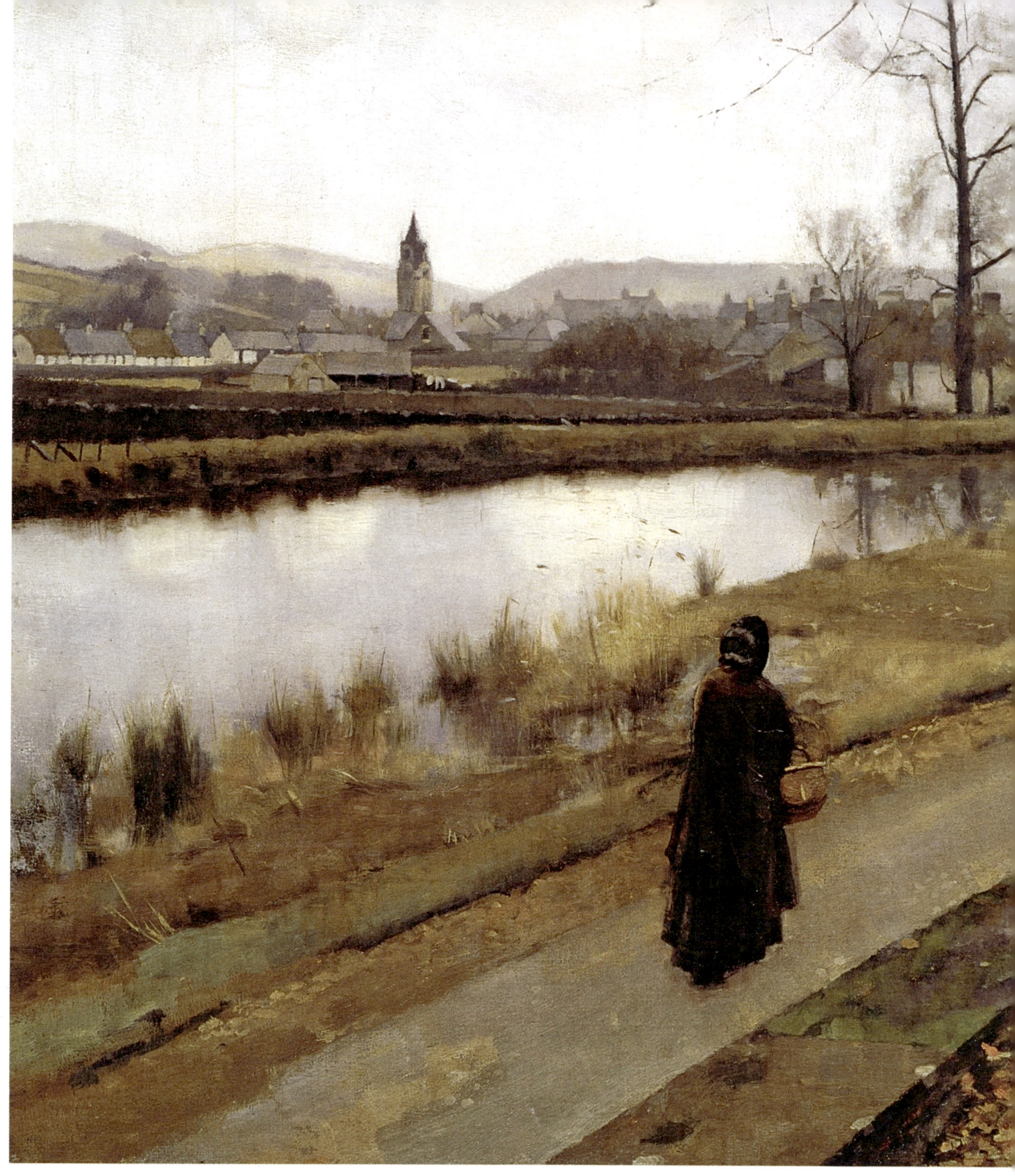

James Paterson (1854–1932)

Oil on canvas, 61.3 x 91.4 cm (24 x 36 in)

• Kelvingrove Art Gallery and Museum, Glasgow

The Last Turning, Winter, 1885 A woman walks along a riverbank towards Moniaive. Paterson's naturalistic style, with strong tonal contrasts, evolved during his years in France, where he studied the work of artists such as Corot, Daubigny, Courbet and Bastien-Lepage.

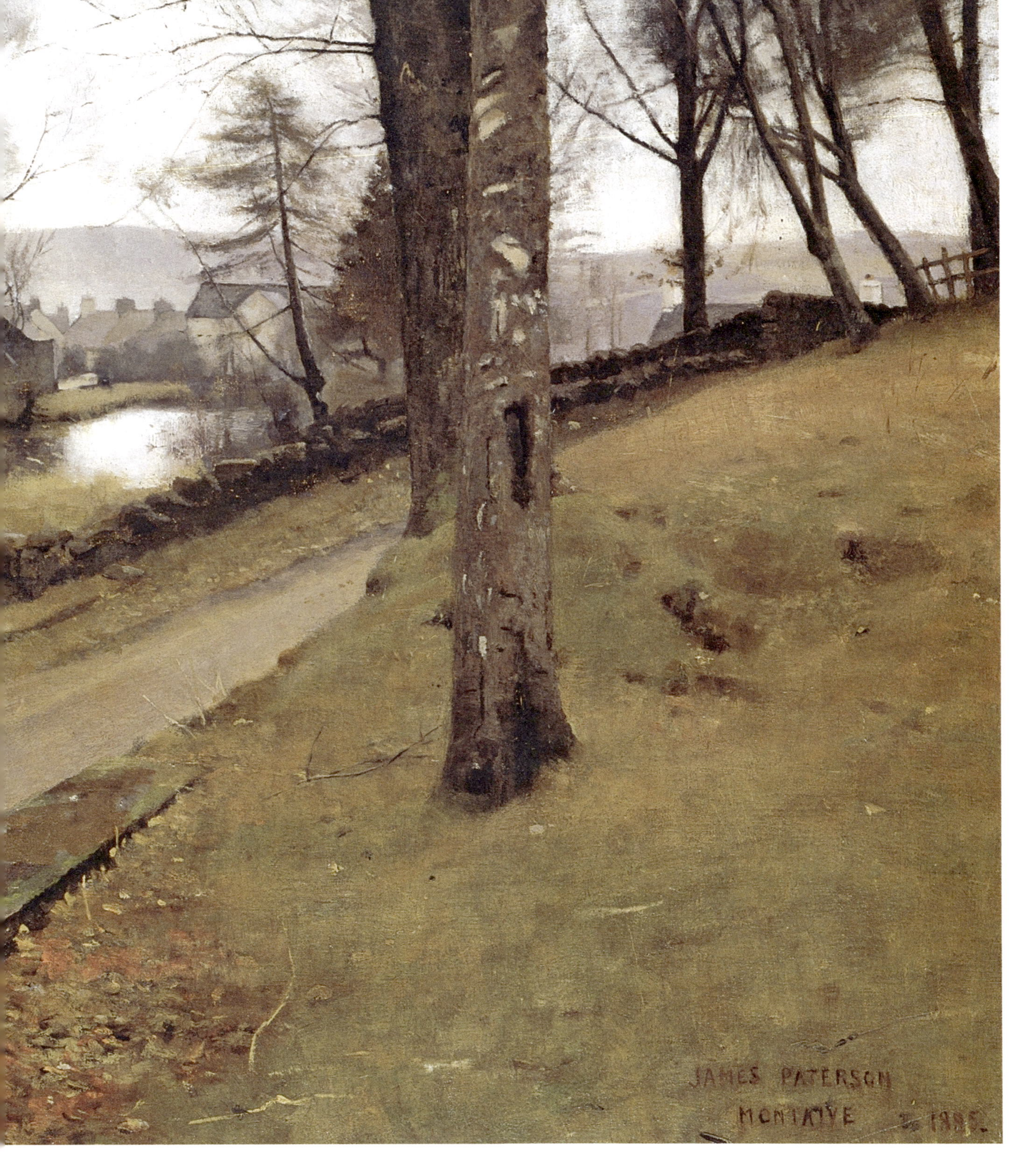

JAMES PATERSON
MONIAIVE   1885

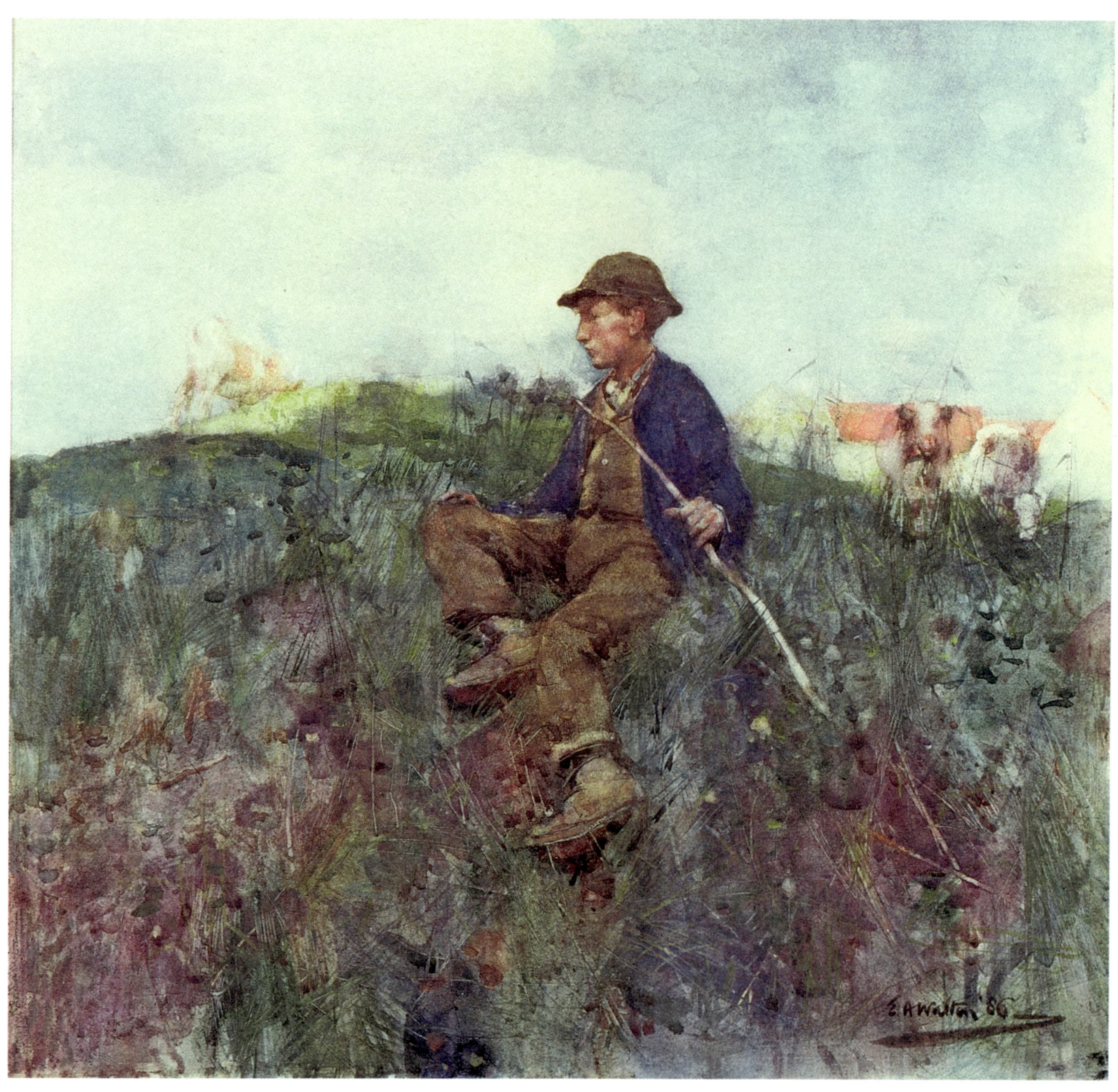

Edward Arthur Walton (1860–1922)
Watercolour with touches of gouache and scraping out on paper,
53.5 x 57 cm (21 x 22⅖ in) • National Galleries of Scotland, Edinburgh

The Herd Boy, 1886 Walton once went to a fancy dress party as the Japanese printmaker
Katsushika Hokusai (1760–1849). Painted from sketches made in Cockburnspath, this
work also shows his admiration of *ukiyo-e* art, emphasizing pattern and colour.

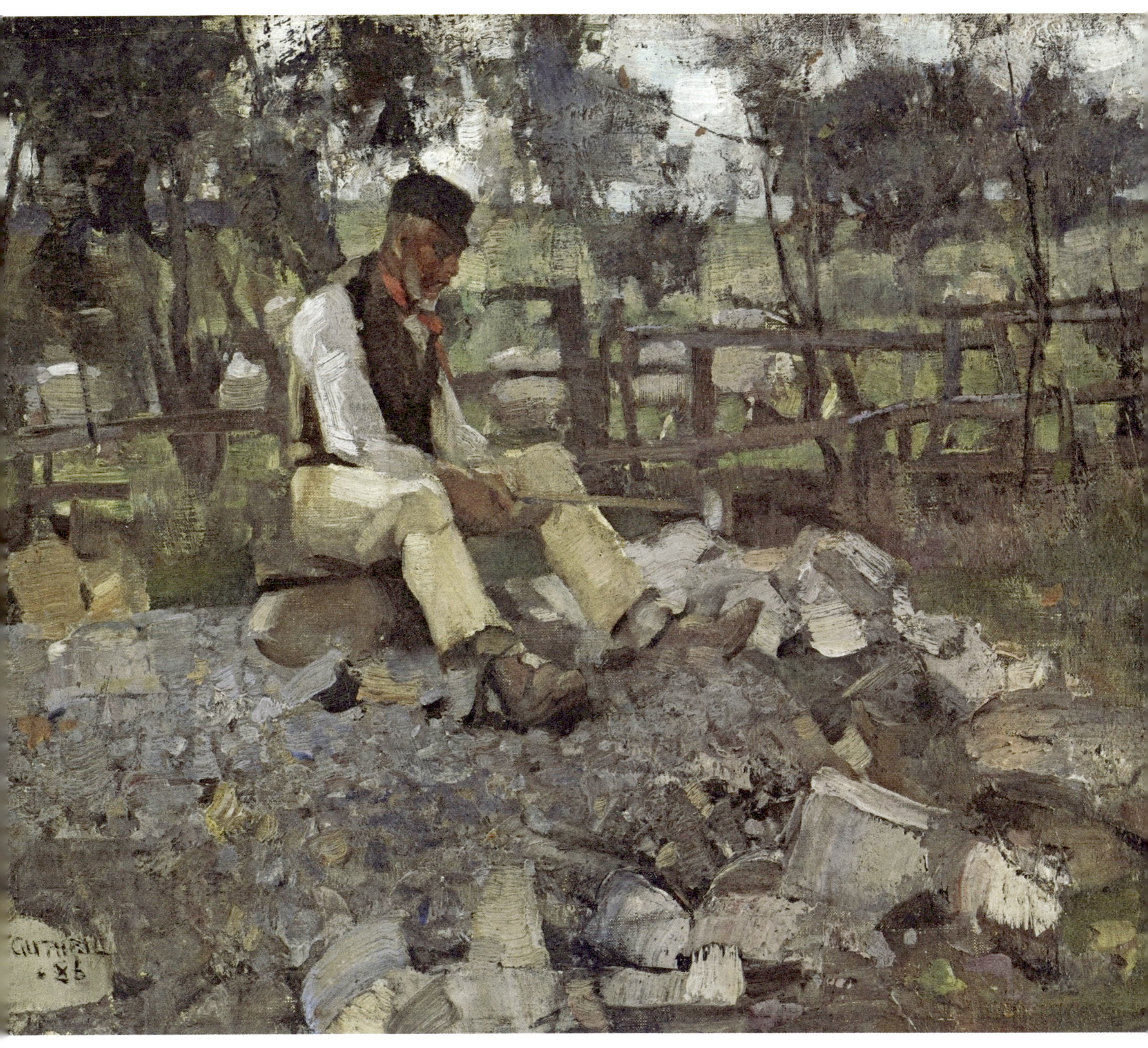

James Guthrie (1859–1930)
Oil on canvas, 30.5 x 38.1 cm (12 x 15 in) • Private collection

The Stone Breaker, 1886 Originally, Guthrie painted this stone breaker talking to a passing farm hand, but in 1923 he cut down the painting. He had witnessed Bastien-Lepage teaching his 'square-brush' technique in 1882, and Guthrie used it from then on.

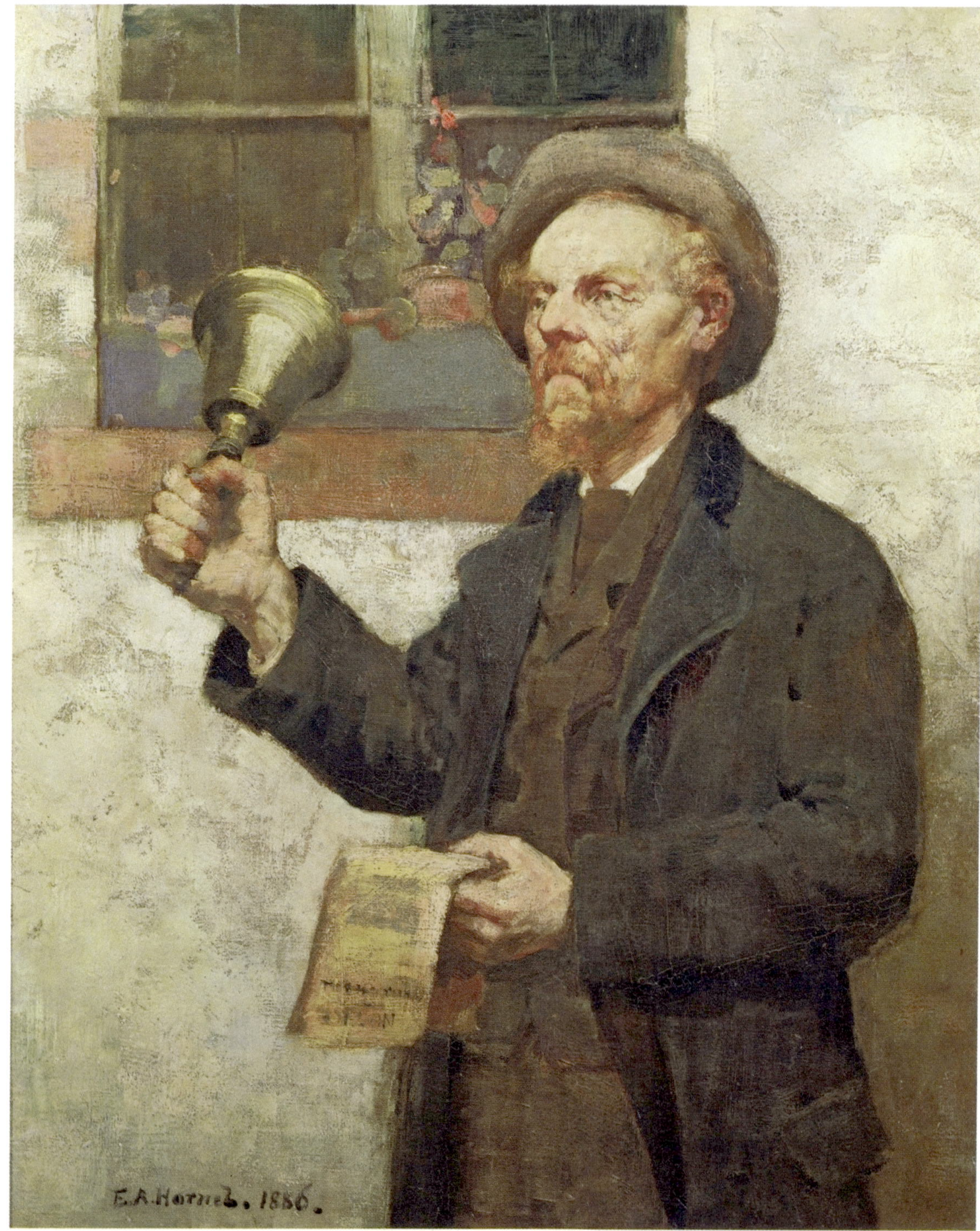

E.A. Hornel (1864–1933)
Oil on canvas, 61 x 50.8 cm (24 x 20 in)
• The Fleming-Wyfold Art Foundation, London

The Bellman, 1886 For most of his life, Hornel lived in Kirkcudbright, where this town crier was a common sight. Although, by now, Hornel was beginning to use elements of Japanese design, this follows his earlier style, showing the influence of Maris, Daubigny and Rousseau.

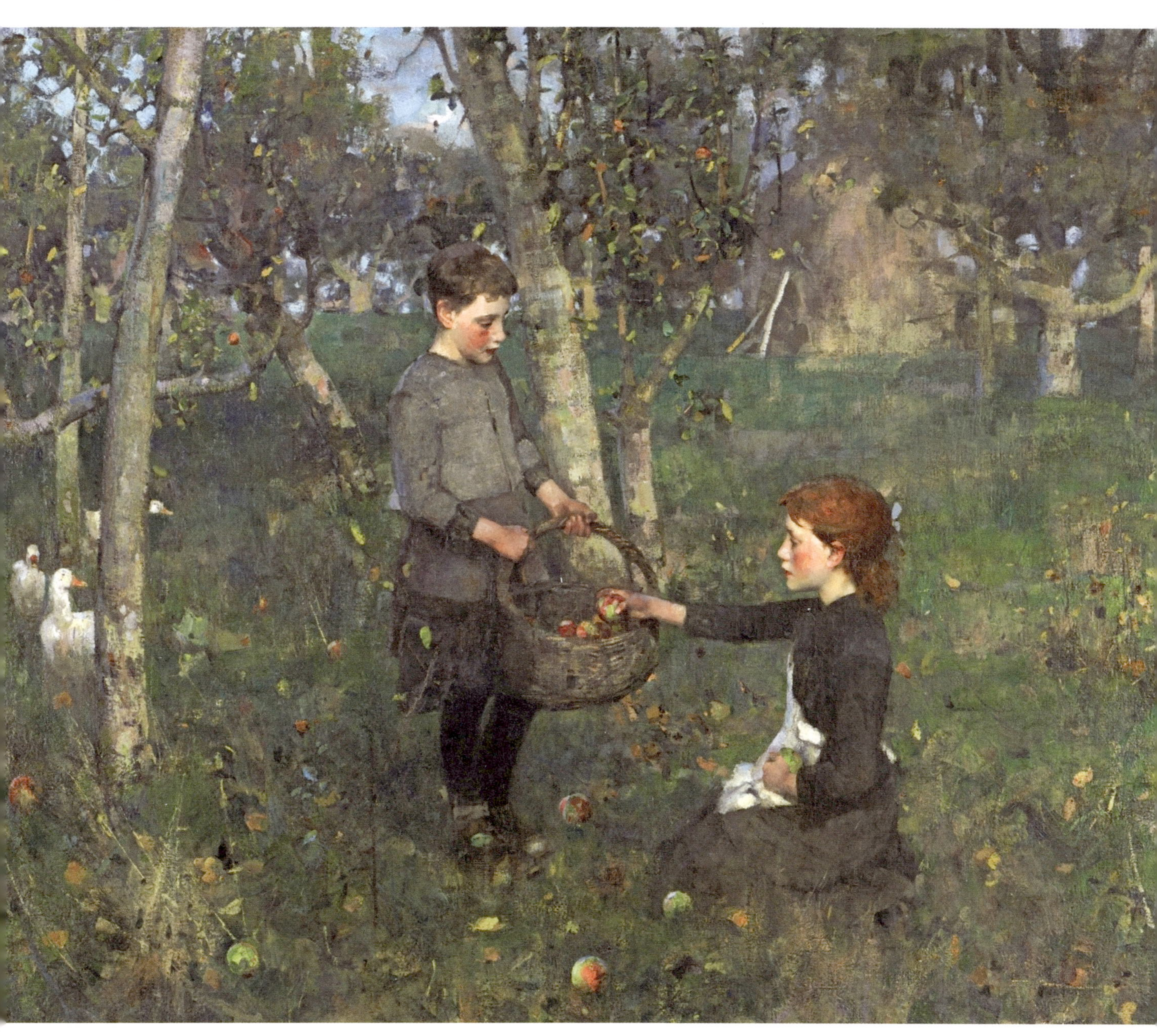

James Guthrie (1859–1930)
Oil on canvas, 152 x 178 cm (59⅗ x 70 in)
• National Galleries of Scotland, Edinburgh

In the Orchard, 1886 A boy and girl collect windfall apples in a sunlit orchard. Guthrie painted this in Cockburnspath, but because it was so large – unusual for such an ordinary subject – he also worked on it in Glasgow and Kirkcudbright.

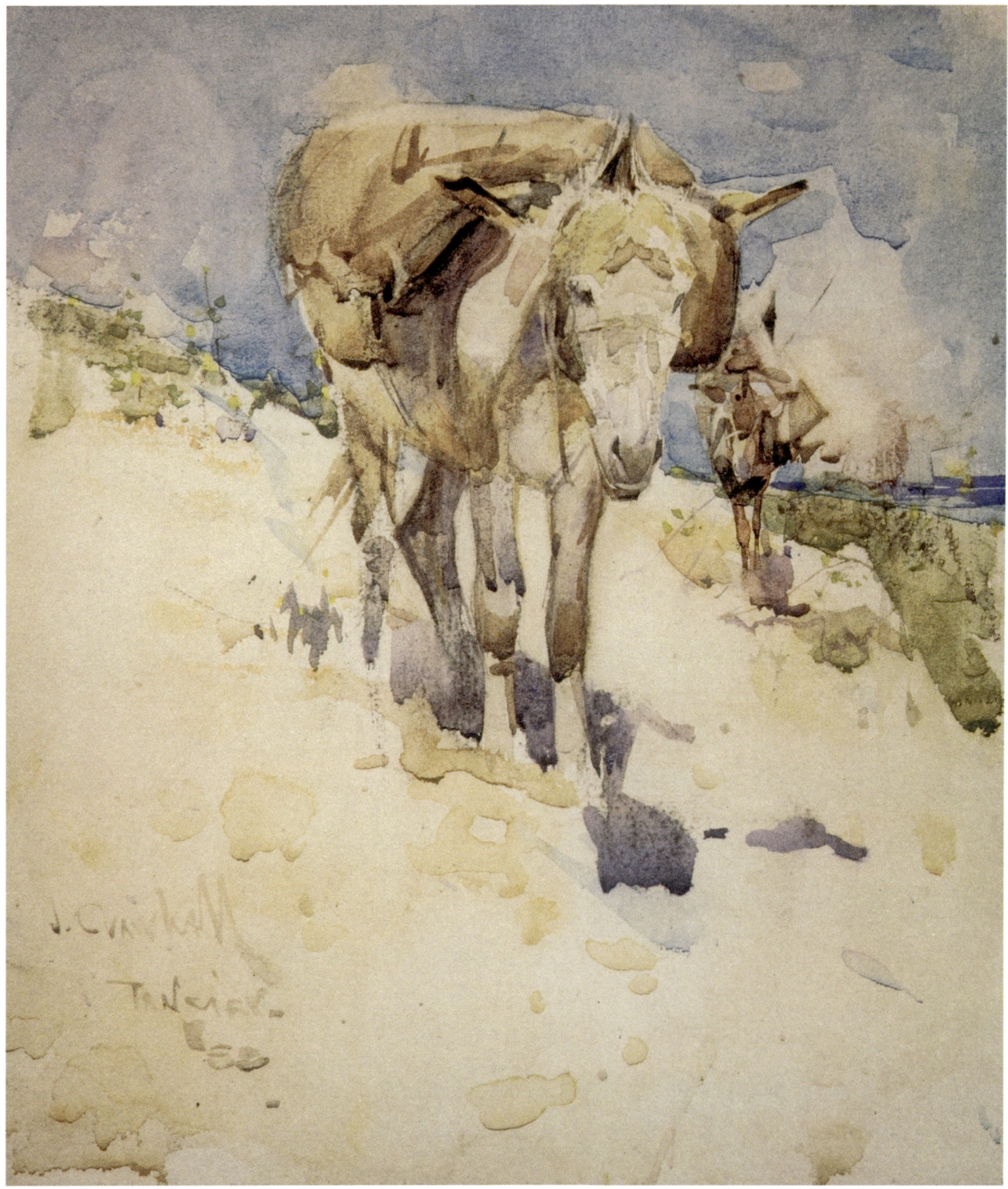

Joseph Crawhall (1861–1913)
Watercolour on paper, 25 x 28 cm (9⅘ x 11 in) • Berwick-upon-Tweed
Borough Museum and Art Gallery, Northumberland

Tangier, 1887 Quite early in his career, Crawhall began painting in watercolour, influenced by Melville but using his own original techniques. On his visit to Tangier in 1884, he depicted these donkeys surrounded by vivid sunlight and deep shadows.

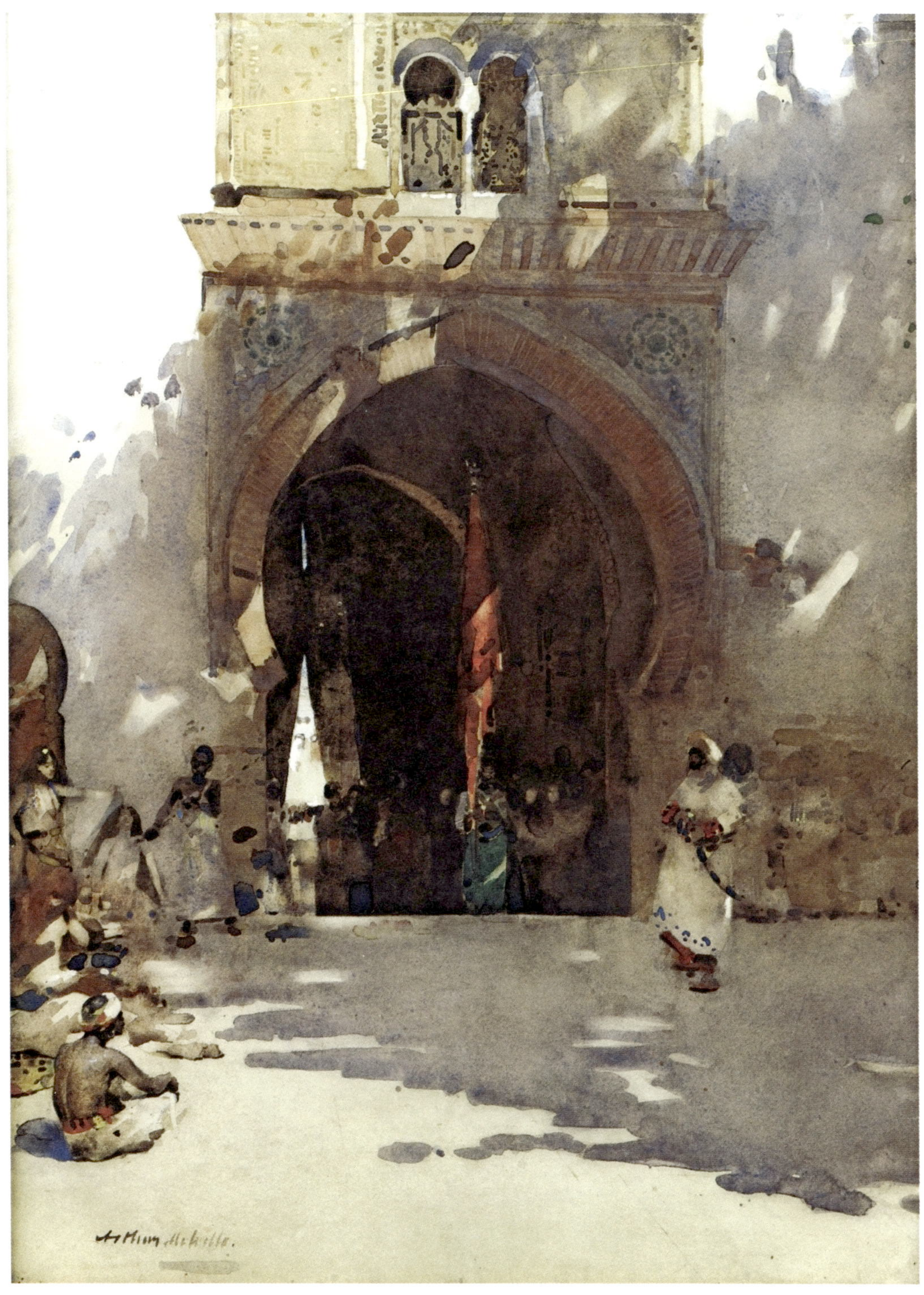

Arthur Melville (1855–1904)
Watercolour on paper, 68.6 x 50.8 cm (27 x 20 in)
• The Ellis Campbell Collection

The Procession, *c.* 1887 A remarkable watercolourist, Melville added dry pigment to wet paper, creating blurred edges, and added accents of pure ultramarine to suggest cool shadows under the arch, from where a procession emerges into the brilliant sunlight.

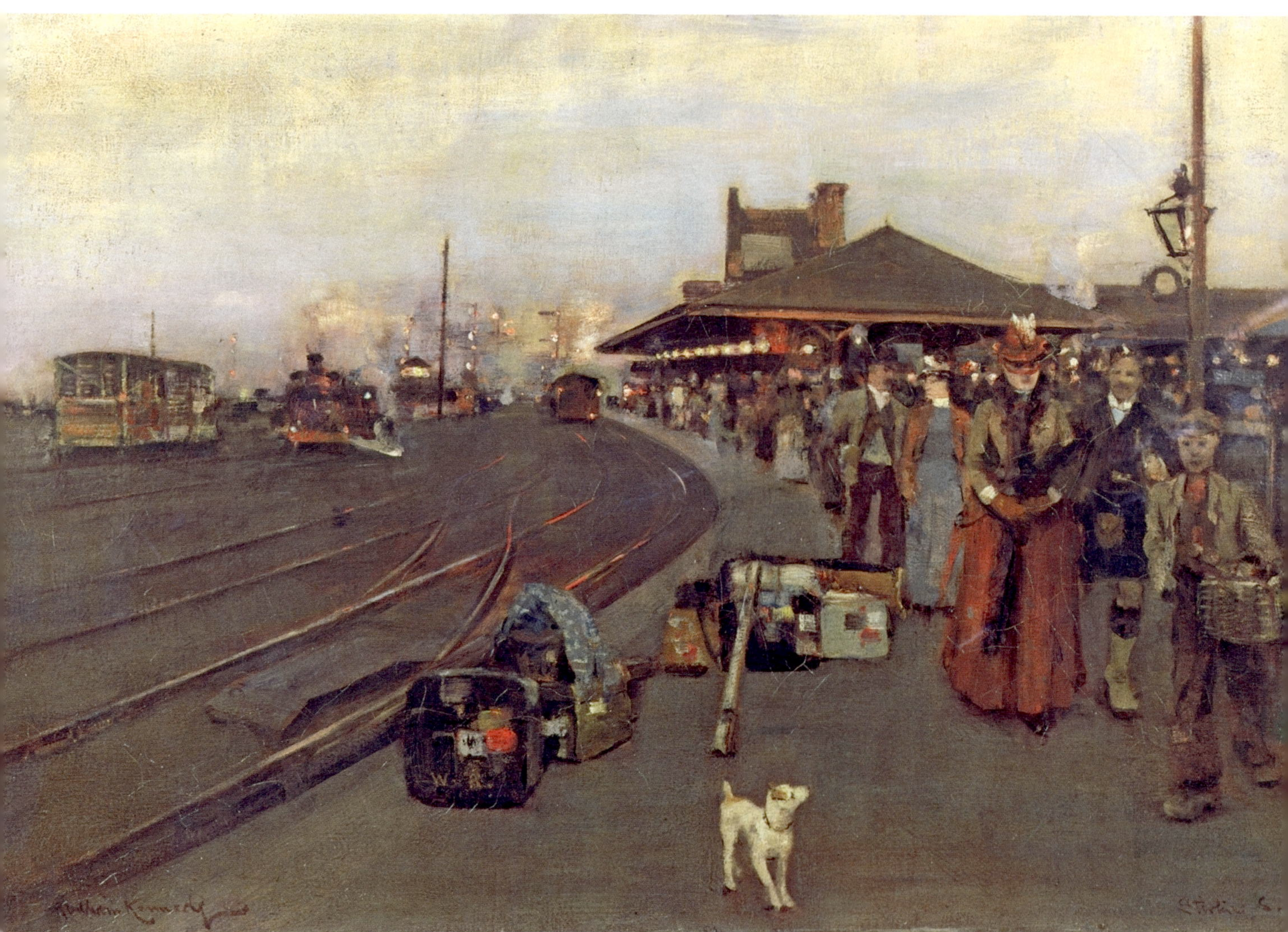

William Kennedy (1859–1918)
Oil on canvas, 52.8 x 79 cm (20¾ x 31 in) • Private collection

Stirling Station, 1888 Influenced by Whistler's 'Nocturnes' and the paintings by Claude Monet (1840–1926) of Gare Saint-Lazare, this depicts modern life – Stirling Station in gathering dusk. The curving platform is crowded, and smoke puffs out of distant locomotives.

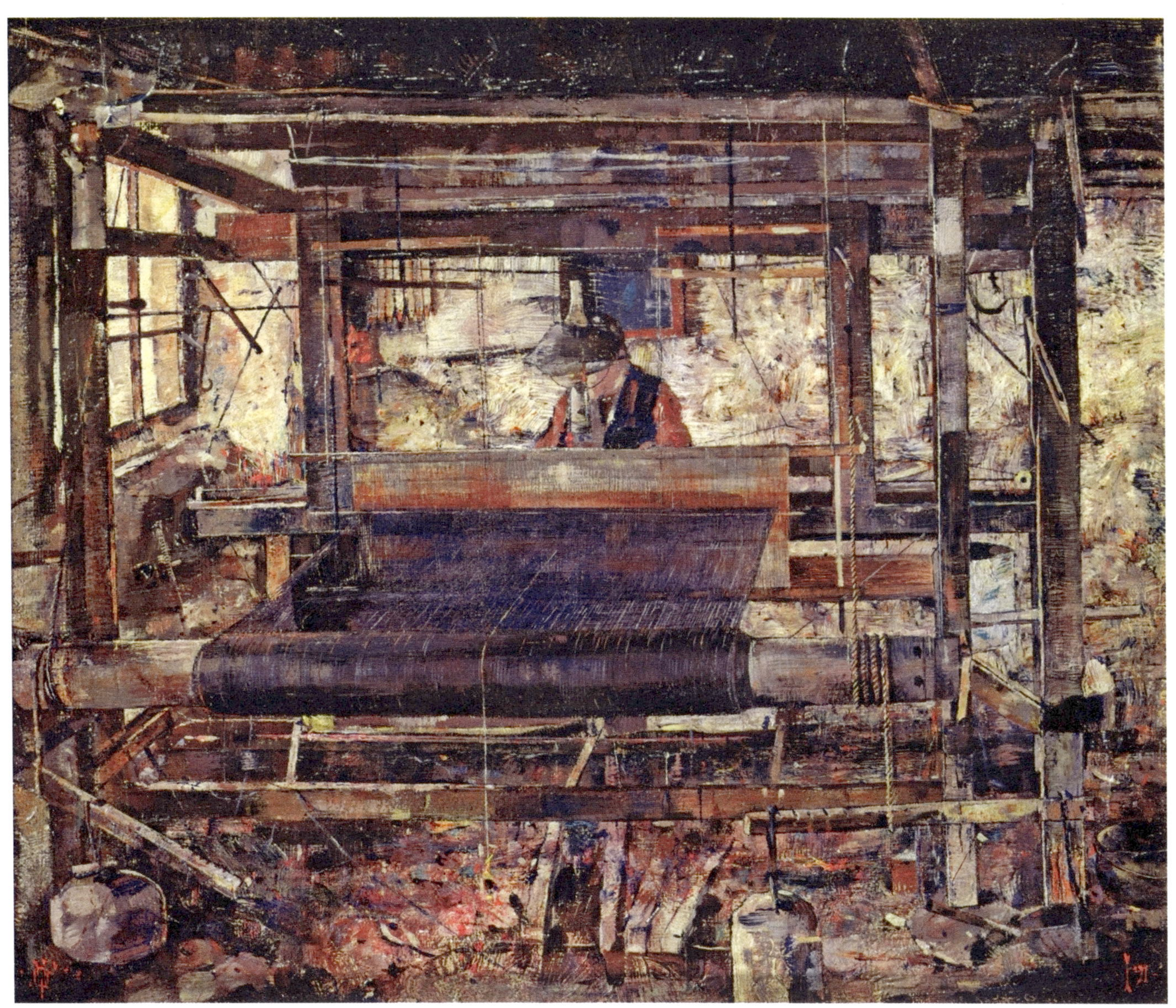

John Quinton Pringle (1864–1925)
Oil on canvas, 30.7 x 37.5 cm (12 x 14¾ in)
• City of Edinburgh Museums and Art Galleries, Edinburgh

The Loom, 1891 This was meticulously painted by Pringle in the year he won the South Kensington National Competition for life drawing. Working in two-hour sessions, the painting, which shows one of the last looms in Glasgow, took him three months to finish.

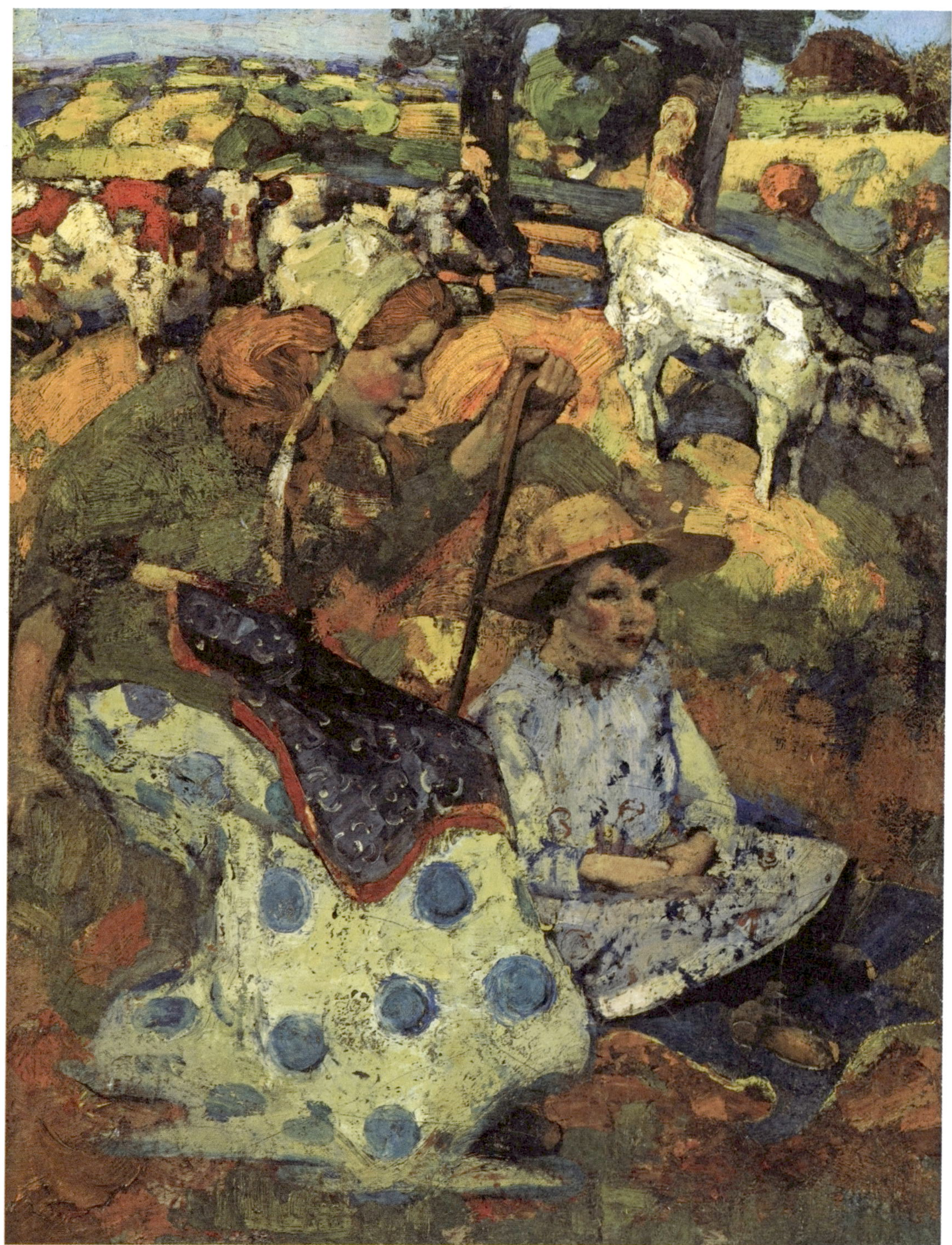

E.A. Hornel (1864–1933)
Oil on canvas, 50.8 x 40.6 cm (20 x 16 in)
• The Ellis Campbell Collection

In Galloway, the Cowherd, *c.* 1890–91 By the 1890s, three years before he went to Japan, Hornel began painting with decorative patches of colour, emphasizing the flatness of the canvas, showing a strong influence of Japanese *ukiyo-e* art. This decade saw him gaining greater recognition.

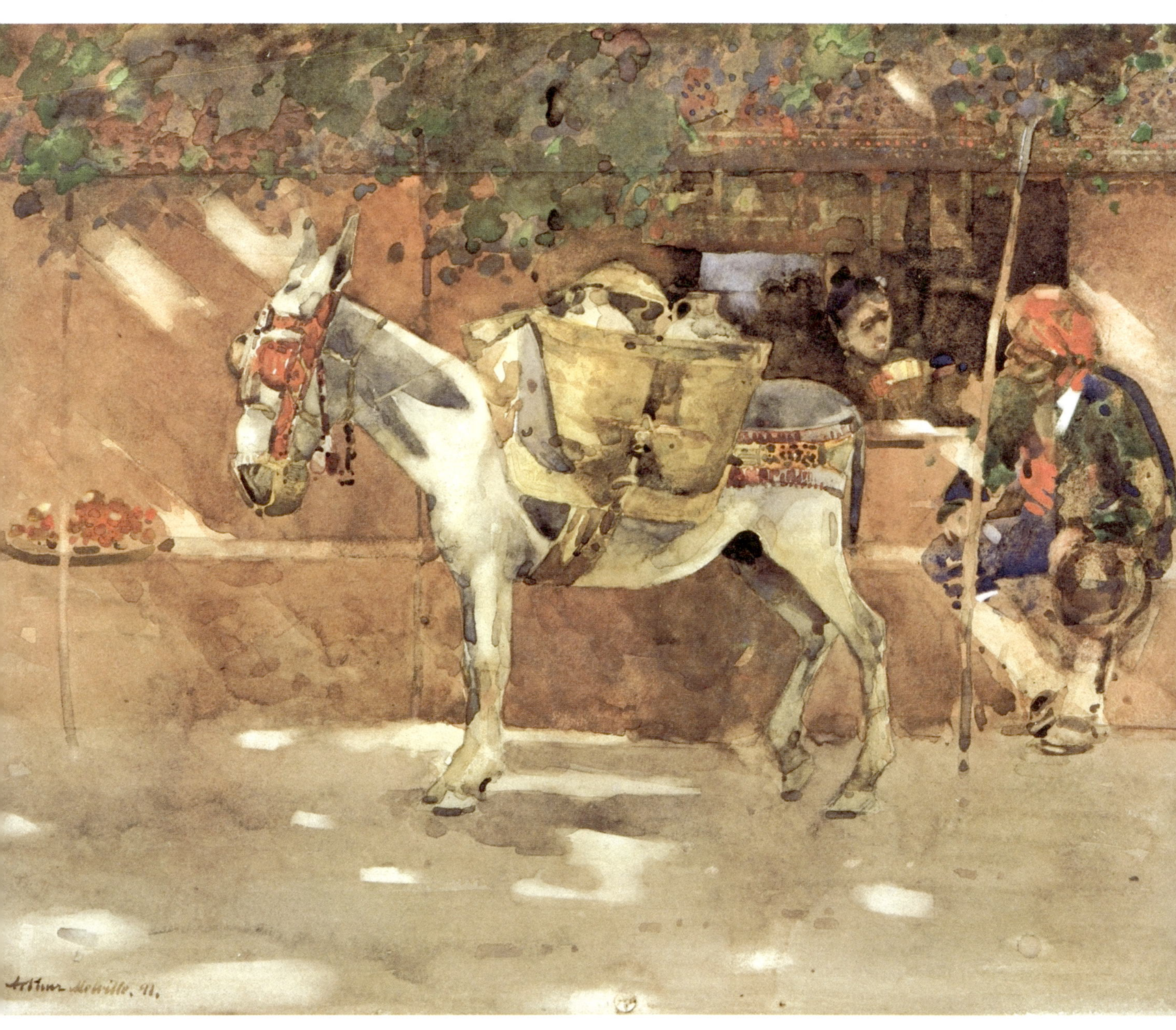

Arthur Melville (1855–1904)
Watercolour on paper, 64.4 x 74 cm (25⅓ x 29 in)
• The Hunterian Art Gallery, Glasgow

A Byway in Granada, 1891 Here, Melville applied wet colour with vigorous brushstrokes,
blotting excess pigment with a sponge. In six visits to Spain, from 1890–99, he used watercolour
to explore ways of capturing the intense colours, blazing light and shimmering heat.

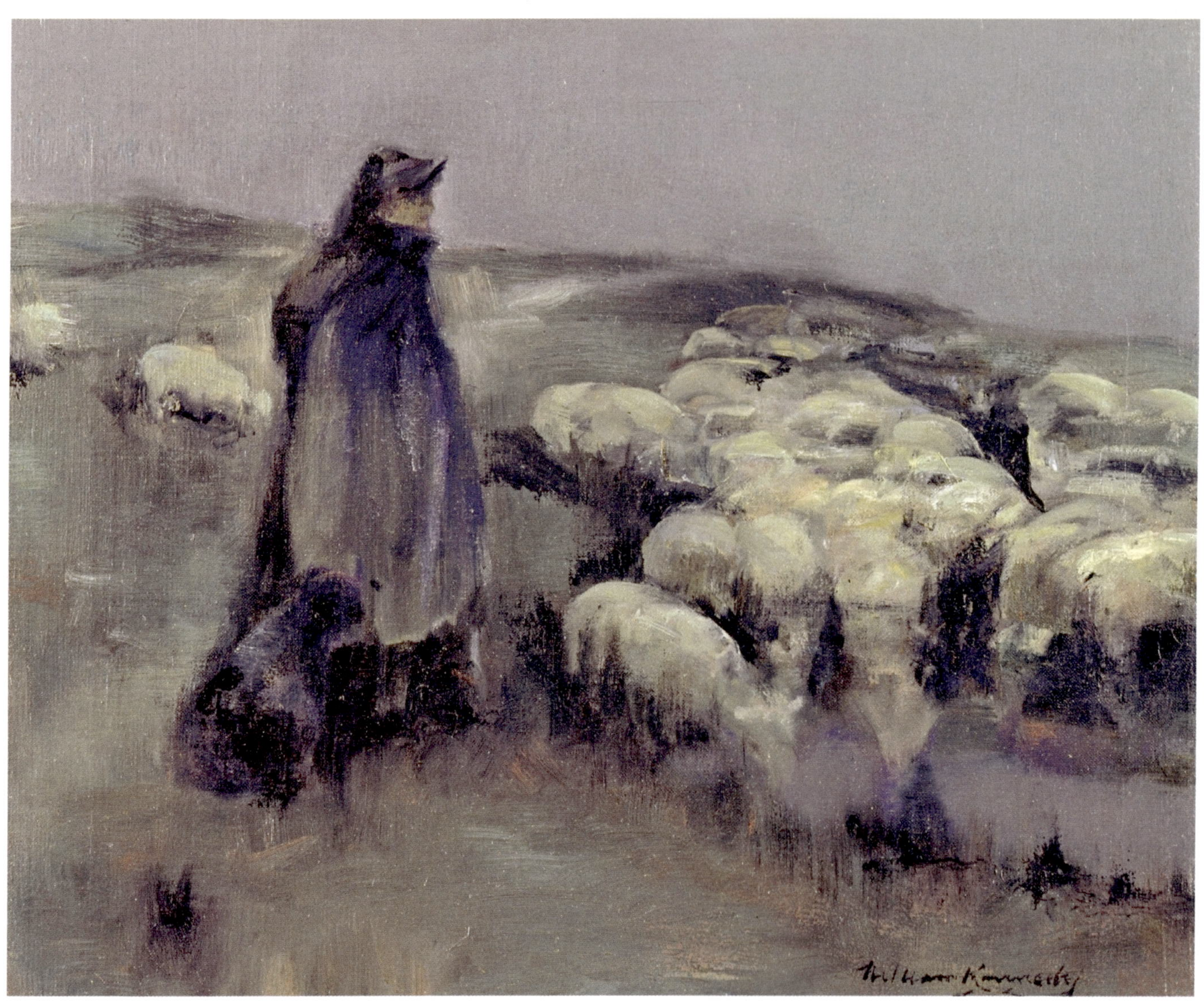

William Kennedy (1859–1918)
Oil on canvas, 40.6 x 50.8 cm (16 x 20 in)
• Yale Center for British Art, Connecticut

A Shepherdess, 1890–95 In Berkshire, Kennedy painted atmospheric, rural landscapes
in soft focus. This twilight scene of a shepherdess leading her sheep through a field was
influenced by Guthrie, Whistler, the Hague School painters and especially Anton Mauve.

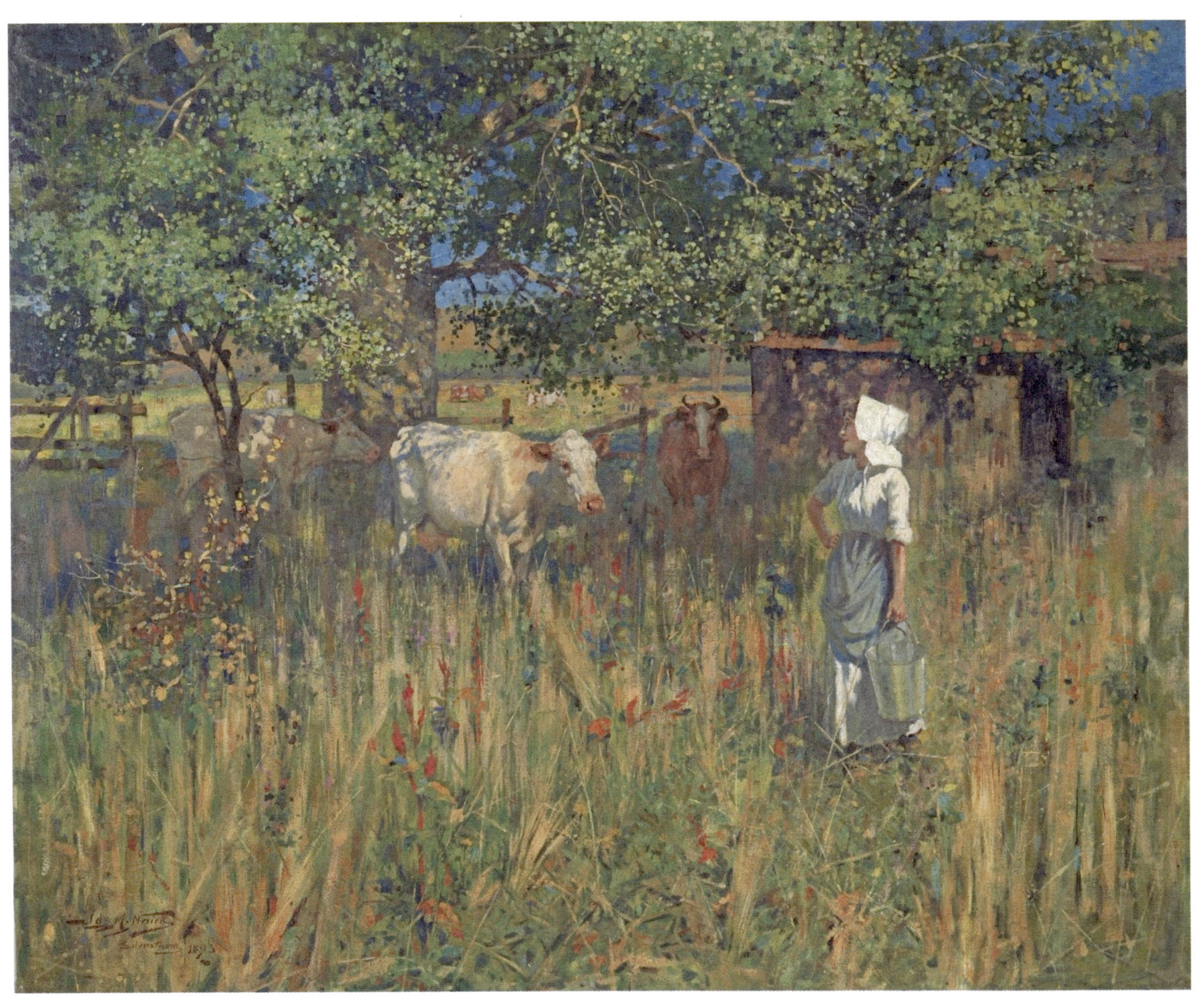

James Nairn (1859–1904)
Oil on canvas, 123.5 x 153.5 cm (48⅔ x 60⅔ in)
• Museum of New Zealand Te Papa Tongarewa, Wellington

Tess, 1893 Modelled by a 16-year-old farmer's daughter, this represents Tess of the d'Urbervilles, the heroine of Thomas Hardy's novel. Using broken brushwork and warm and cool tones, Nairn builds up the effects of the strong New Zealand sunlight.

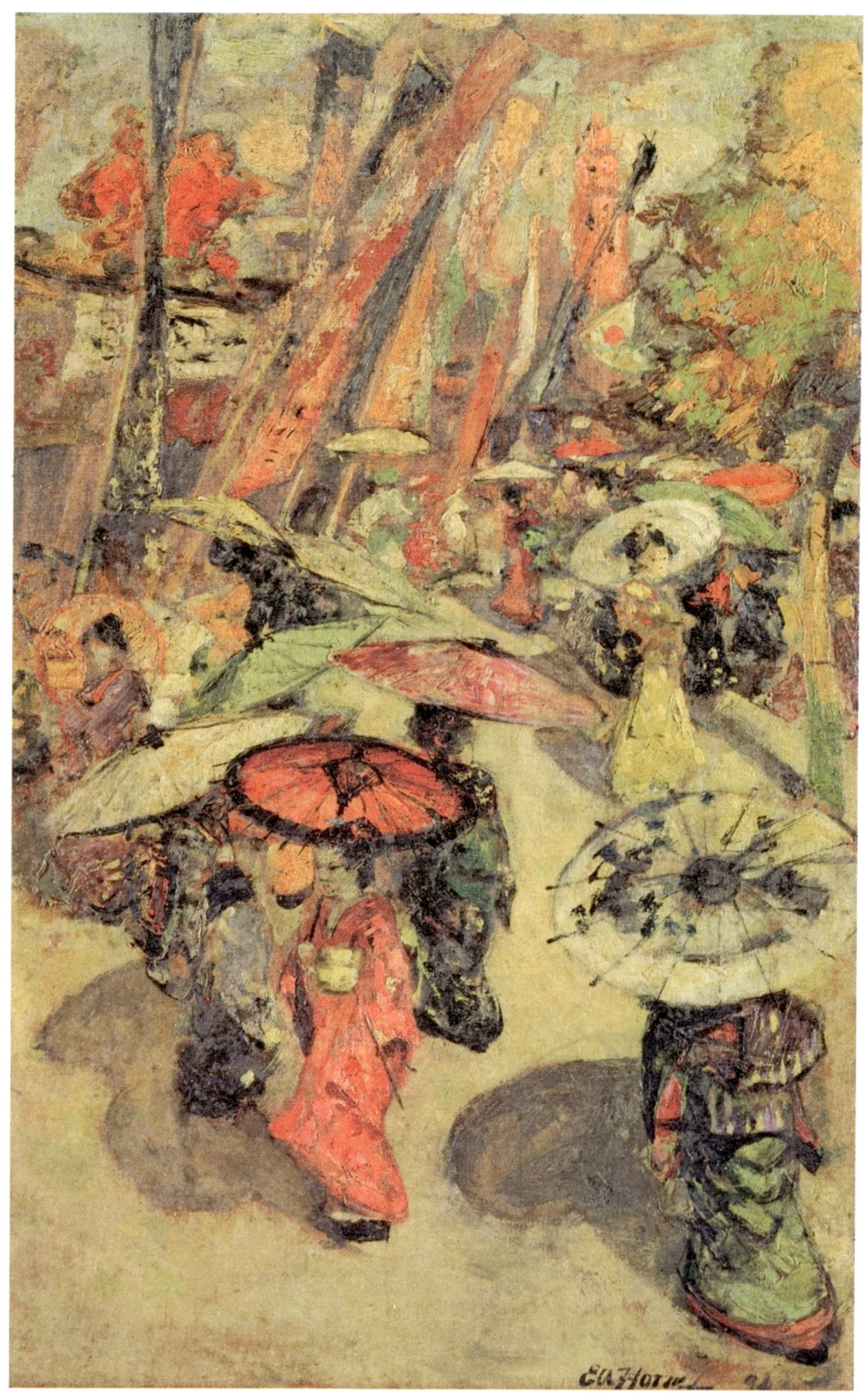

E.A. Hornel (1864–1933)
Oil on canvas, 75.9 x 47.6 cm (29⅔ x 18¾ in)
• Yale Center for British Art, Connecticut

Street Scene, Tokyo, 1894 Hornel and Henry were among the first European artists to visit Japan. Portrayed from a high, slanting angle, this street in Tokyo is crowded with colourful kimonos and parasols, created with soft, harmonious colours and shapes.

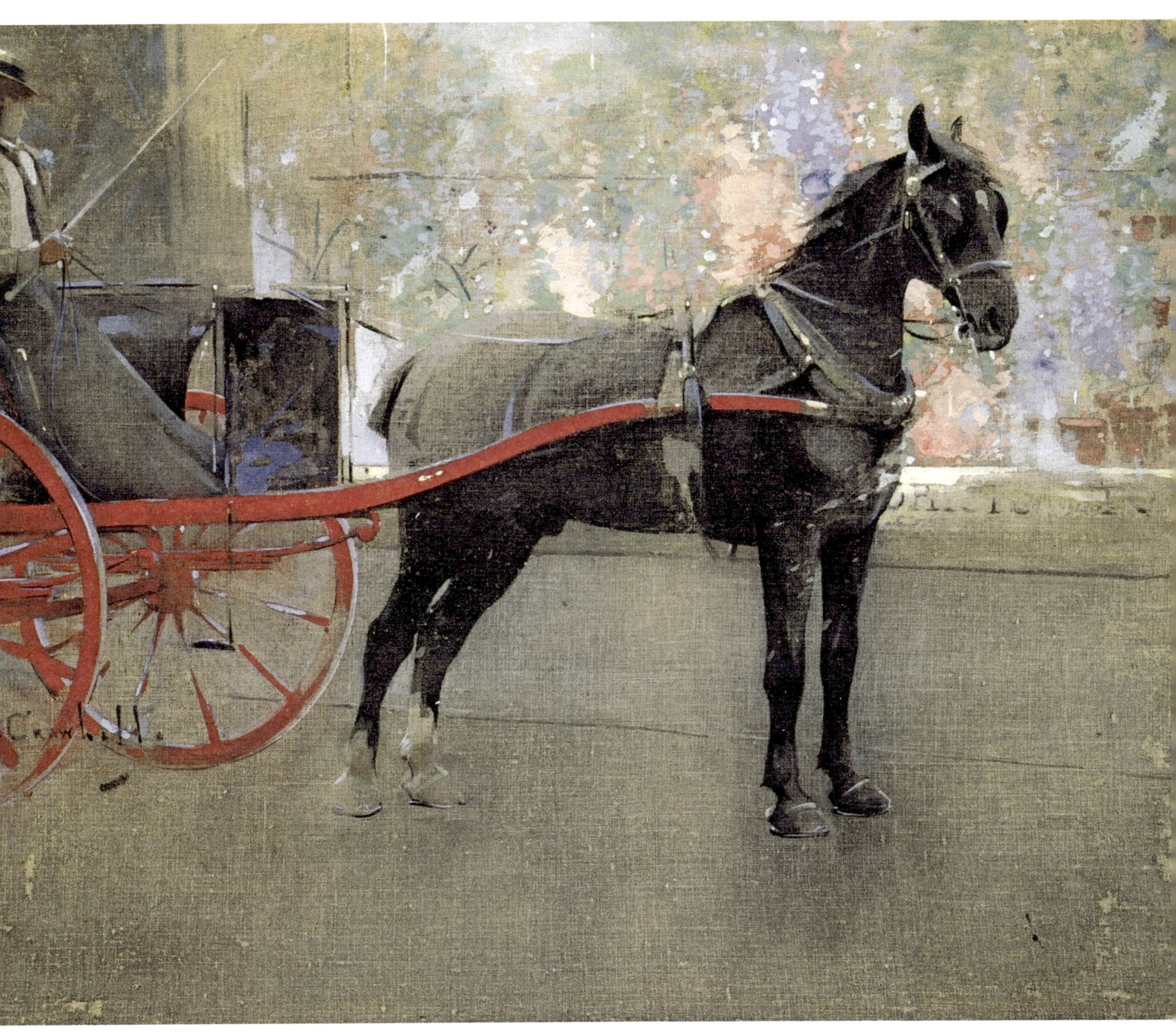

Joseph Crawhall (1861–1913)
Gouache on linen, 27.3 x 34.3 cm (10¾ x 13½ in)
• Kelvingrove Art Gallery and Museum, Glasgow

The Flower Shop, *c.* 1894–1900 Crawhall's style became more fluid when he began using gouache on linen, as here. Rather than relying on the art market, he painted only when he was inspired, often painting animals and focusing on light, colour and Japanese-inspired compositions.

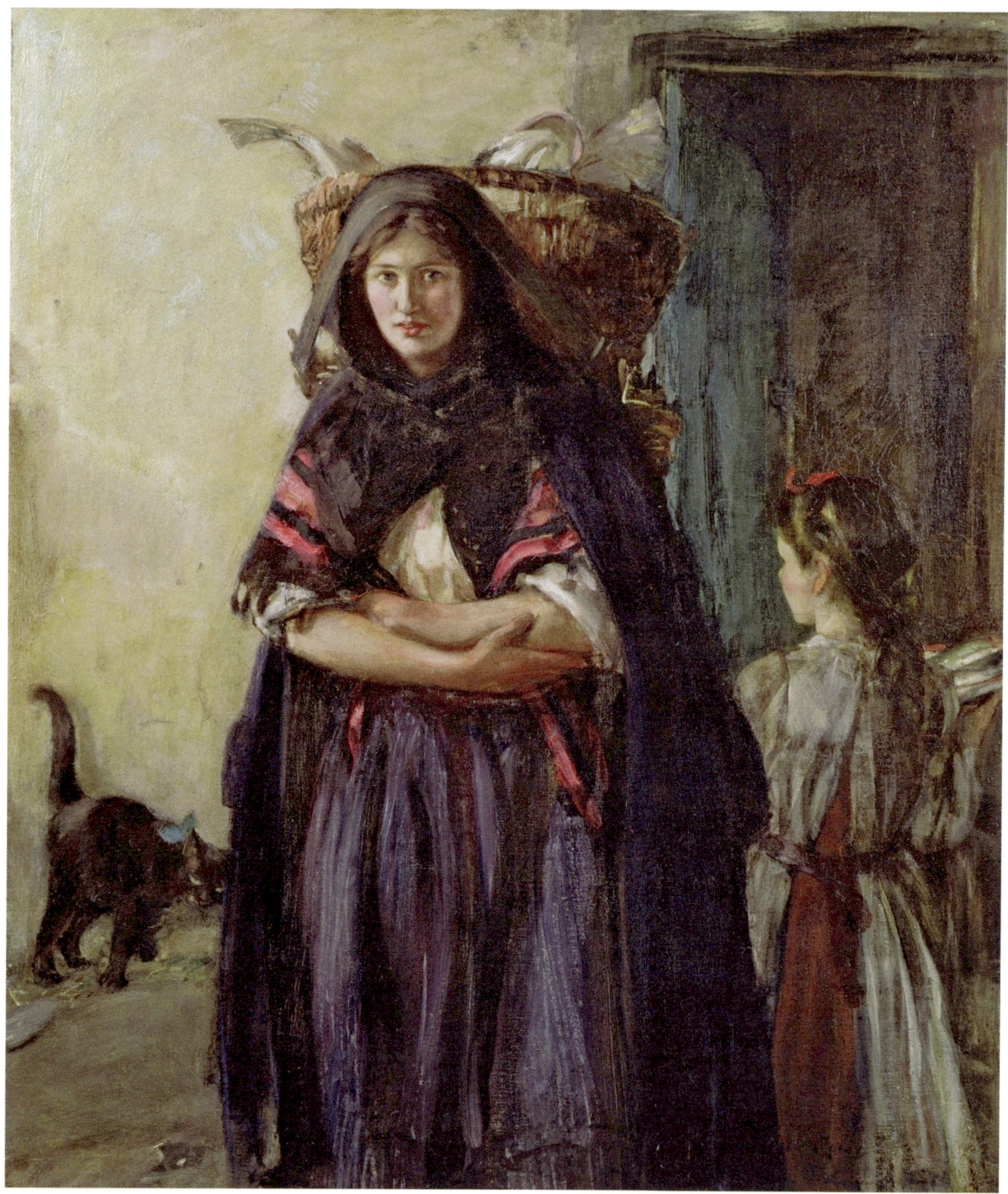

Alexander Ignatius Roche (1861–1921)
Oil on canvas, 127 x 111.8 cm (50 x 44 in)
• The Fleming-Wyfold Art Foundation, London

A Newhaven Fishwife, date unknown Fishwives from Newhaven in Edinburgh were famous for their flamboyance, brightly coloured traditional outfits and sharp tongues. They were renowned for driving hard bargains, so many fishermen employed them to sell their catches.

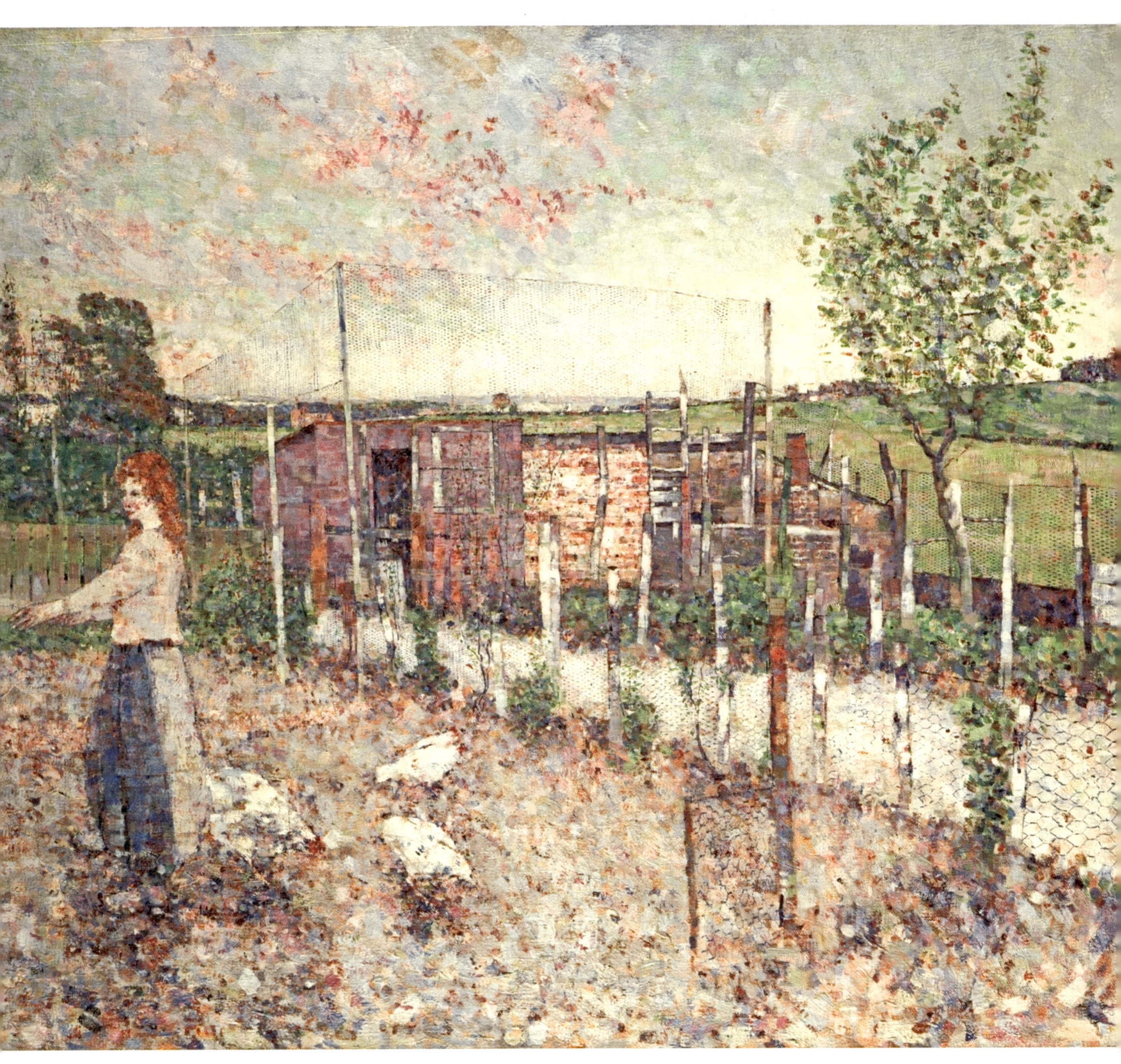

John Quinton Pringle (1864–1925)
Oil on canvas, 63.77 x 76.4 cm (25 x 30 in)
• National Galleries of Scotland, Edinburgh

Poultry Yard, Gartcosh, 1906 Painted during the year that Pringle lived away from Glasgow, rather than painting in the square brushmarks of Bastien-Lepage, for once, he applied small brushstrokes in myriad colours, resembling Pissarro's paintings of the 1890s.

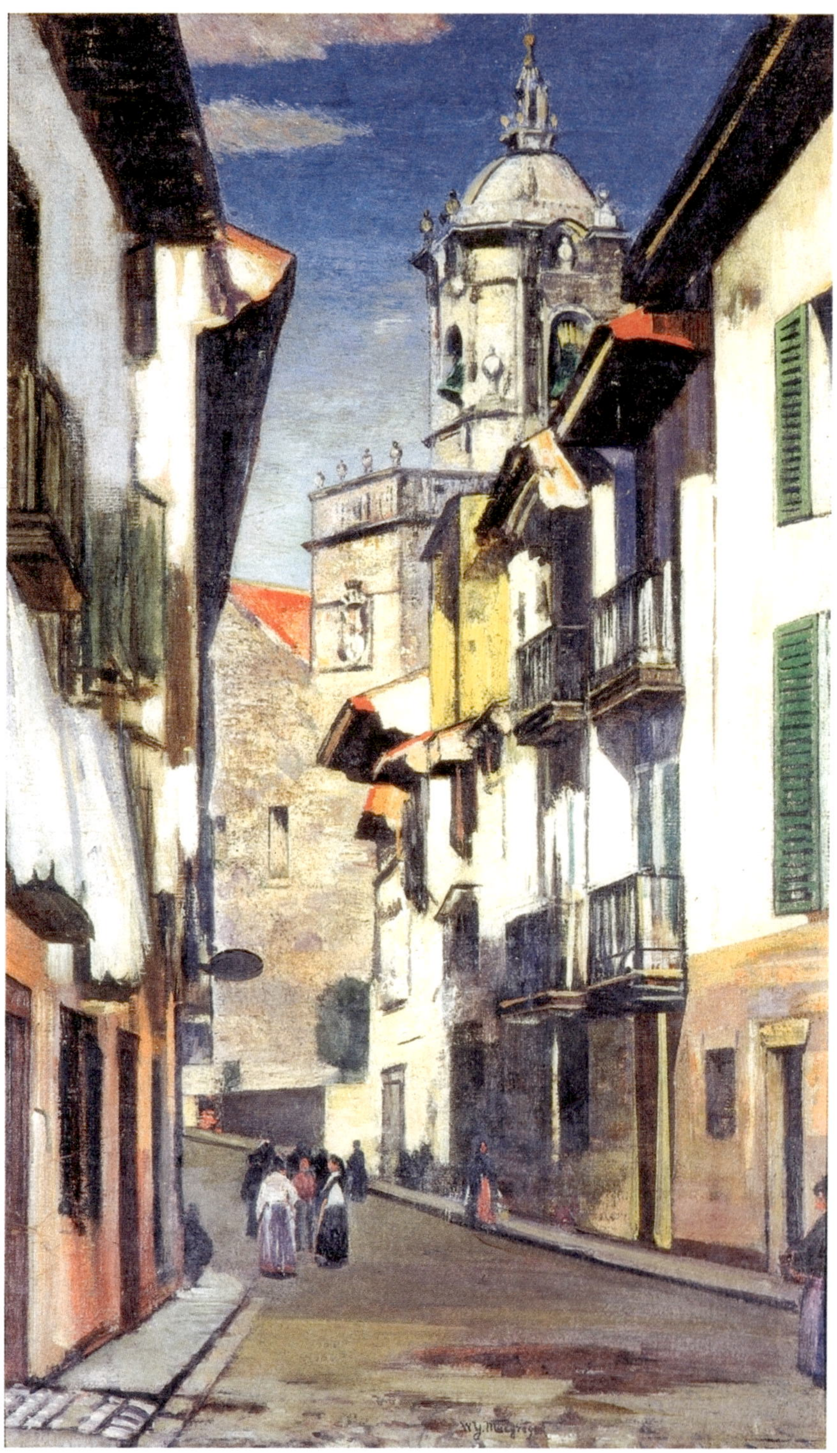

William York Macgregor (1855–1923)
Oil on canvas, 91.2 x 55.8 cm (36 x 22 in)
• Laing Art Gallery, Newcastle-upon-Tyne

A Street in Fuenterrabia, *c.* **1908** Bathed in brilliant sunlight, this is Fuenterrabia, a Spanish fishing village near the French border. After his return to Scotland from South Africa, with much-improved health, Macgregor visited Spain and painted several light-filled views.

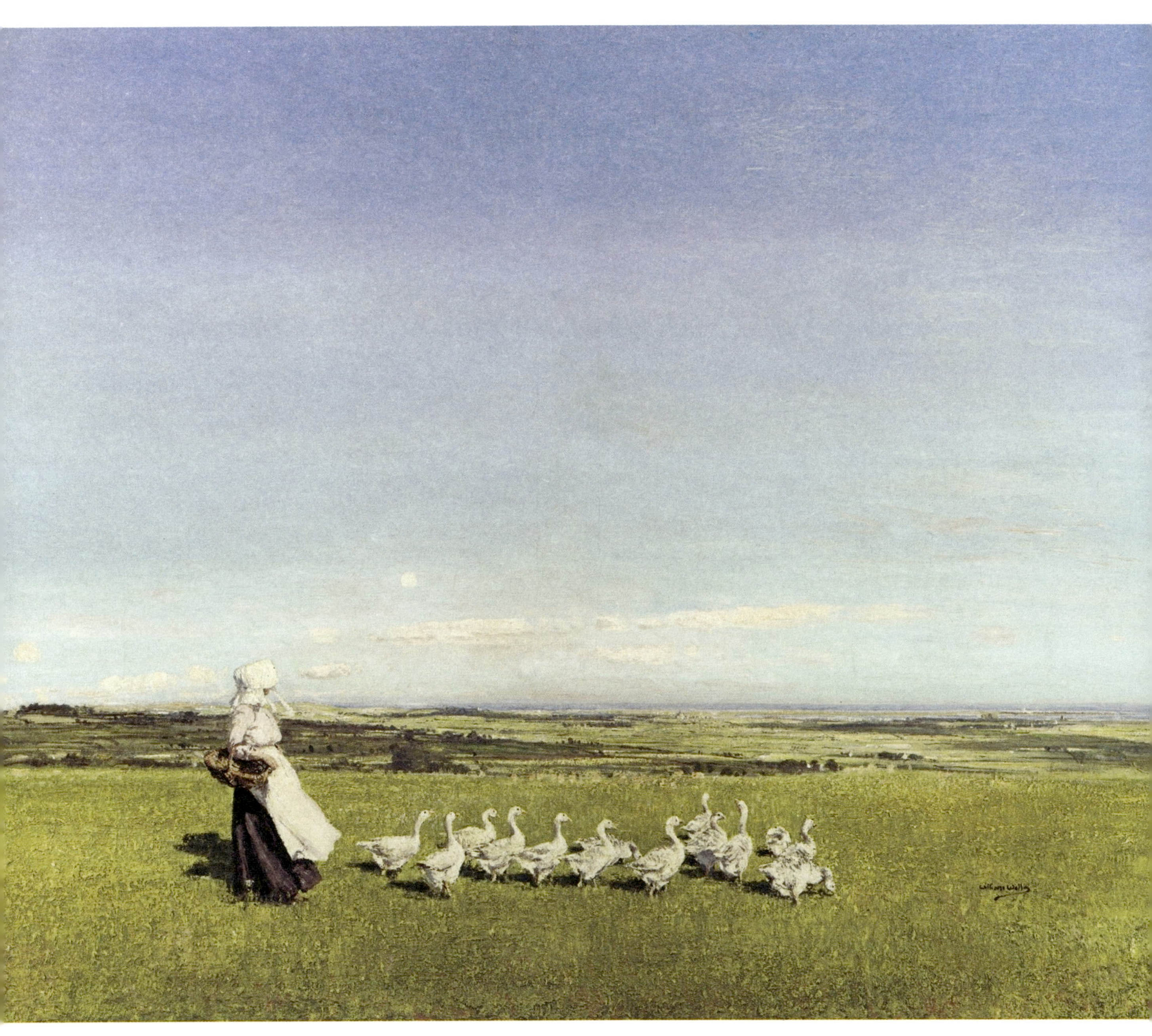

William Page Atkinson Wells (1872–1923)
Oil on canvas, 102.2 x 127.6 cm (40¼ x 50¼ in)
• The Ellis Campbell Collection

The Uplands of Arbory, Isle of Man, 1911 Painted after Atkinson Wells left Preston and lived
on the Isle of Man, this summer scene is created with an extremely restricted palette. The
goose girl's skirt blows in the breeze, while she and her geese are bathed in bright sunlight.

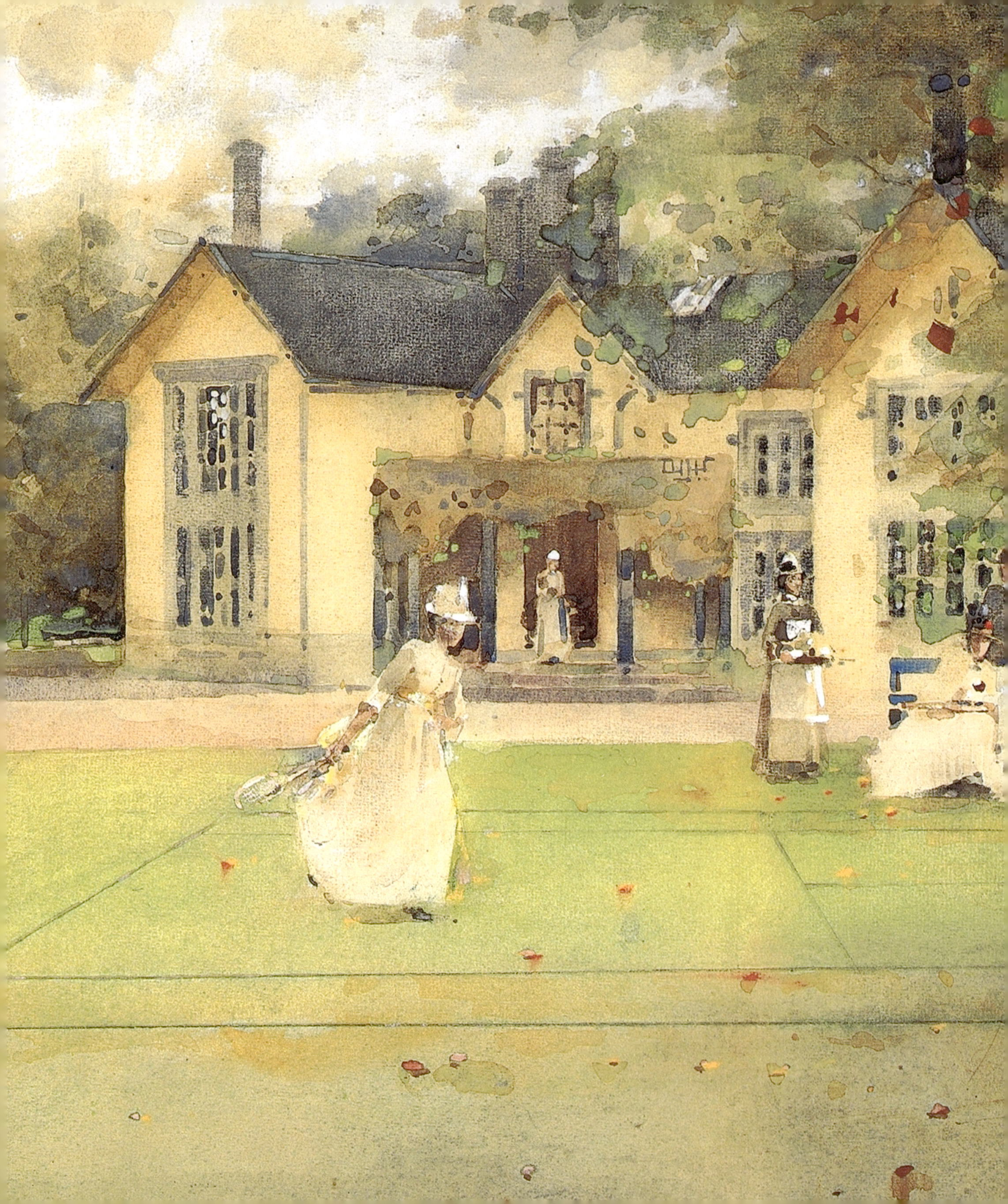

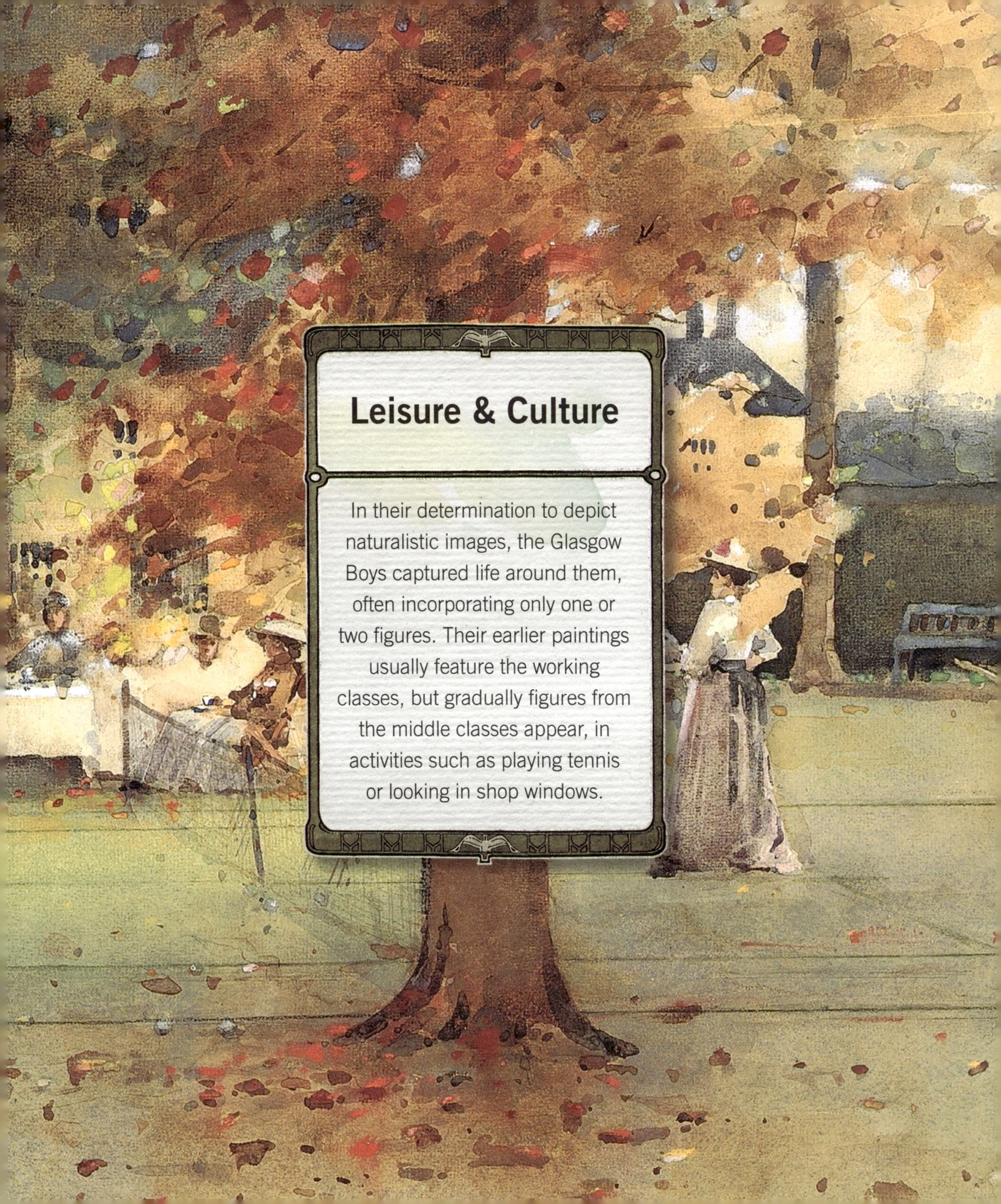

Leisure & Culture

In their determination to depict naturalistic images, the Glasgow Boys captured life around them, often incorporating only one or two figures. Their earlier paintings usually feature the working classes, but gradually figures from the middle classes appear, in activities such as playing tennis or looking in shop windows.

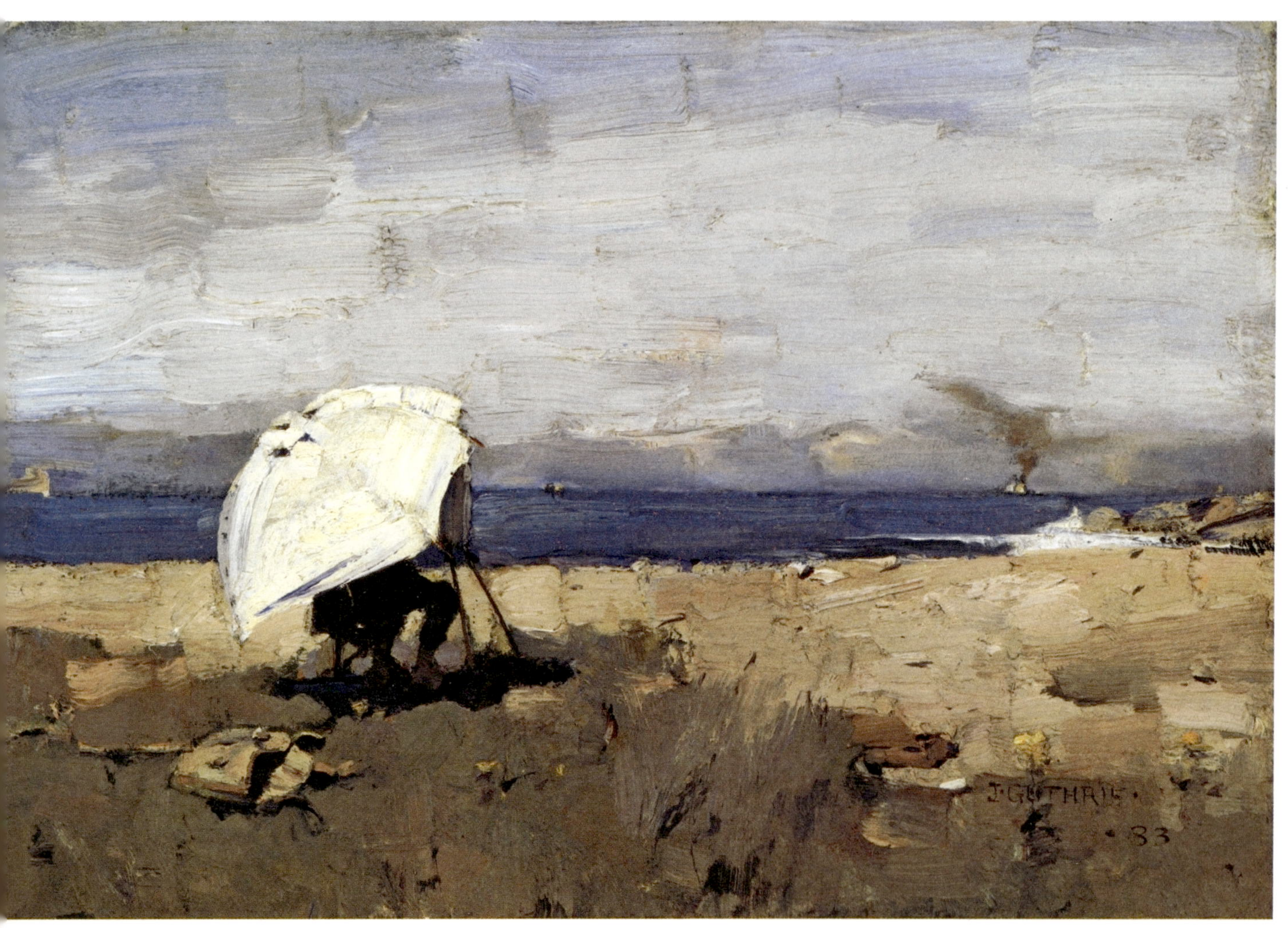

James Guthrie (1859–1930)
Oil on canvas, 31.1 x 46 cm (12¼ x 18 in)
• Kelvingrove Art Gallery and Museum, Glasgow

Hard At It, 1883 Created with impasto paint applied with a palette knife, this portrays an artist working *en plein air,* with an umbrella to protect him from the wind on the Scottish coast and to block any shadows from shading his canvas.

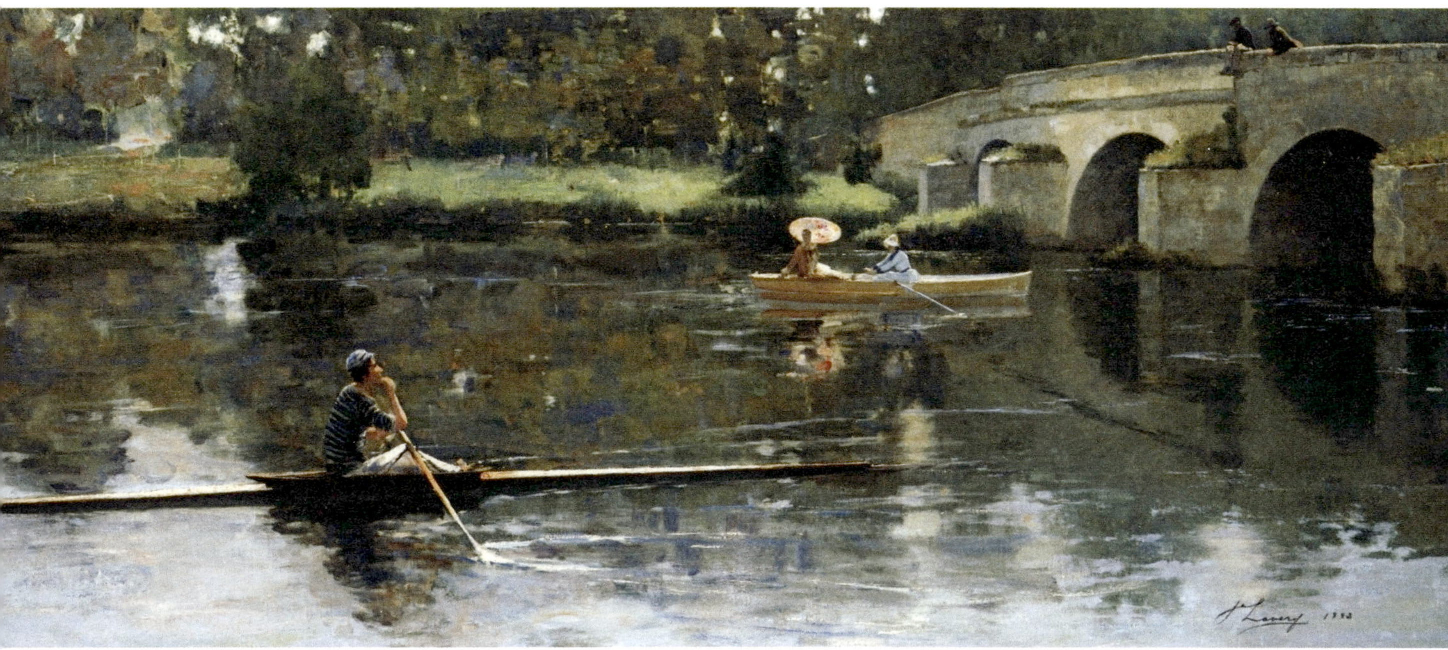

John Lavery (1856–1941)
Oil on canvas, 76.2 x 183.5 cm (30 x 72¼ in) • Private collection

The Bridge at Grez, 1883 The ancient village of Grez-sur-Loing had already become an international artists' colony when the Glasgow Boys first began painting there in the 1880s. Lavery painted this alongside his friend, the painter Frank O'Meara (1853–88).

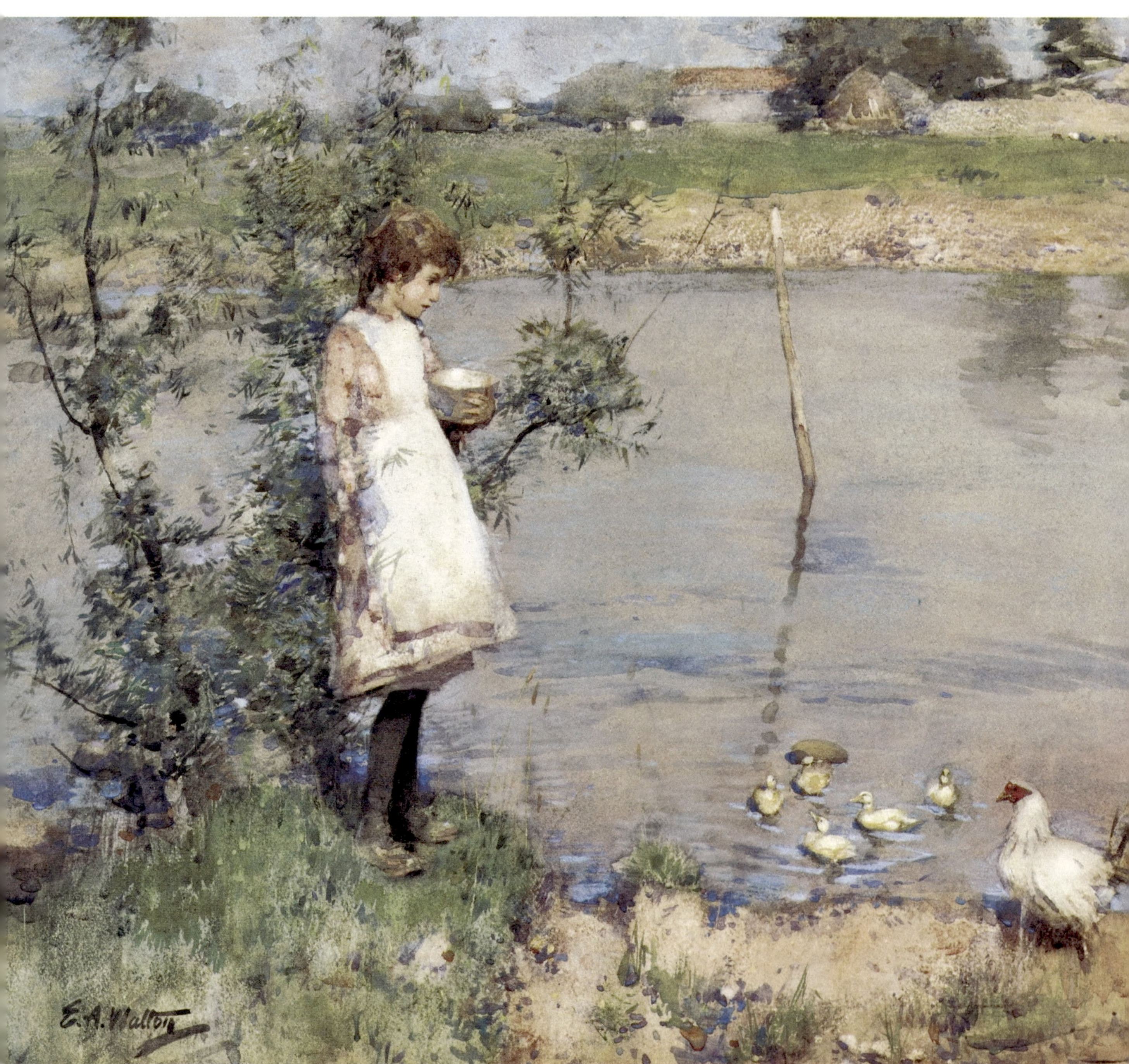

Edward Arthur Walton (1860–1922)
Watercolour and body colour on paper, 48 x 56 cm (18⅘ x 22 in)
• The Ellis Campbell Collection

Girl Feeding the Ducklings, Cockburnspath, *c.* 1883–84 As in most of Walton's Cockburnspath paintings, this is depicted in full sunlight. An example of the importance some of the Glasgow Boys put on watercolours, it is a bold composition, with the duck pond taking up most of the picture.

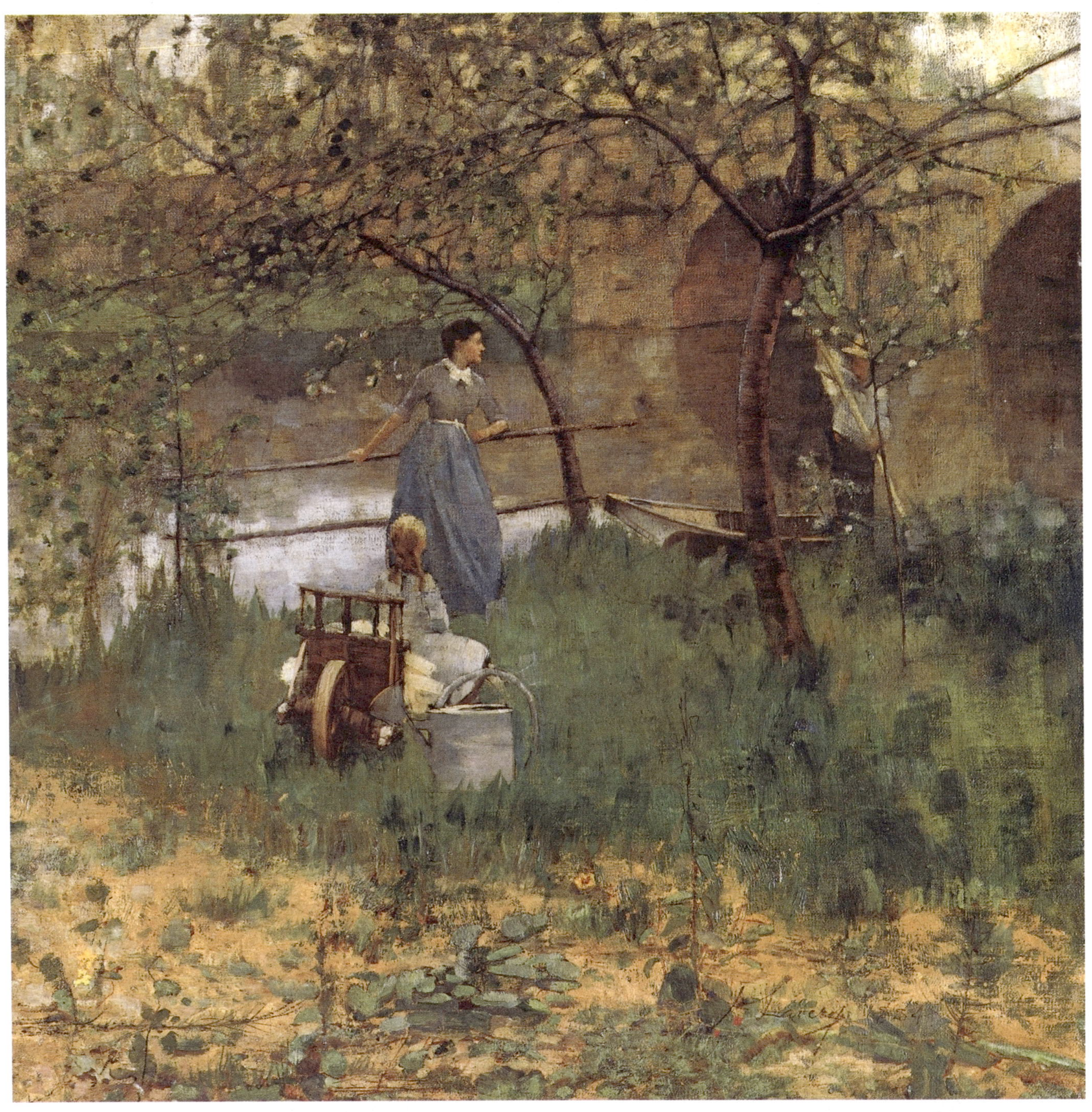

John Lavery (1856–1941)
Oil on canvas, 79 x 76 cm (31 x 30 in) • Private collection

On the Loing, 1884 In 1884, Lavery stayed for nine months at the reasonably priced Hôtel Chevillon, in Grez-sur-Loing, where he met Frank O'Meara, who had been living there for a while. In this composition, the sky can mainly only be seen in water reflections.

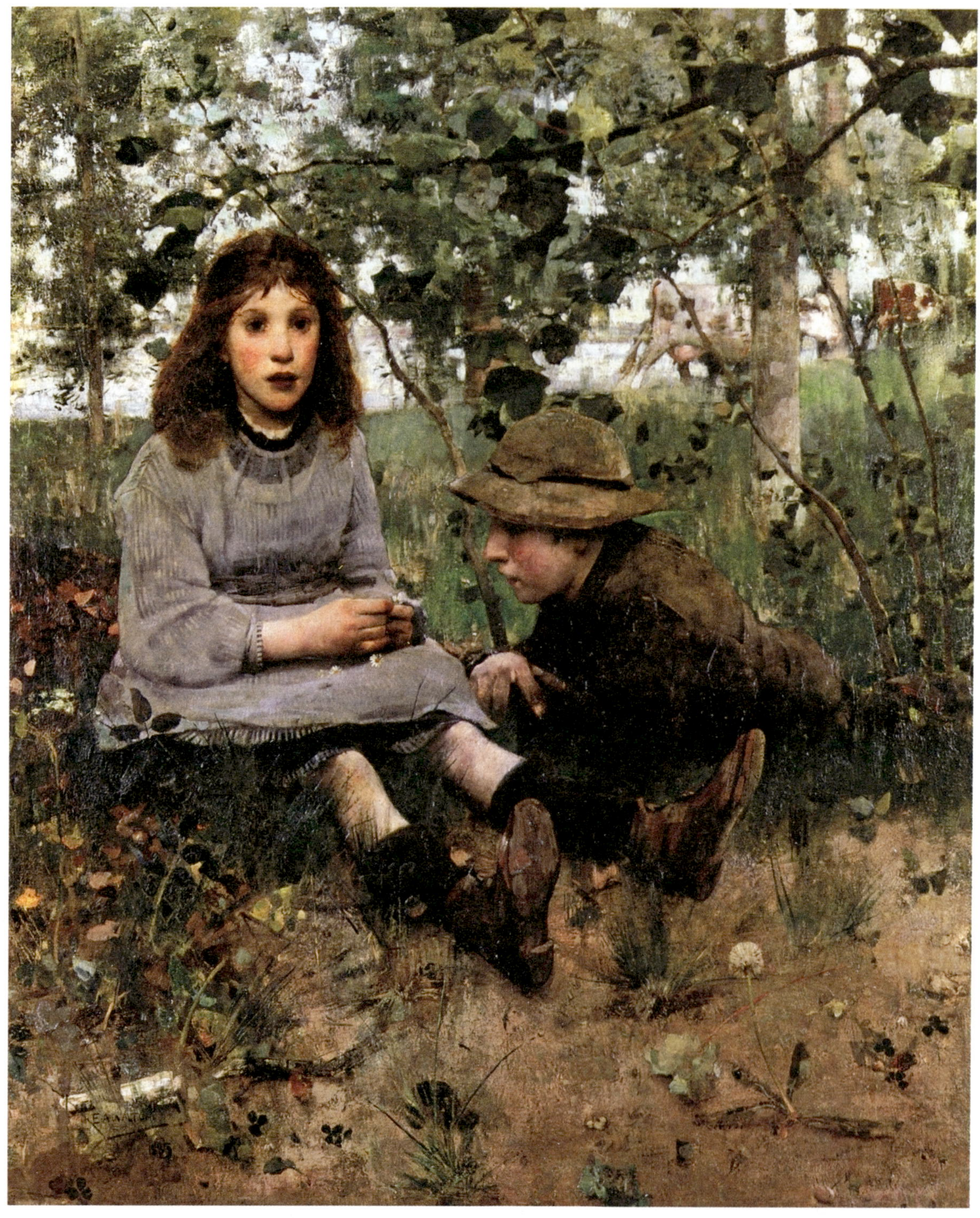

Edward Arthur Walton (1860–1922)
Oil on canvas, 139.7 x 116 cm (55 x 45⅔ in)
• Collection of Andrew McIntosh Patrick, UK

The Daydream, 1885 By the mid-1880s, Walton was creating more decorative compositions. Here, a peasant girl and boy seem to be close to the front of the picture plane as they relax in woodland. From the title, the girl is clearly dreaming of a better life.

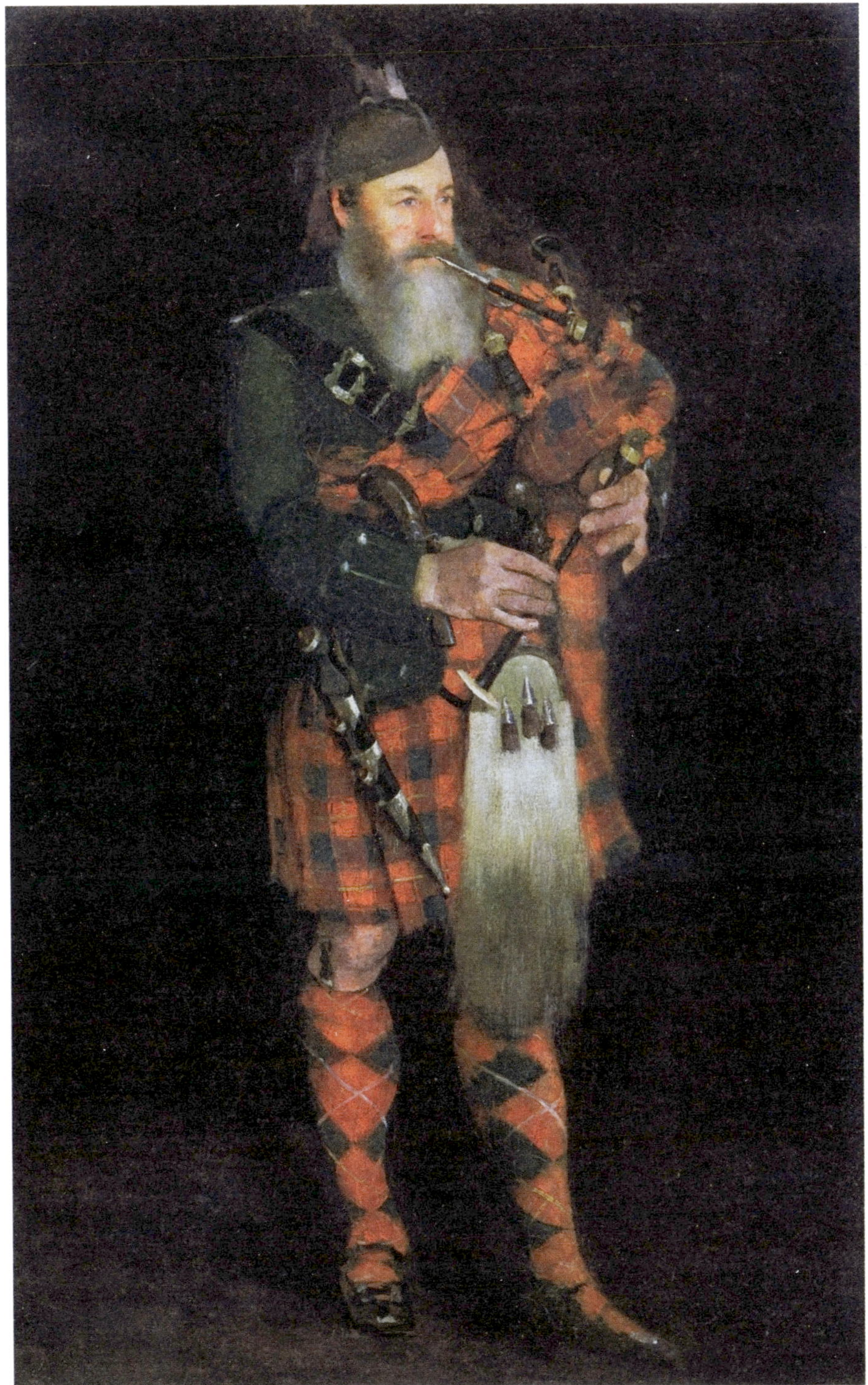

William Kennedy (1859–1918)
Oil on canvas, 45 x 29 cm (17¾ x11⅓ in) • Private collection

A Piper, 1885 Illuminated against a dark background, the bold colours, soft brushstrokes, reduced tonal contrasts and simple composition echo elements of Whistler's painting style. Kennedy painted this when he first moved back to Scotland.

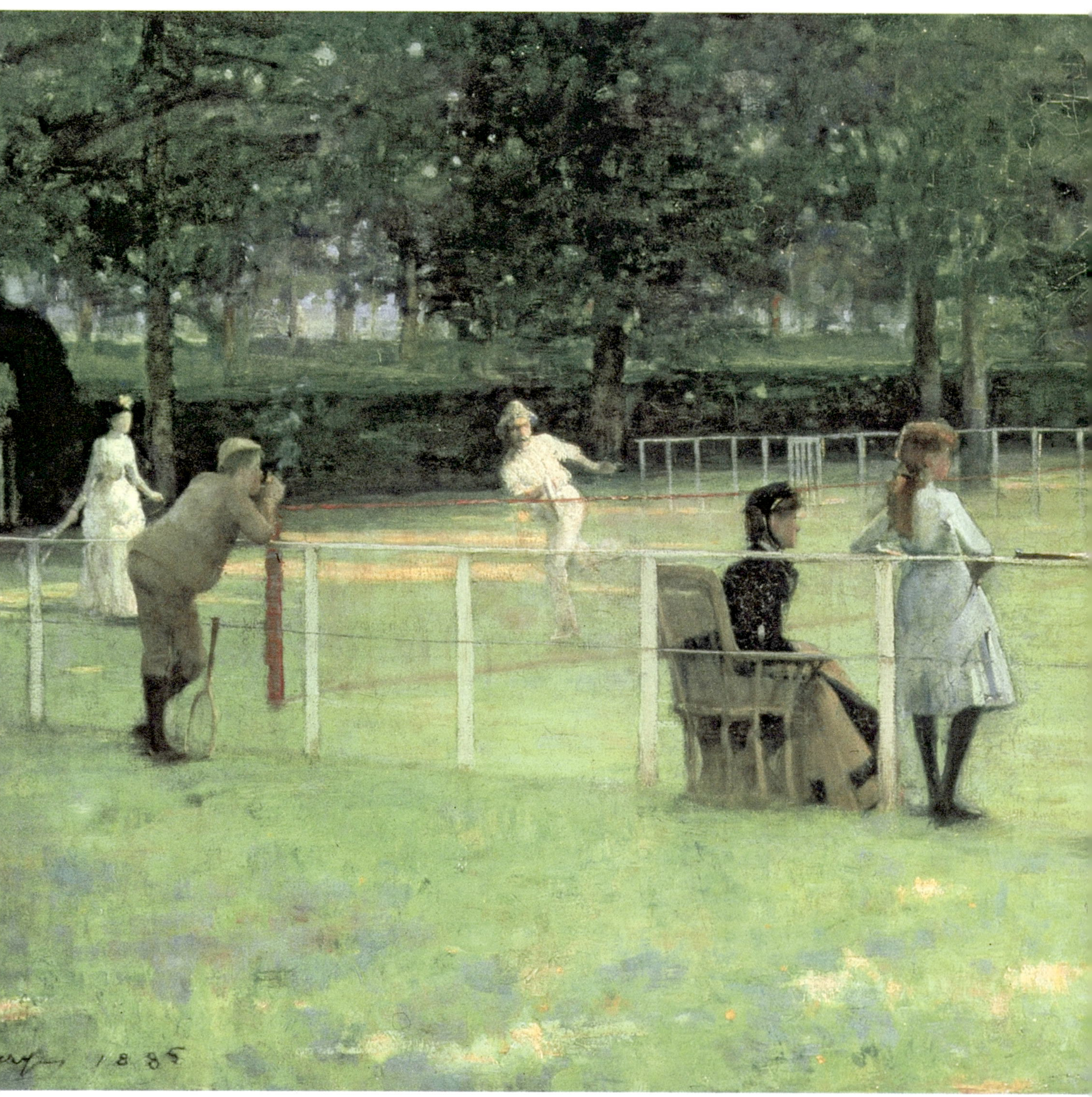

John Lavery (1856–1941)
Oil on canvas, 76.2 x 183 cm (30 x 72 in)
• Aberdeen Art Gallery and Museums, Aberdeen

The Tennis Party, 1885 One of the earliest depictions of a game of tennis, Lavery painted his friends Alexander and Elizabeth MacBride playing tennis in their Glasgow garden. That summer, he, Guthrie, Melville and Walton met there often. He recalled, 'I became obsessed by figures in movement.'

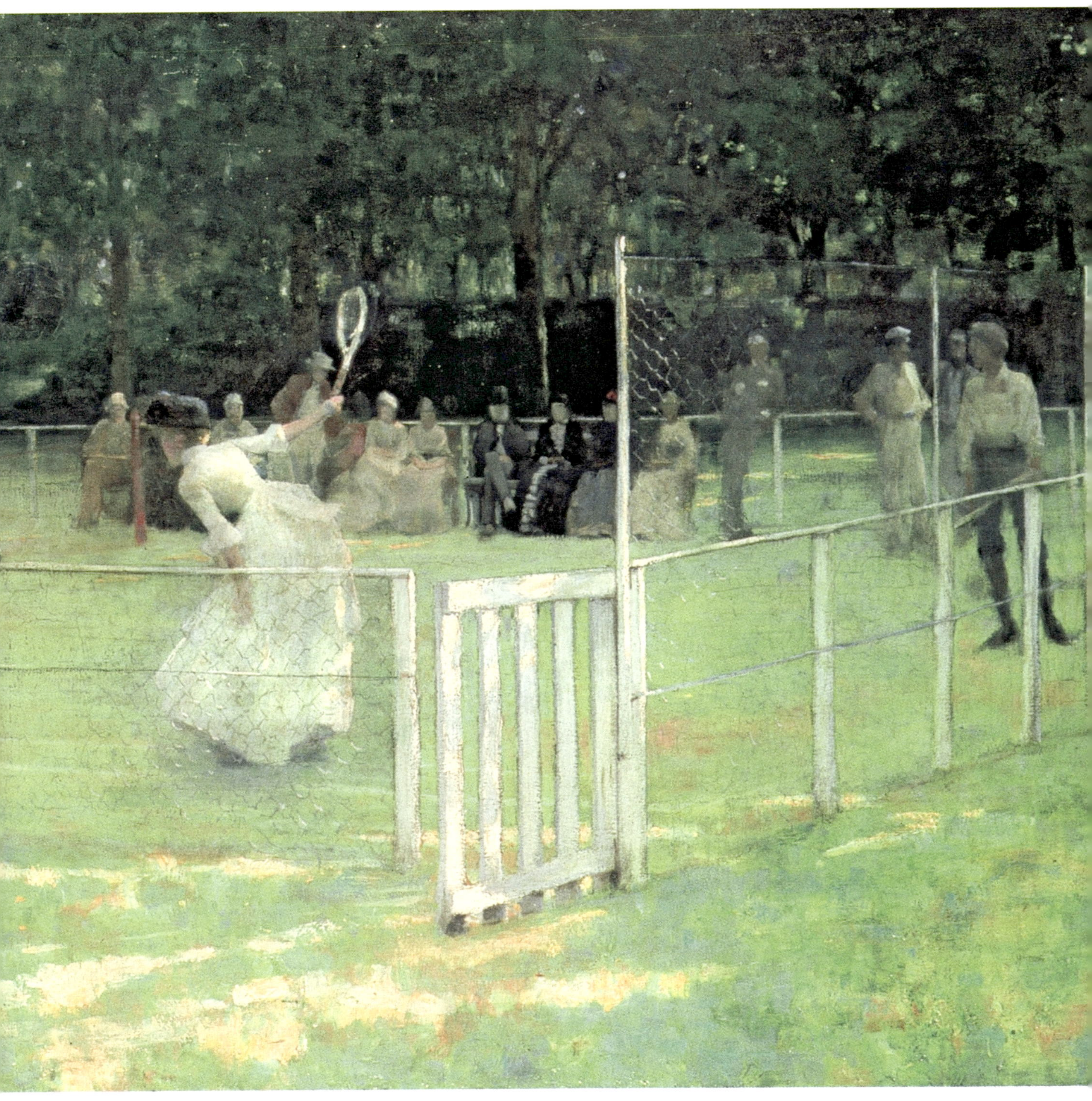

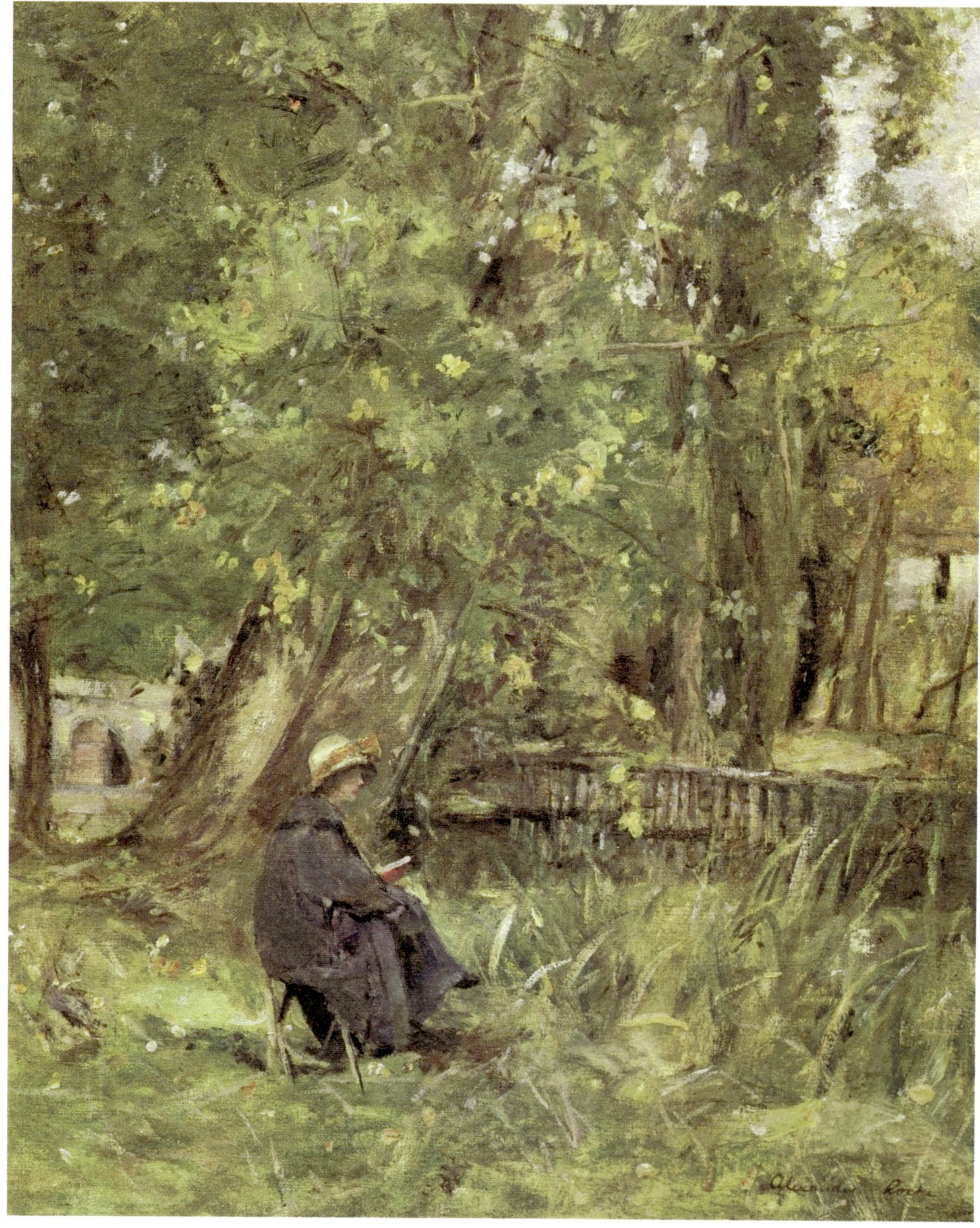

Alexander Ignatius Roche (1861–1921)
Oil on canvas, 45.7 x 38 cm (18 x 15 in)
• The Fleming-Wyfold Art Foundation, London

Early Autumn, Grez, date unknown Probably produced between 1881 and 1885,
when Roche was in Grez-sur-Loing, this displays the free paint application he used while
working there, inspired by both the landscape and the like-minded artists painting there.

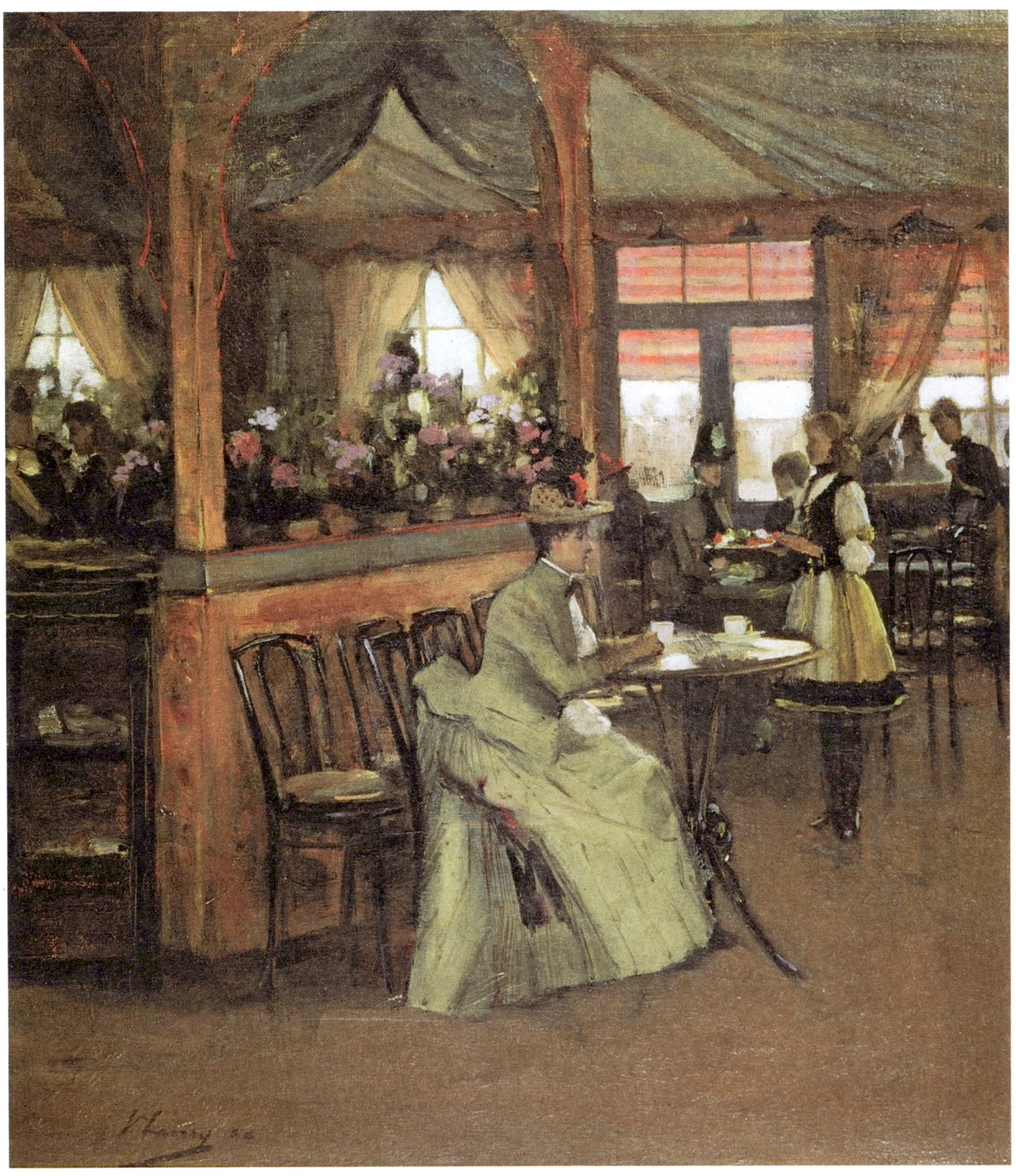

John Lavery (1856–1941)
Oil on canvas, 50.8 x 45.7 cm (20 x 18 in) • Private collection

A Cup of Chocolate, 1888 In 1882, in Paris, Lavery possibly saw *Young Peasant Girl Having Her Coffee,* painted by Camille Pissarro in 1881. The subjects are similar, but Lavery's composition and fashionable young woman completely contrast with Pissarro's work.

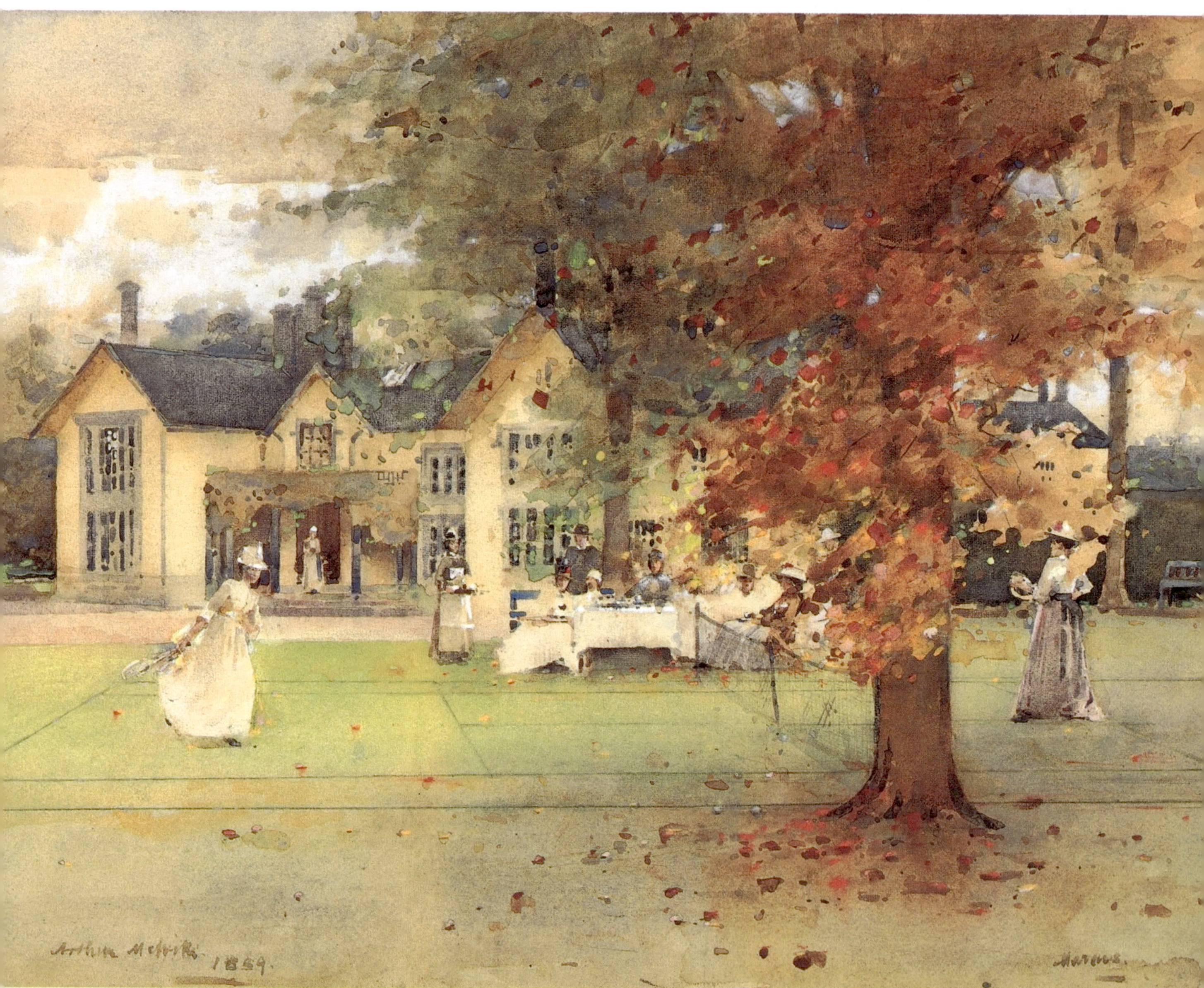

Arthur Melville (1855–1904)
Pencil, watercolour and body colour on paper, 54.7 x 72.5 cm
(21½ x 28½ in) • Private collection

The Lawn Tennis Party at Marcus, 1889 Melville painted this at the home of his friend
John Robertson, who sits at the table under a tree with the Reverend John Herkless.
In the foreground, their wives play tennis – the game had been invented in 1874.

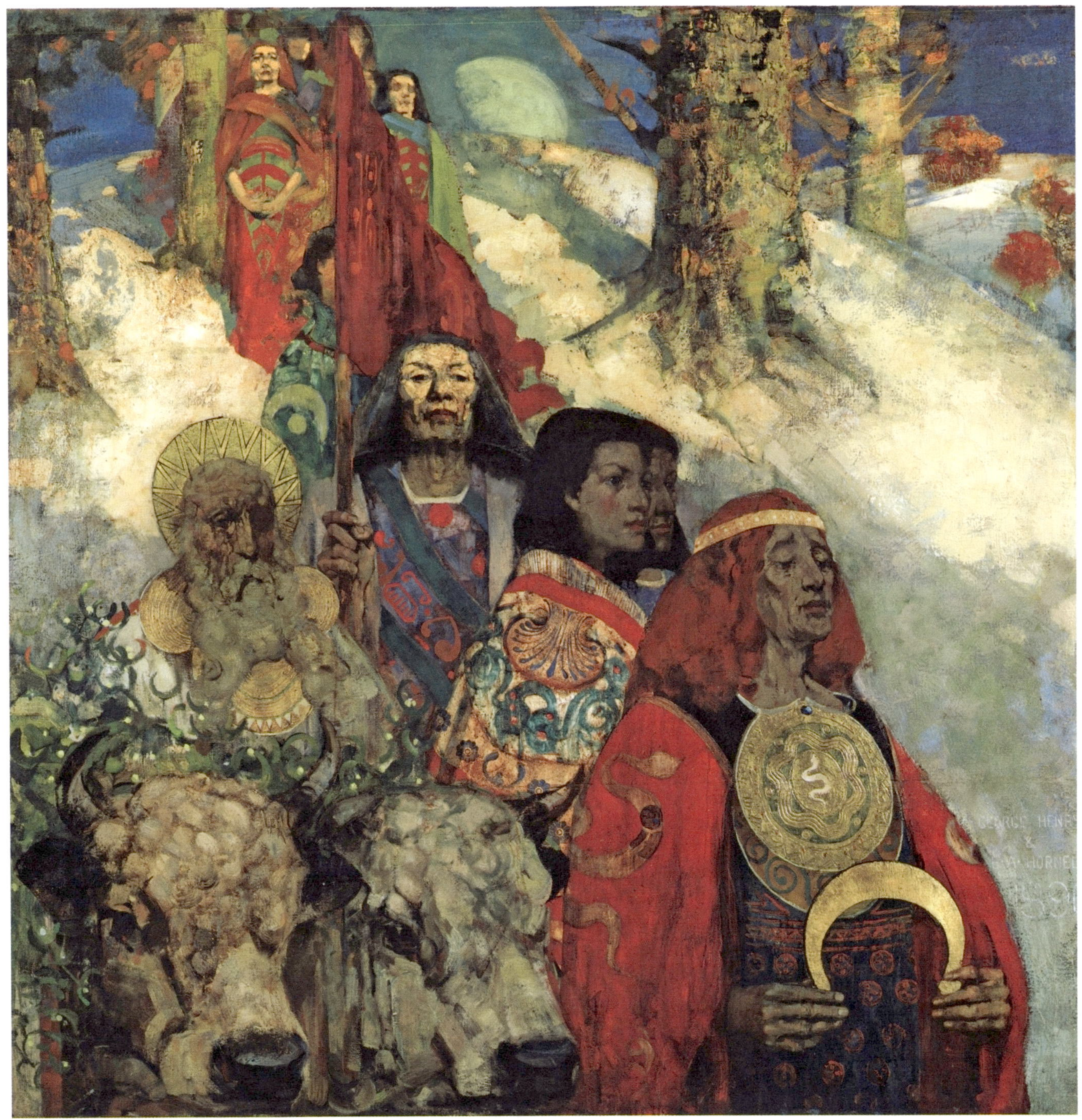

George Henry (1858–1943) and E.A. Hornel (1864–1933)
Oil, gold leaf and gesso on canvas, 152.4 x 152.4 cm (60 x 60 in)
• Kelvingrove Art Gallery and Museum, Glasgow

The Druids – Bringing in the Mistletoe, 1890 In ceremonial robes, druids and two white bulls file down a snowy hill. One of two collaborative works painted by Henry and Hornel, this depicts the Celtic ritual of taking mistletoe inside. Mistletoe was sacred and believed to have medicinal powers.

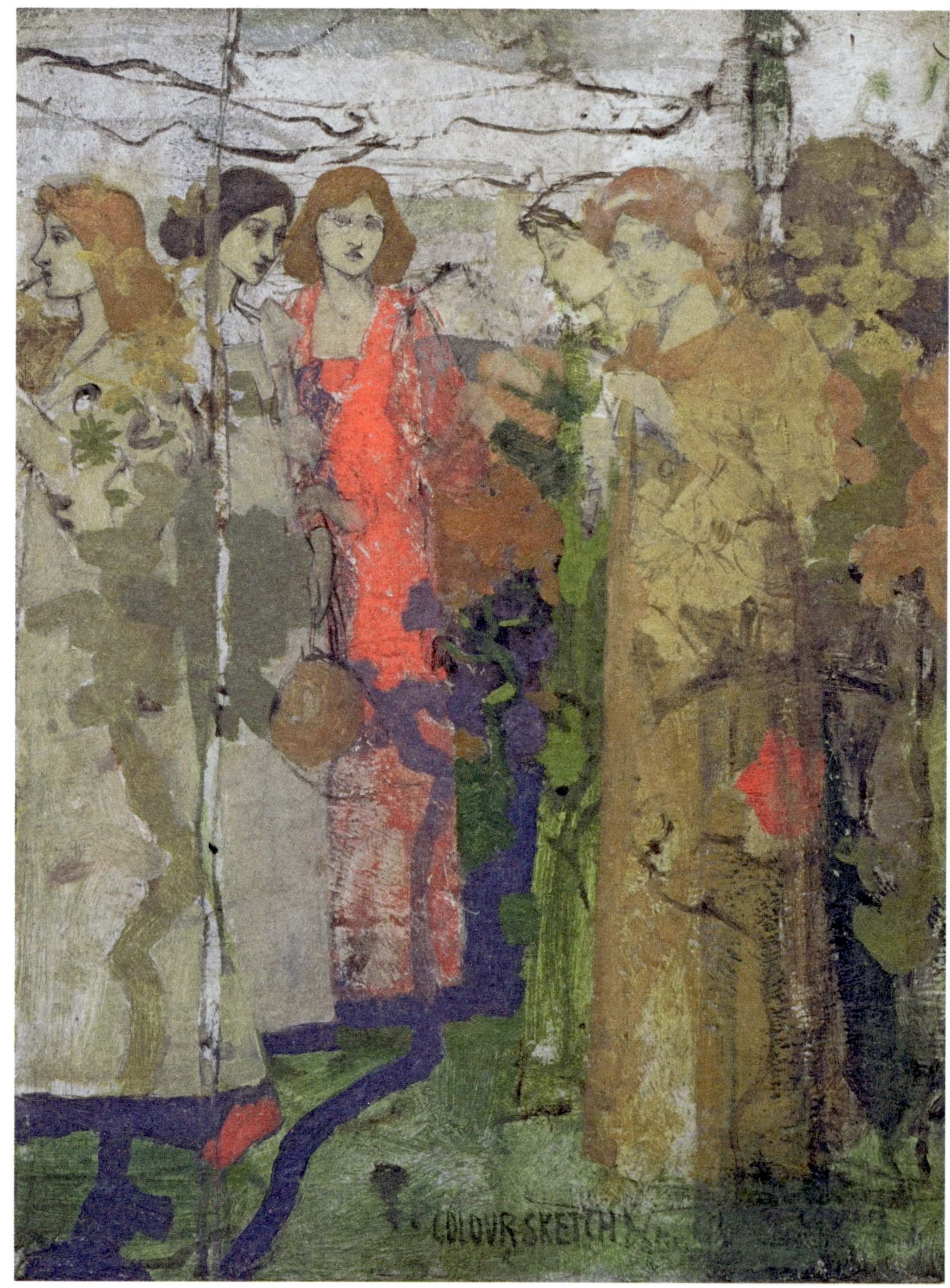

David Gauld (1865–1936)
Oil on paper, 50.8 x 40.6 cm (20 x 16 in)
• The Fleming-Wyfold Art Foundation, London

Colour Sketch, 1890 Inspired by the colours and themes of the Pre-Raphaelite Brotherhood, as well as the bold colours and flattened space of medieval art, Gauld went against the *plein-air* naturalism of the other Glasgow Boys, and here, his painting approach can be discerned.

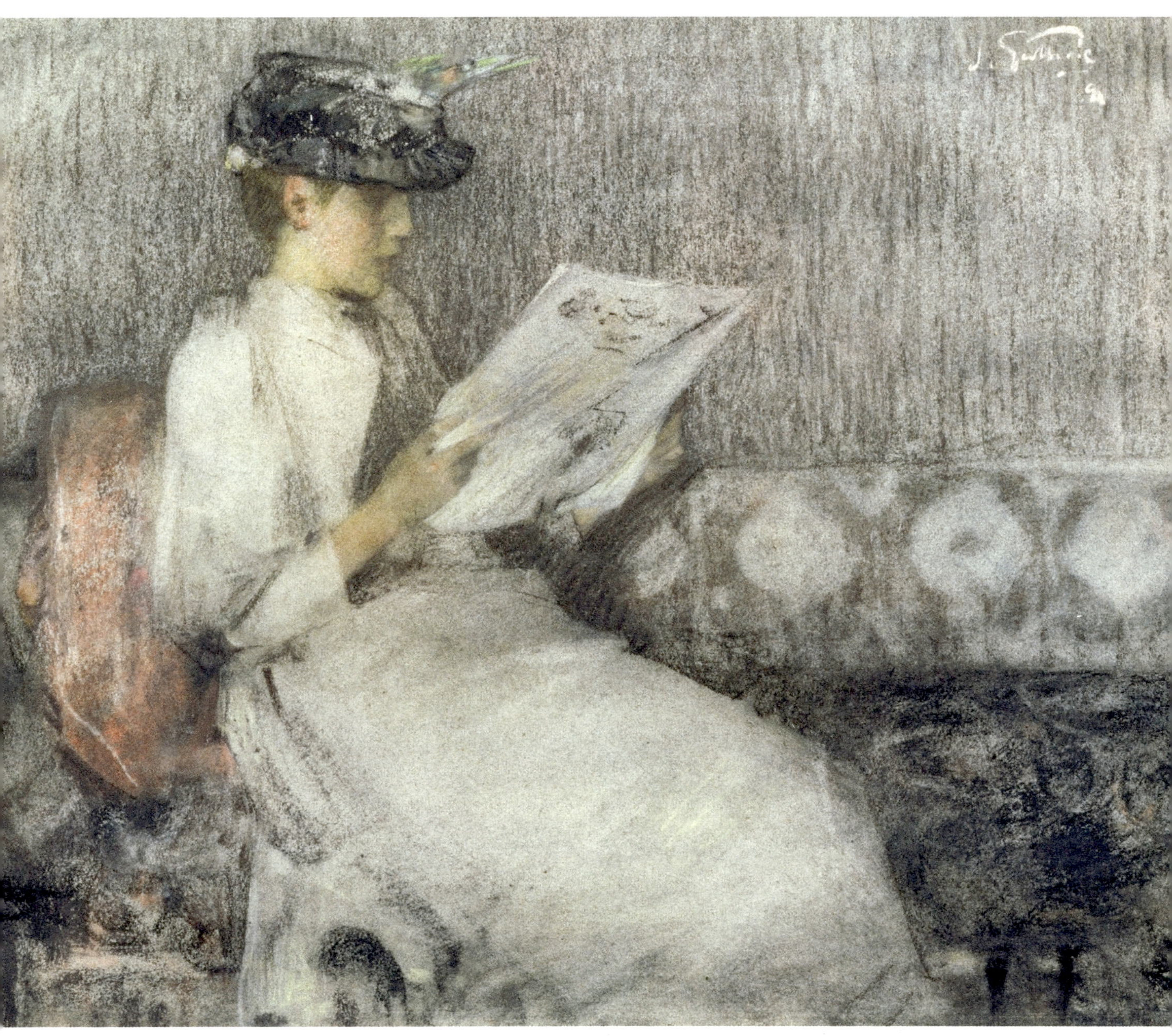

James Guthrie (1859–1930)
Pastel on paper, 48 x 61 cm (18⅓ x 24 in)
• The Fine Art Society, London

The Morning Paper, *c.* **1890–91** After the mid-1880s, Guthrie painted more portraits, and featured the middle classes, rather than the poor. Working with pastels, using a similar technique to Edgar Degas (1834–1917), this interior depicts a fashionable young woman reading the newspaper.

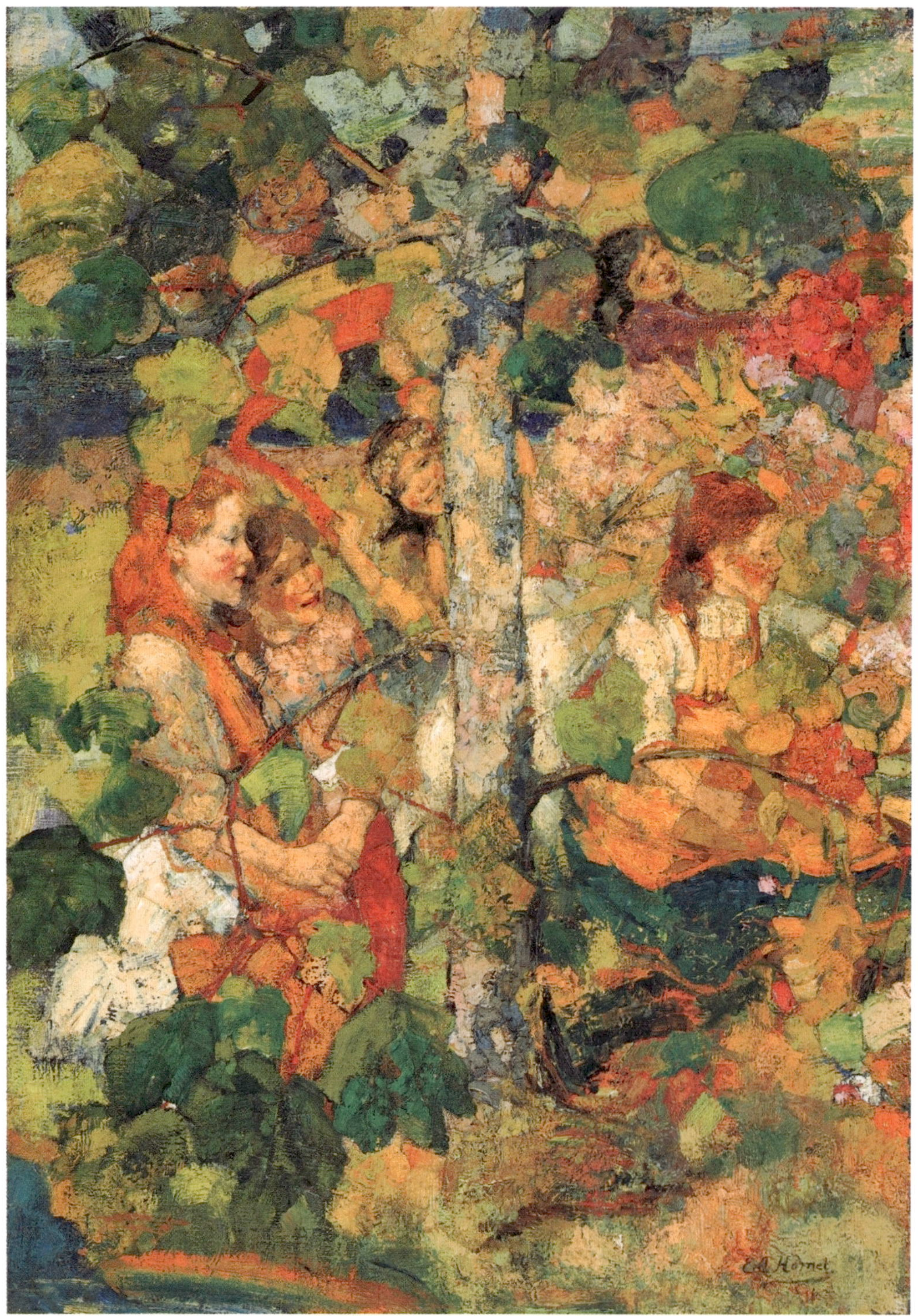

E.A. Hornel (1864–1933)
Oil on canvas, 84.5 x 116.8 cm (33¼ x 46 in)
• Private collection

Children Dancing Around a Tree, 1891 Criticized when it was first exhibited, just before Hornel left for Japan, this painting contrasted directly with the other Glasgow Boys' naturalistic styles. Among other criticisms, it was compared to patchwork, but it shows his fascination with shape and colour.

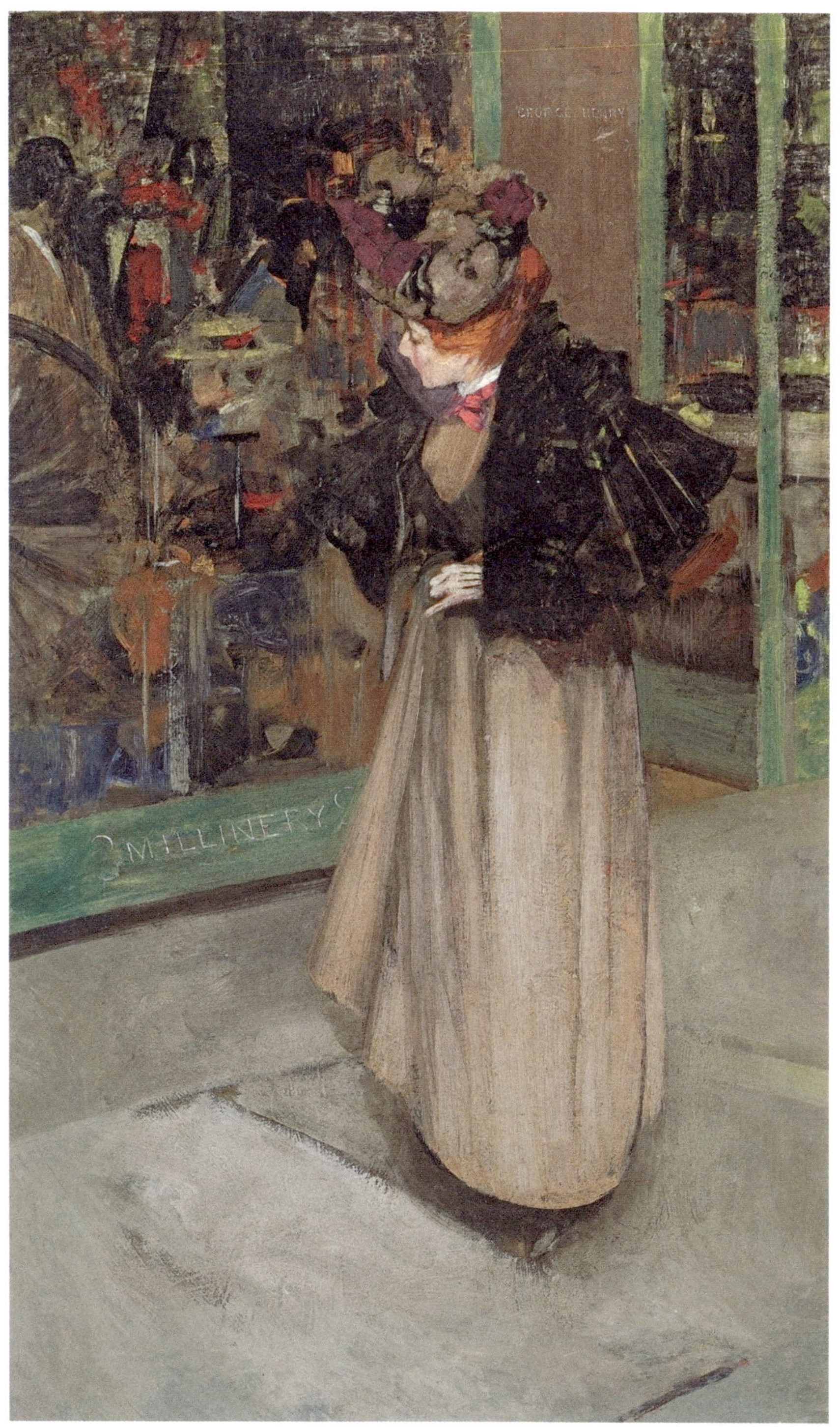

George Henry (1858–1943)
Oil on canvas, 88 x 54.1 cm (34⅔ x 21¼ in)
• Private collection

The Milliner's Window, 1894 A middle-class woman glances in a hat shop window. On his return from Japan, Henry was full of new ideas, and this image embraces modern life in a seemingly simple composition, recalling the work of Degas and Japanese *ukiyo-e* images.

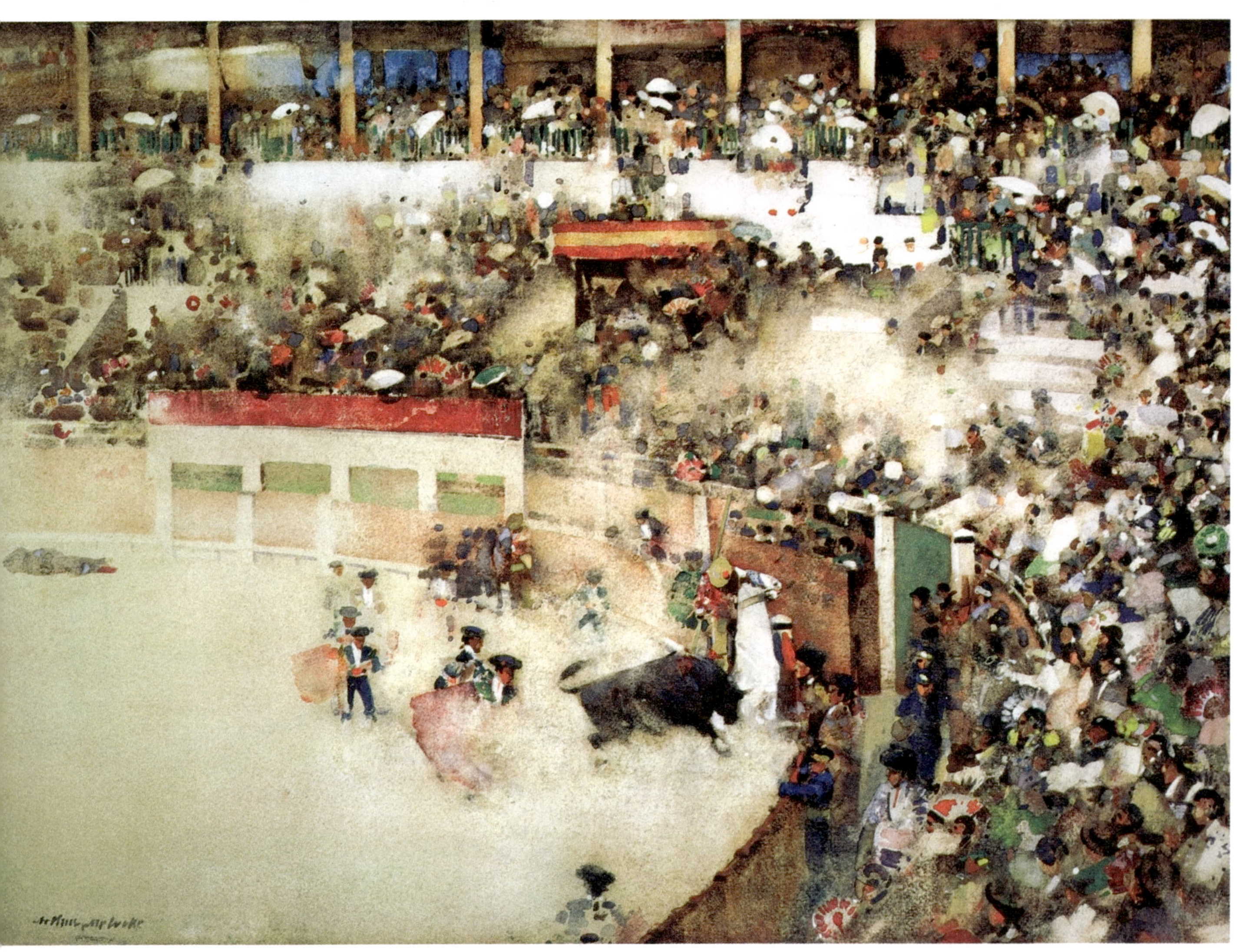

Arthur Melville (1855–1904)
Watercolour on paper, 55.9 x 77.5 cm (22 x 30½ in)
• The V&A Museum, London

The Little Bull, 'Bravo Toro!', 1894 Using his technique of soaking paper and dropping pigment over line drawings, plus applying areas of Chinese white, Melville captures the heat, colour and dynamism of a Spanish bullfight. The method was derided by critics as 'blottesque and stainy'.

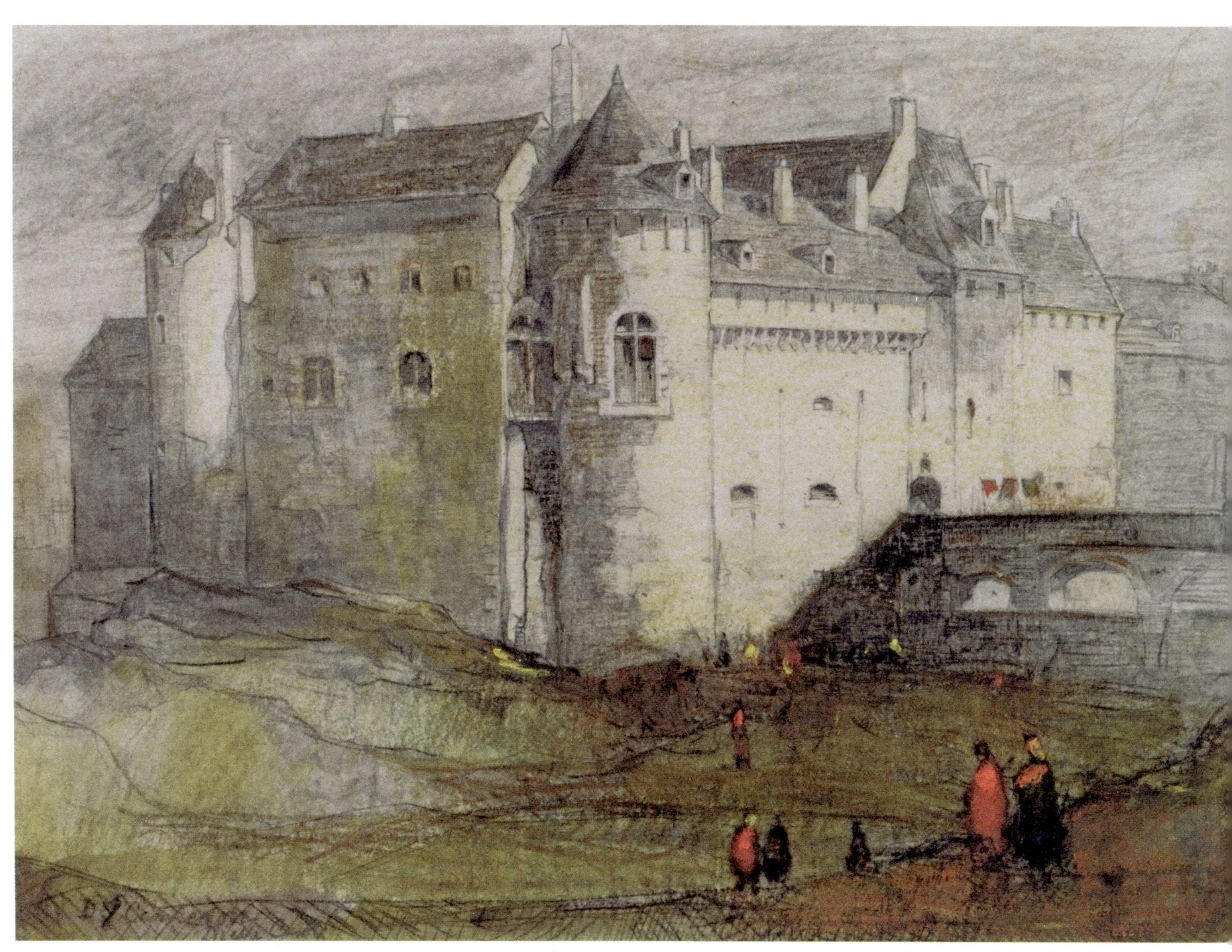

David Young Cameron (1865–1945)
Wash and pencil on paper, 27.9 x 38.1 cm (11 x 15 in)
• The Fleming-Wyfold Art Foundation, London

Dieppe Castle, 1896 Cameron painted this view of Dieppe Castle in 1896, in France, and later produced etchings of the image. The view of a familiar French landmark, while skilful, shows little resemblance to the work of the other Glasgow Boys.

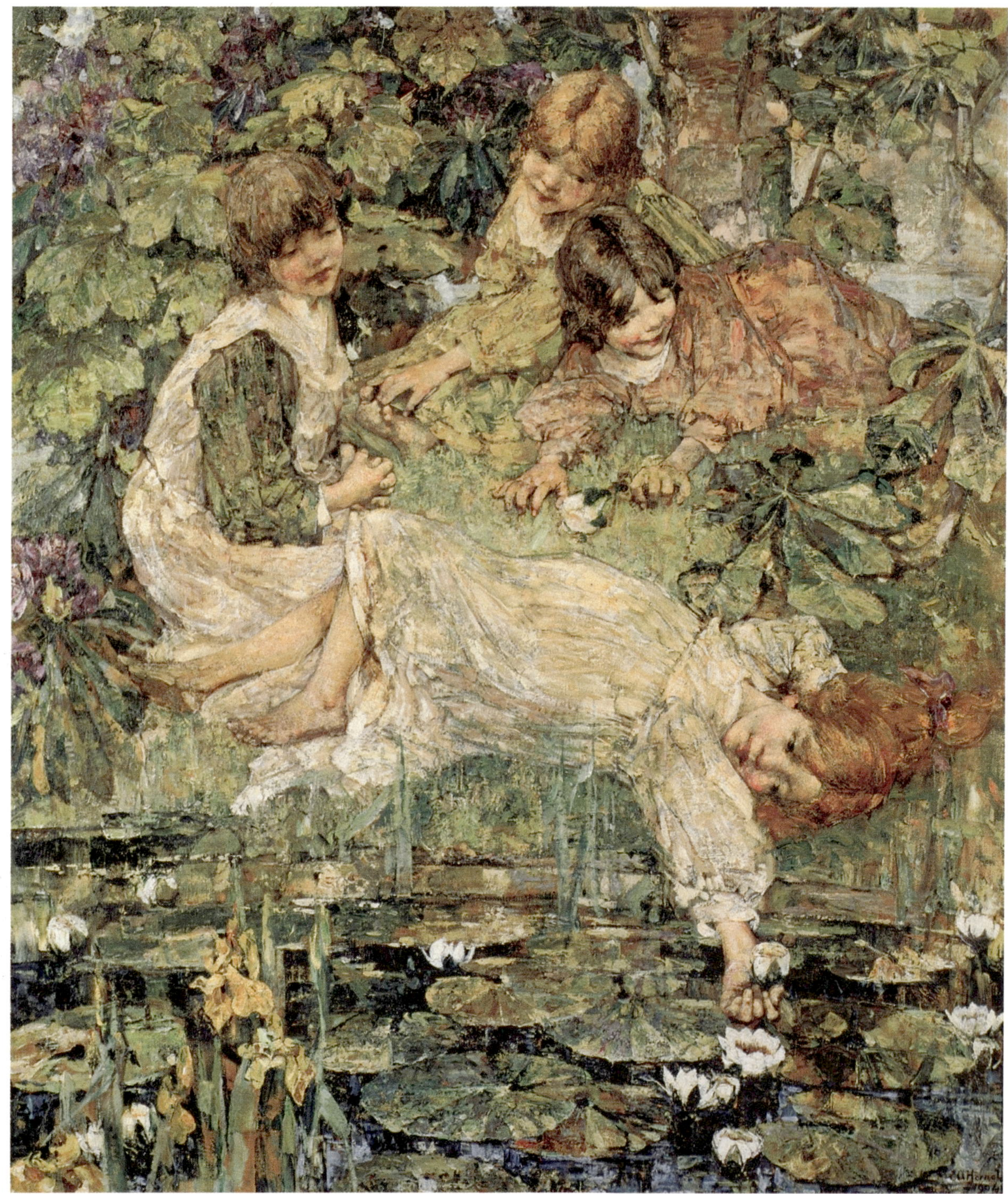

E.A. Hornel (1864–1933)
Oil on canvas, 117 x 102 cm (46 x 40 in)
• Bradford Art Galleries and Museums, Yorkshire

The Pool, 1904 One of several paintings of girls beside a pool of water, seemingly embedded in the leaves, this piece explores colour and shape. Departing from the naturalism of the Glasgow Boys' early paintings, it follows the linear styles and decorative aspects of Art Nouveau.

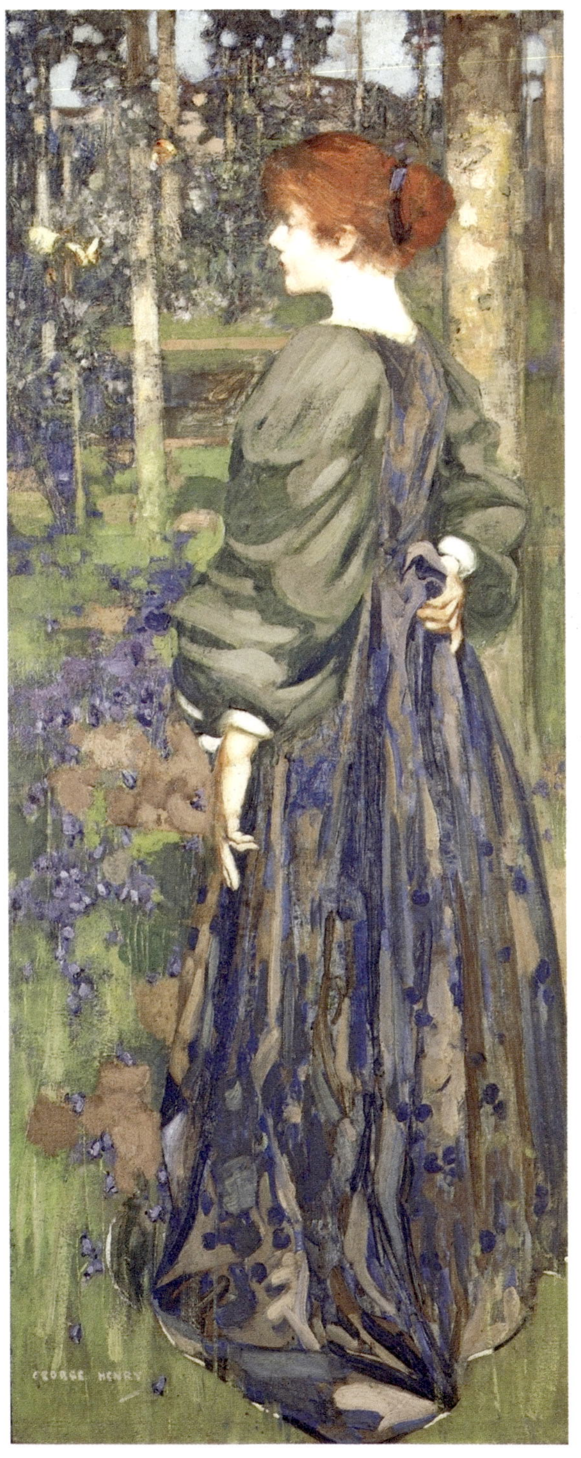

George Henry (1858–1943)
Oil on canvas, 147.4 x 61 cm (58 x 24 in)
• Private collection

In the Bluebell Wood, *c.* 1904 Painted while Henry was living in an artists' community in Chelsea, London, when he became a founding member of the Chelsea Arts Club, this shows influences of Whistler, Dante Gabriel Rossetti (1828–82) and Edward Coley Burne-Jones (1833–98).

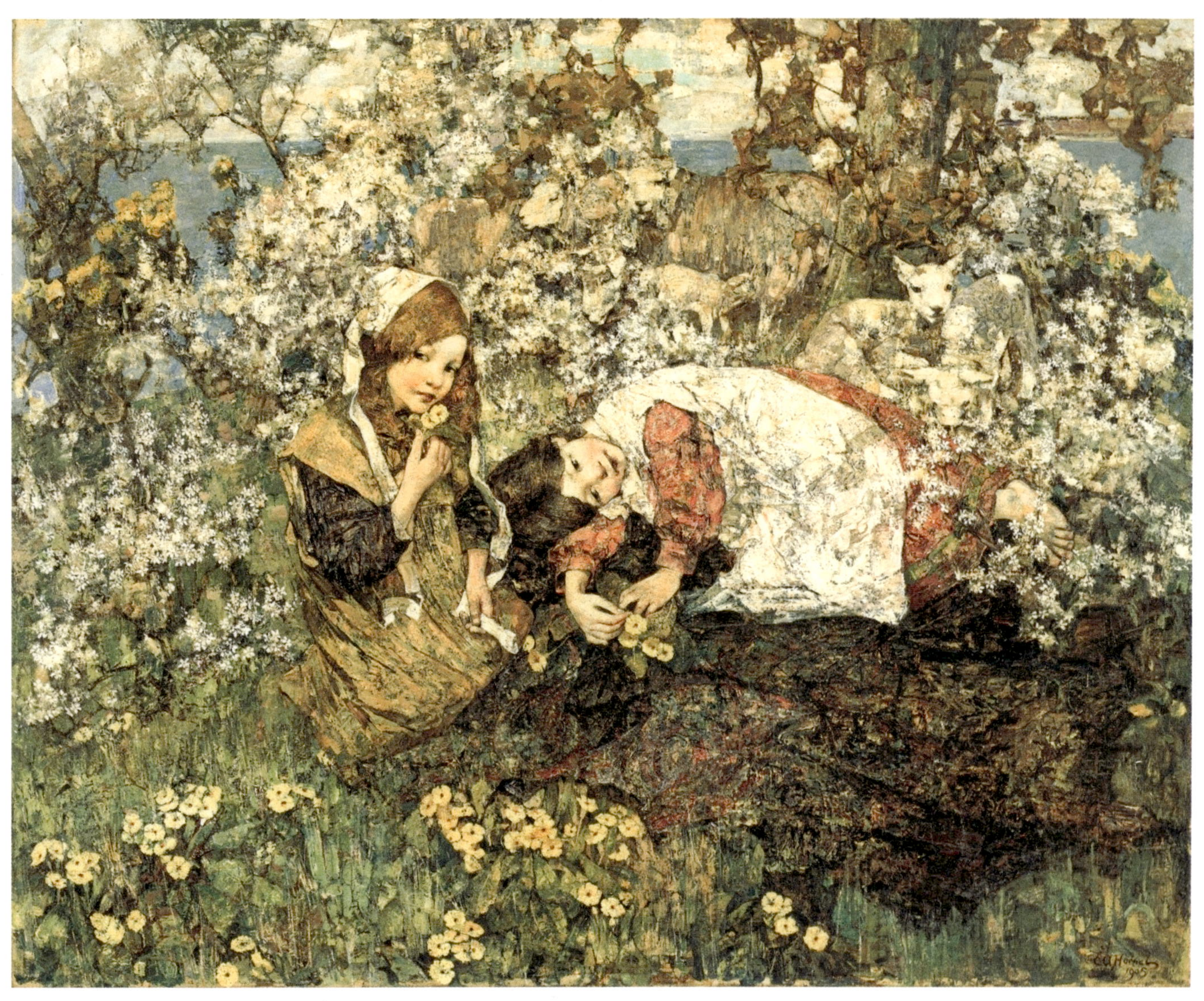

E.A. Hornel (1864–1933)
Oil on canvas, 124.2 x 153.6 cm (48⅘ x 60⅖ in)
• Museum of Fine Arts, Ghent

Spring Idyll, 1905 Extremely successful during his career, Hornel used a more graphic approach after his Japanese trip and, by the early twentieth century, featured more 'British' subjects, such as children and flowers, with a glimpse of blue water in the distance.

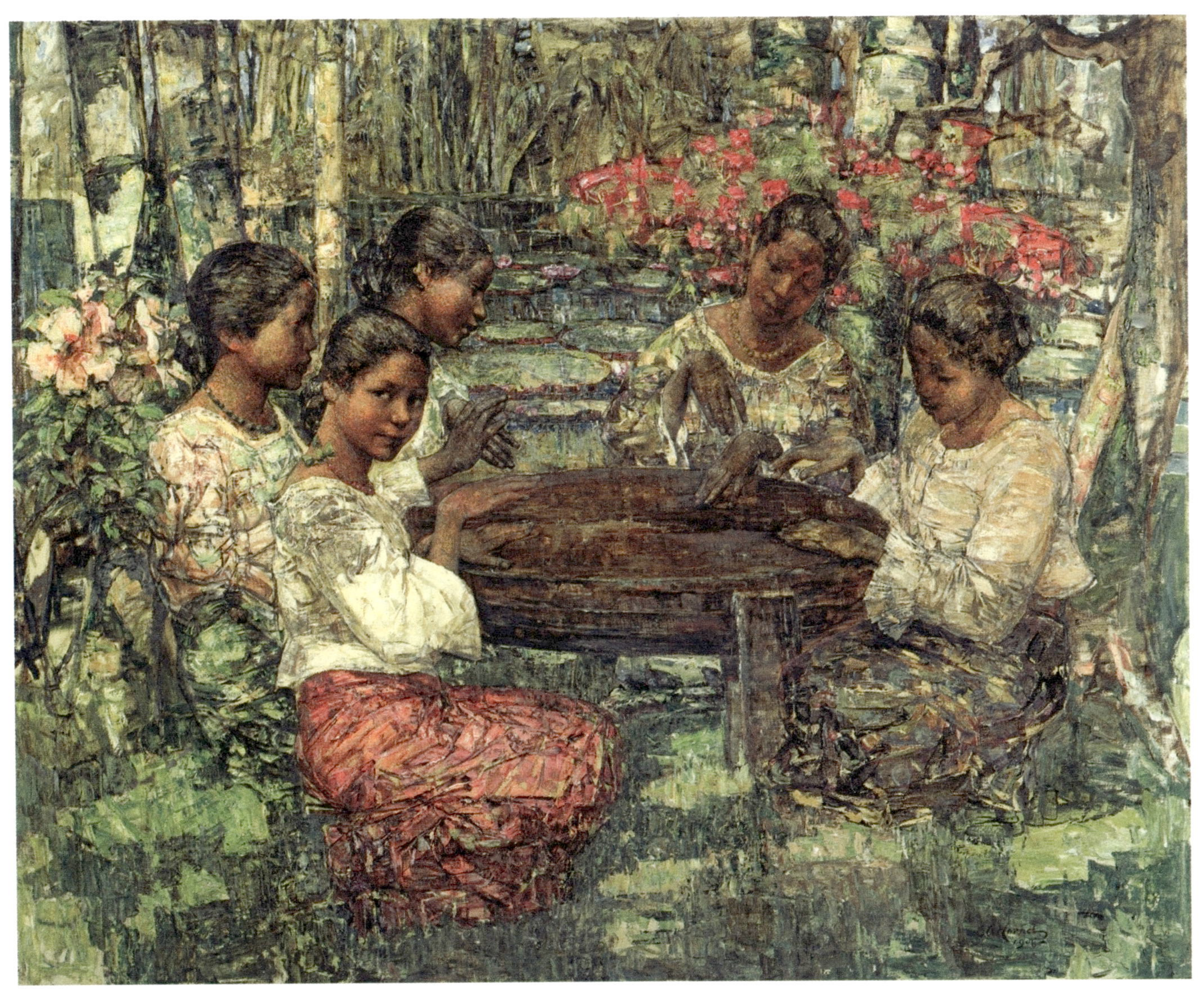

E.A. Hornel (1864–1933)
Oil on canvas, 122.1 x 152.9 cm (48 x 60 in)
• Manchester Art Gallery, Manchester

Tom-Tom Players, Ceylon, 1908 In 1907, Hornel visited Ceylon (now Sri Lanka) with his sister. Using sketches and photographs from the trip, Hornel painted this on his return, with his unique textural paint application. Five young girls sit around a drum, surrounded by flowers and trees in dappled sunlight.

Portraits
& Still Life

With their diverse influences and approaches, each of the Glasgow Boys made quite different contributions, especially after their early realist phase. Some of their most significant works were portraits, still lifes, and paintings of animals or flowers.

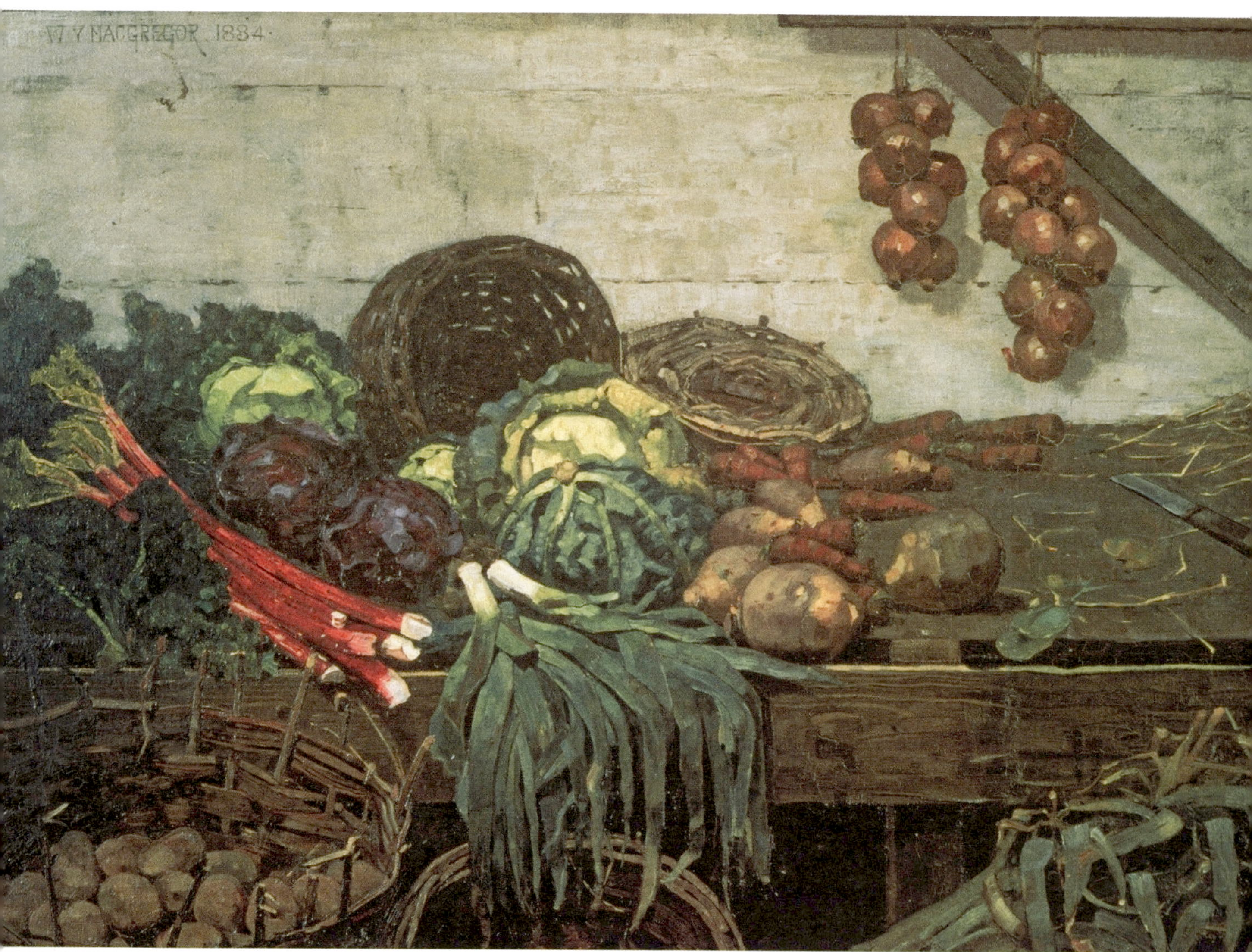

William York Macgregor (1855–1923)
Oil on canvas, 106.5 x 153 cm (42 x 60¼ in)
• National Galleries of Scotland, Edinburgh

The Vegetable Stall, 1884 This richly coloured still life was created while Macgregor was living in Crail, and is one of the first urban subjects painted by any of the Boys. The knife and onions were painted later, to cover a female stallholder counting her takings.

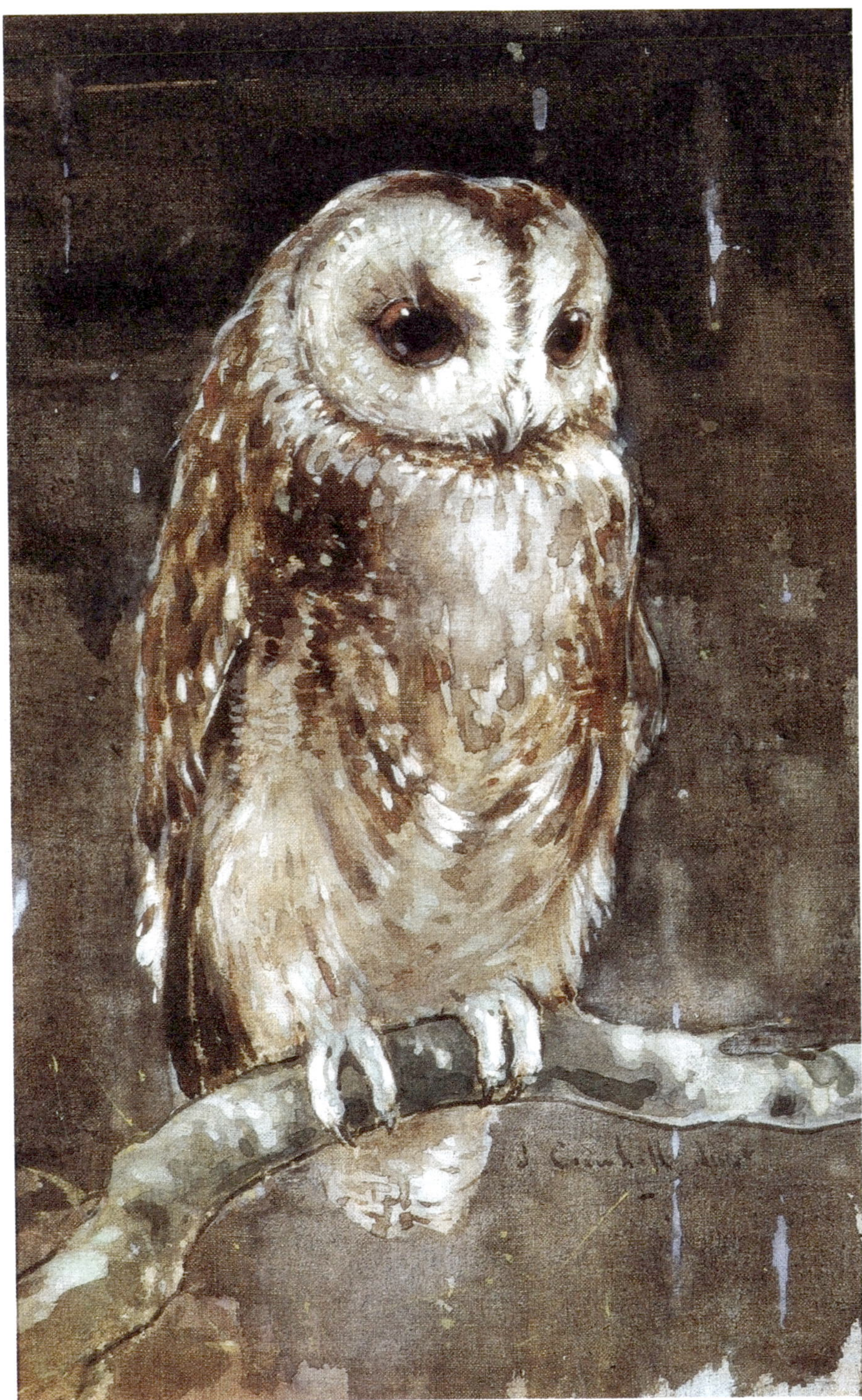

Joseph Crawhall (1861–1913)
Body colour and watercolour on textile, 18.2 x 25.5 cm (7 x 10 in)
• Laing Art Gallery, Newcastle-upon-Tyne

Tawny Owl, *c.* 1885–1910 Crawhall turned to watercolour early in his career, and often painted with gouache on brown holland, a buff-coloured linen. This owl is an example of his method of painting from memory after careful observation.

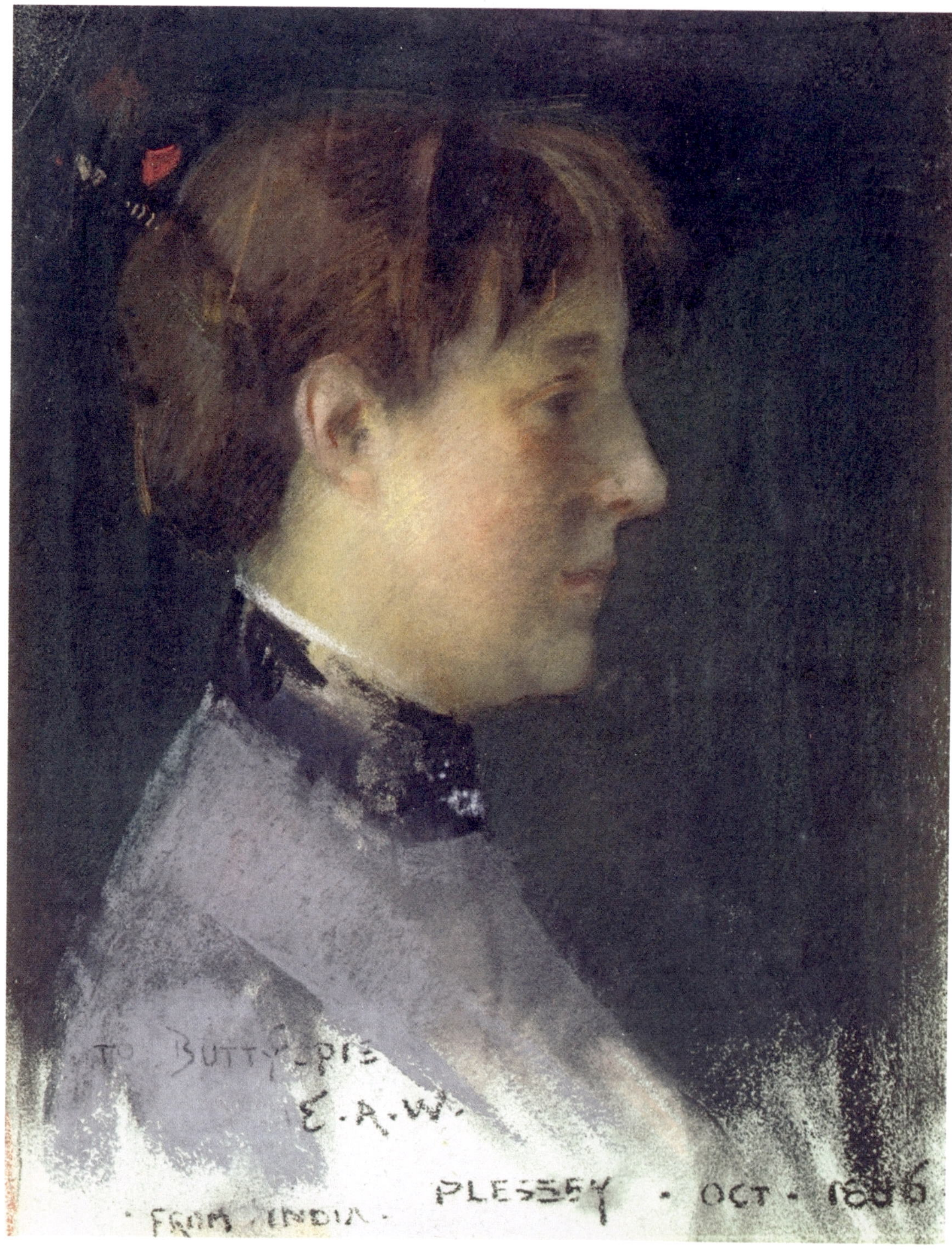

Edward Arthur Walton (1860–1922)
Pastel on paper, 36.8 x 30.5 cm (14⅖ x 12 in)
• Private collection

Portrait of Beatrice Crawhall, 1886 Beatrice Crawhall was Joseph Crawhall's sister.
Another sister was married to Walton's brother, so the families were closely connected.
Walton's profile of Beatrice is created with soft contours, colours and tonal contrasts.

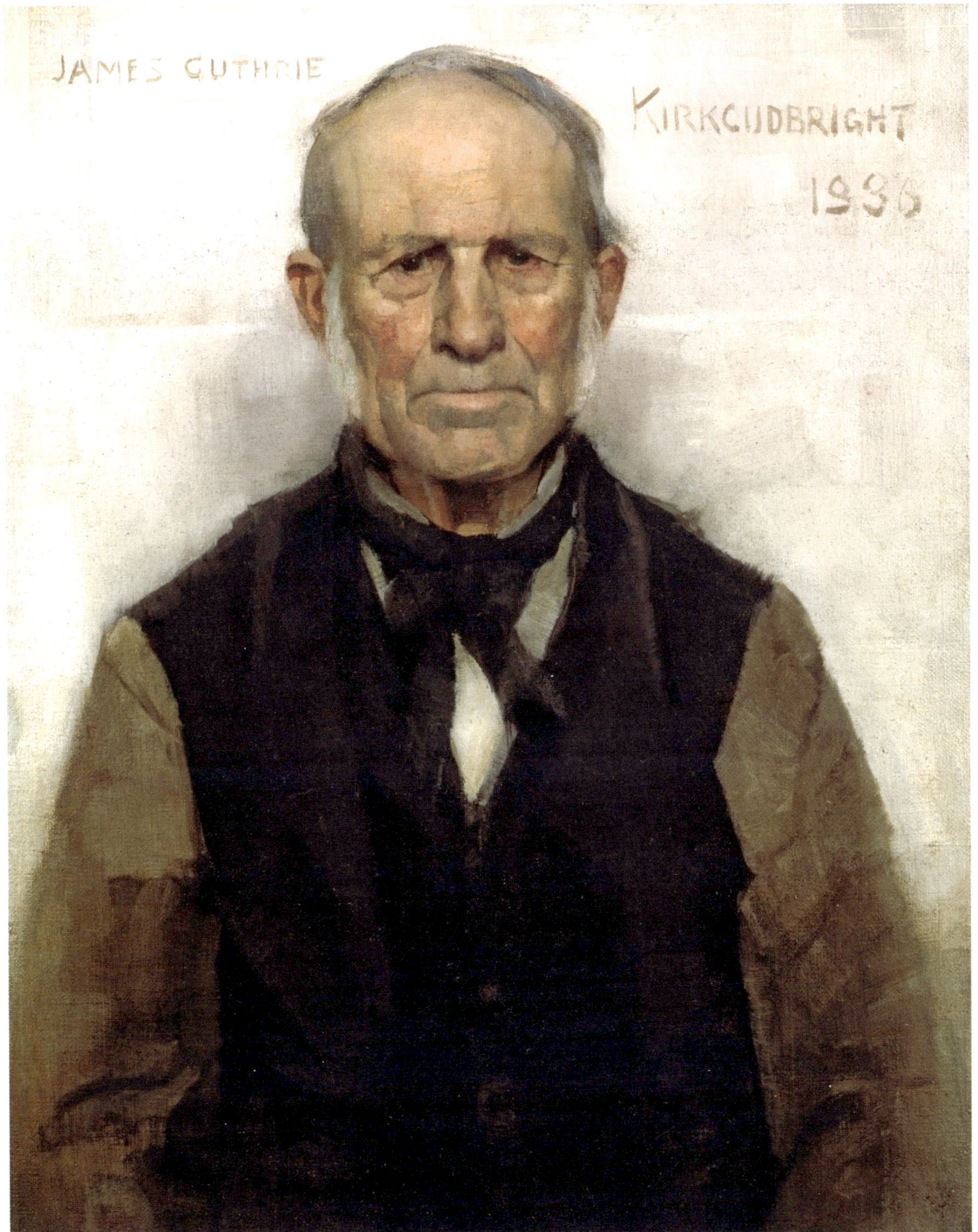

James Guthrie (1859–1930)
Oil on canvas, 60.8 x 50.8 cm (24 x 20 in)
• Kelvingrove Art Gallery and Museum, Glasgow

Old Willie – the Village Worthy, 1886 The weather-beaten face of a local man from Kirkcudbright looking directly at viewers and standing against a whitewashed wall demonstrates Guthrie's skill in portraying character, dignity and a sense of realism in the glow of subtle light.

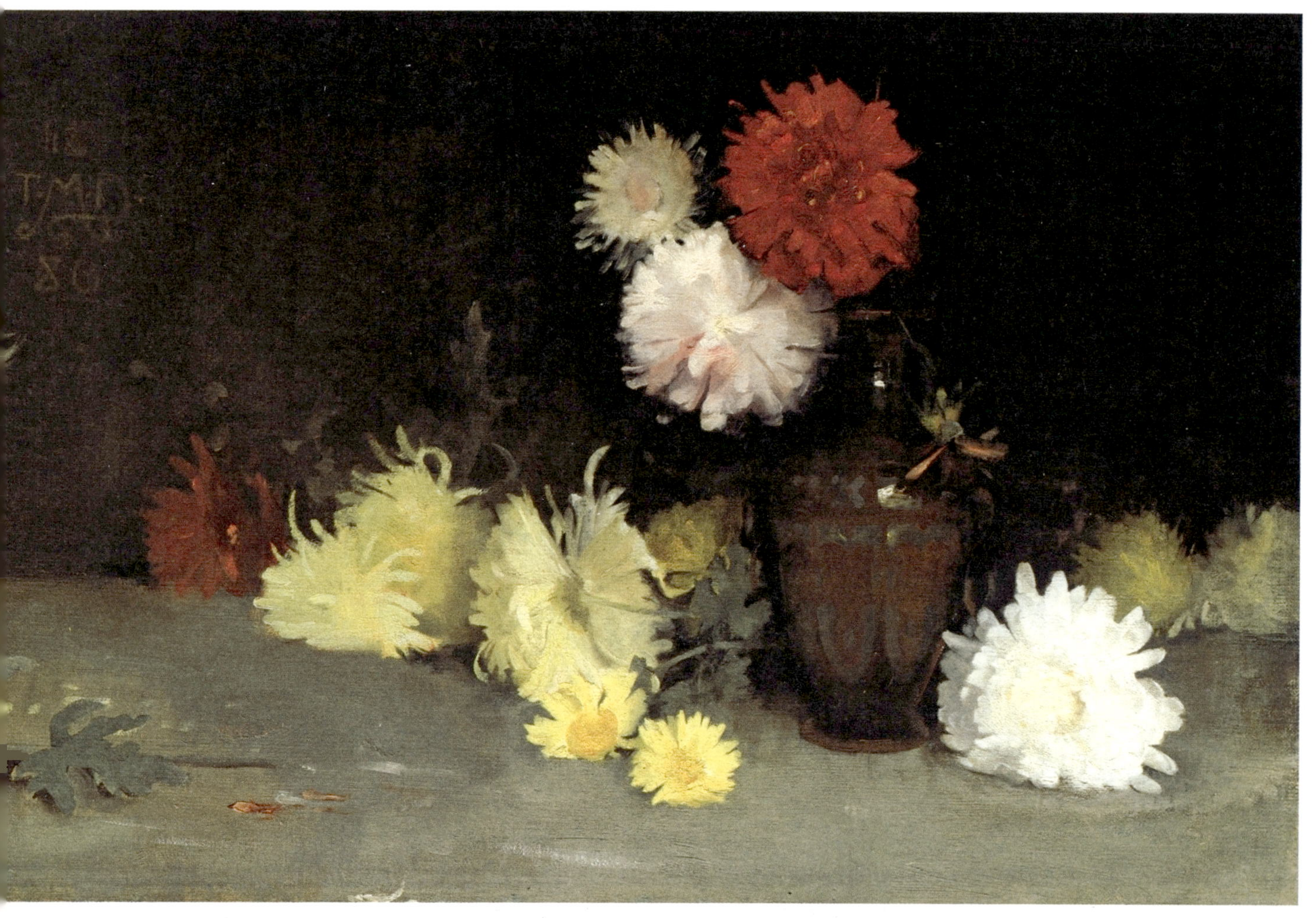

Thomas Millie Dow (1848–1919)
Oil on canvas, 35.7 x 53.3 cm (14 x 21 in)
• Private collection

Flowers in a Vase, 1886 Influenced by, among others, his friend William Stott, the Impressionists and Anton Mauve, who was a great colourist, Dow produced many naturalistic paintings of seemingly casually arranged flowers, set against plain, dark backgrounds.

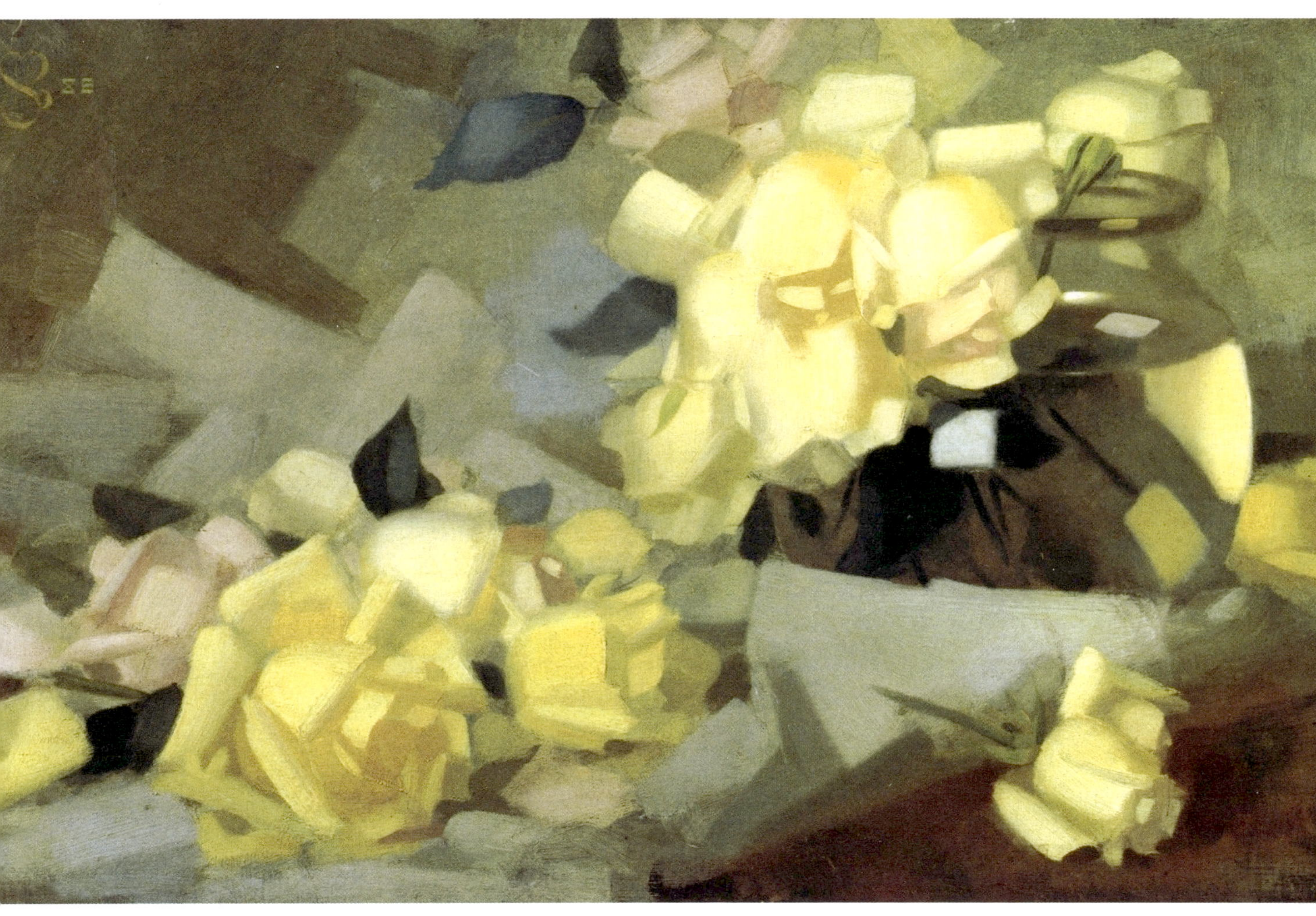

James Stuart Park (1862–1933)
Oil on canvas, 40.6 x 66 cm (16 x 26 in)
• Kelvingrove Art Gallery and Museum, Glasgow

Roses, 1889 An abstract element emerged in Park's flower paintings through his emphasis on design and avoidance of details. Here, the lemon-, pink-, white- and cream-coloured petals are almost prismatic, seeming fresh and different from traditional flower paintings.

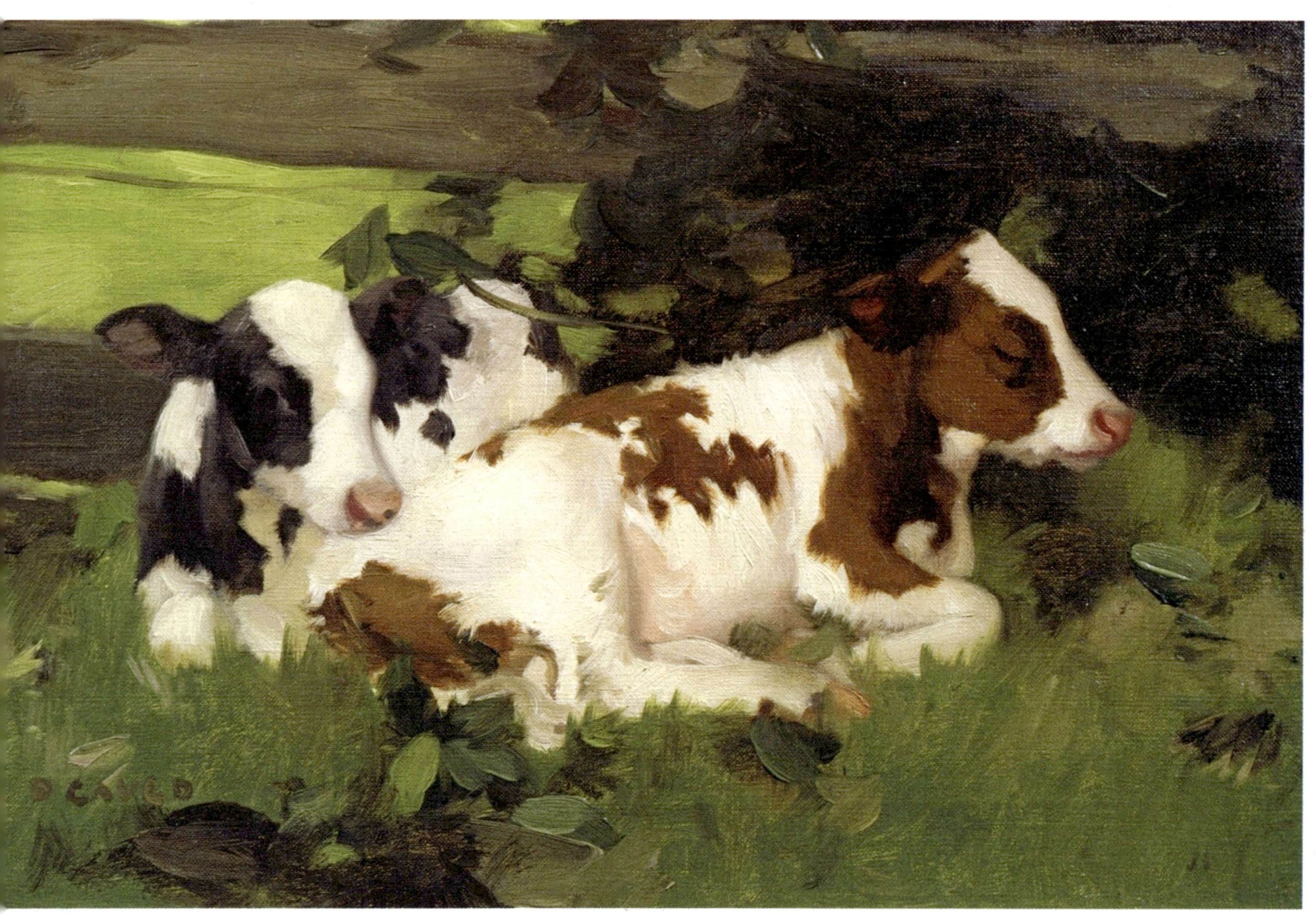

David Gauld (1865–1936)
Oil on canvas, 50.7 x 76.2 cm (20 x 30 in)
• The Ellis Campbell Collection

Ayrshire Calves, 1890 At variance with the Glasgow Boys' beliefs, Gauld's paintings of cattle in the Ayrshire countryside had been pioneered by the Scottish artists they all disdained. Yet Gauld's approach was innovative, with seemingly spontaneous brushmarks and flat areas of colour.

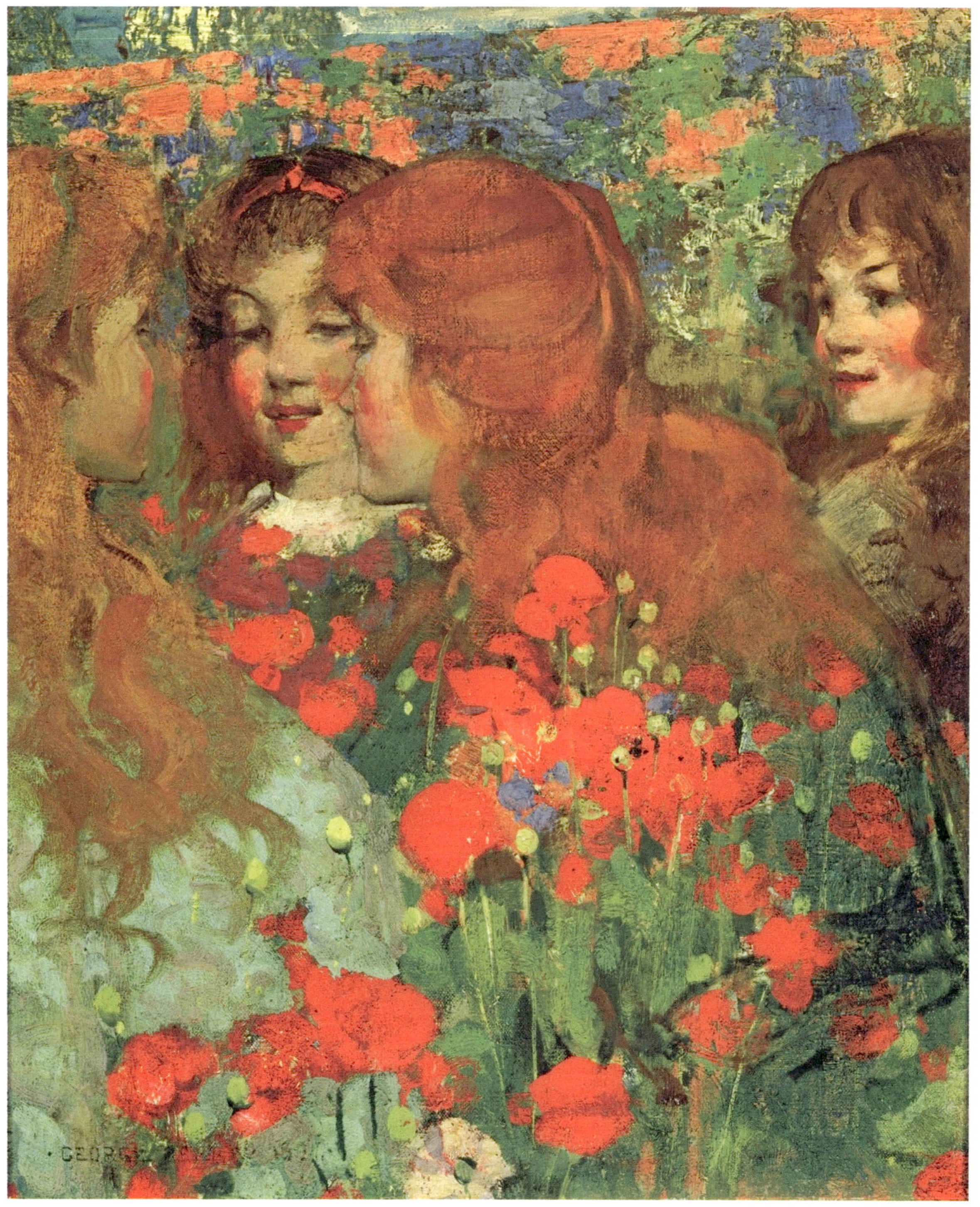

George Henry (1858–1943)
Oil on canvas, 61 x 50.8 cm (24 x 20 in)
• City of Edinburgh Museums and Art Galleries, Edinburgh

The Poppies, 1891 Going against the naturalism of the Boys' early work, the vivid palette and decorative quality of Henry's compositions influenced several of them. This unusual painting is enhanced by the juxtaposition of complementary colours.

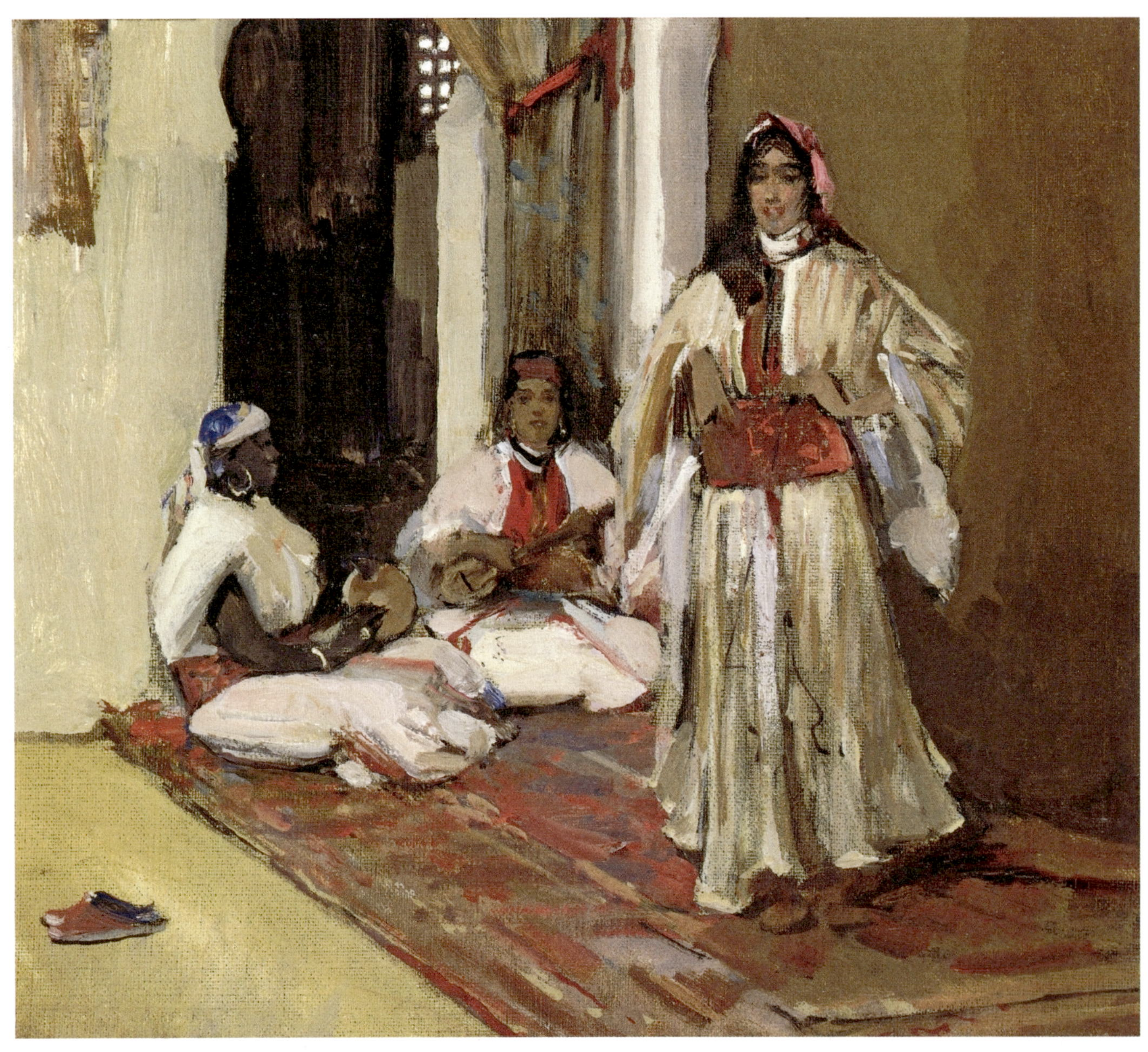

John Lavery (1856–1941)
Oil on canvas, 24 x 27 cm (9½ x 10⅔ in)
• Private collection

Habiba, 1892 Like many artists, Lavery was fascinated by North Africa, especially Morocco, and since 1890, he had spent the winters there. Accompanied by musicians, one with a tambourine and the other with an oud, this Moroccan woman is about to dance.

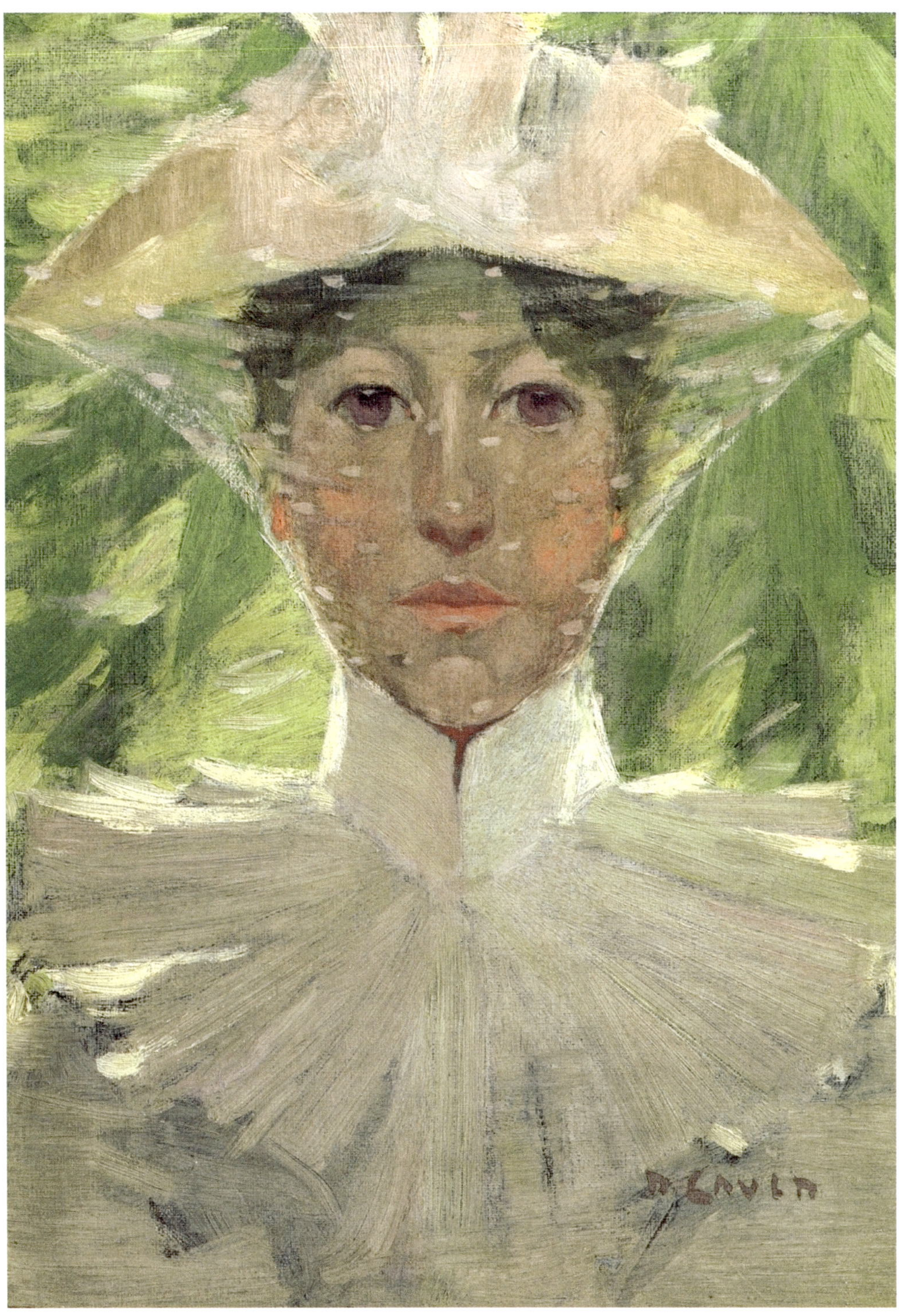

David Gauld (1865–1936)
Oil on board, 35.5 x 25 cm (14 x 9⅘ in)
• Private collection

The New Bonnet, *c.* 1893–94 Although best known for his studies of cattle, Gauld's portraits, emphasizing surface textures and patterns, were also highly regarded. This simple composition, with soft brushmarks and a reduced palette, demonstrates his modernist outlook.

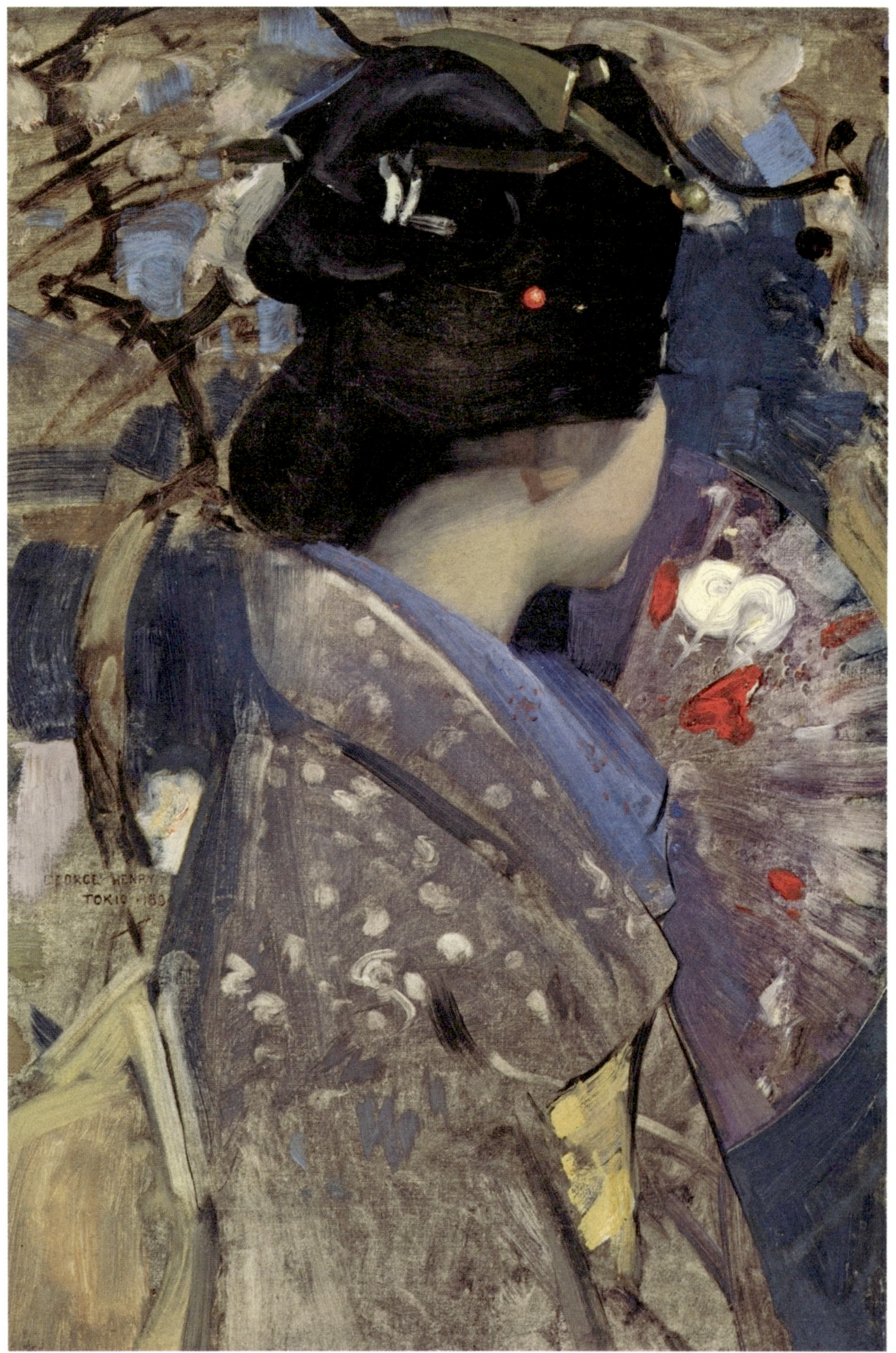

George Henry (1858–1943)
Oil on canvas, 61 x 40.6 cm (24 x 16 in)
• Kelvingrove Art Gallery and Museum, Glasgow

Japanese Lady with a Fan, 1894 Most of Henry's Japanese paintings are of single figures.
Probably inspired by Japanese *ukiyo-e* prints and photographs that were produced for foreign
export, this was painted in Tokyo in 1894. The focus is not on realism, but on pattern and colour.

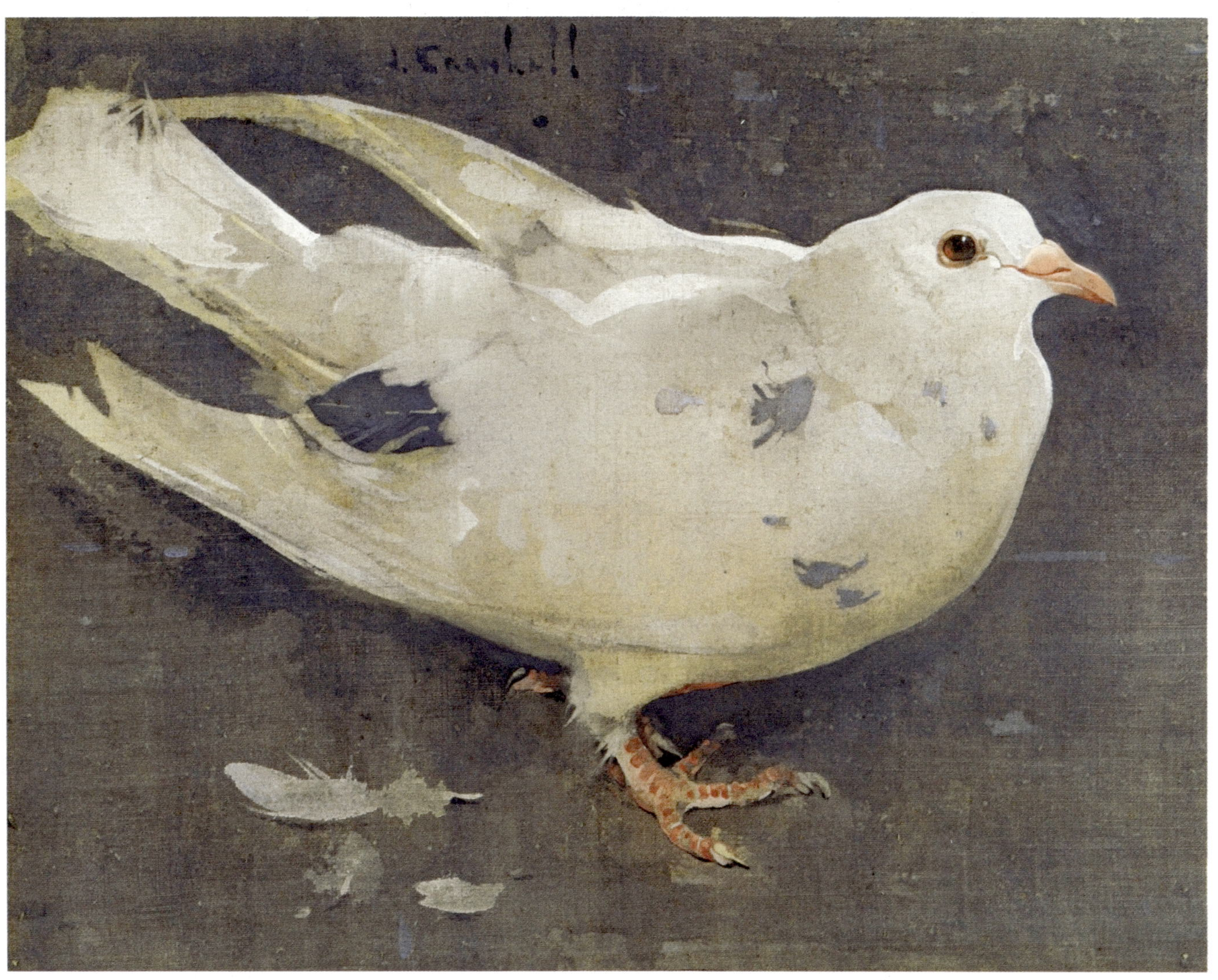

Joseph Crawhall (1861–1913)
Gouache on linen, 23.5 x 31.1 cm (9¼ x 12¼ in)
• Kelvingrove Art Gallery and Museum, Glasgow

The Pigeon, *c.* 1894 Crawhall began painting with gouache on linen from about 1890, and he used the water-based medium to render the feathers of this pigeon with remarkable skill, bathing it in bright light. Using the tip of the brush in some places, he applied the paint judiciously.

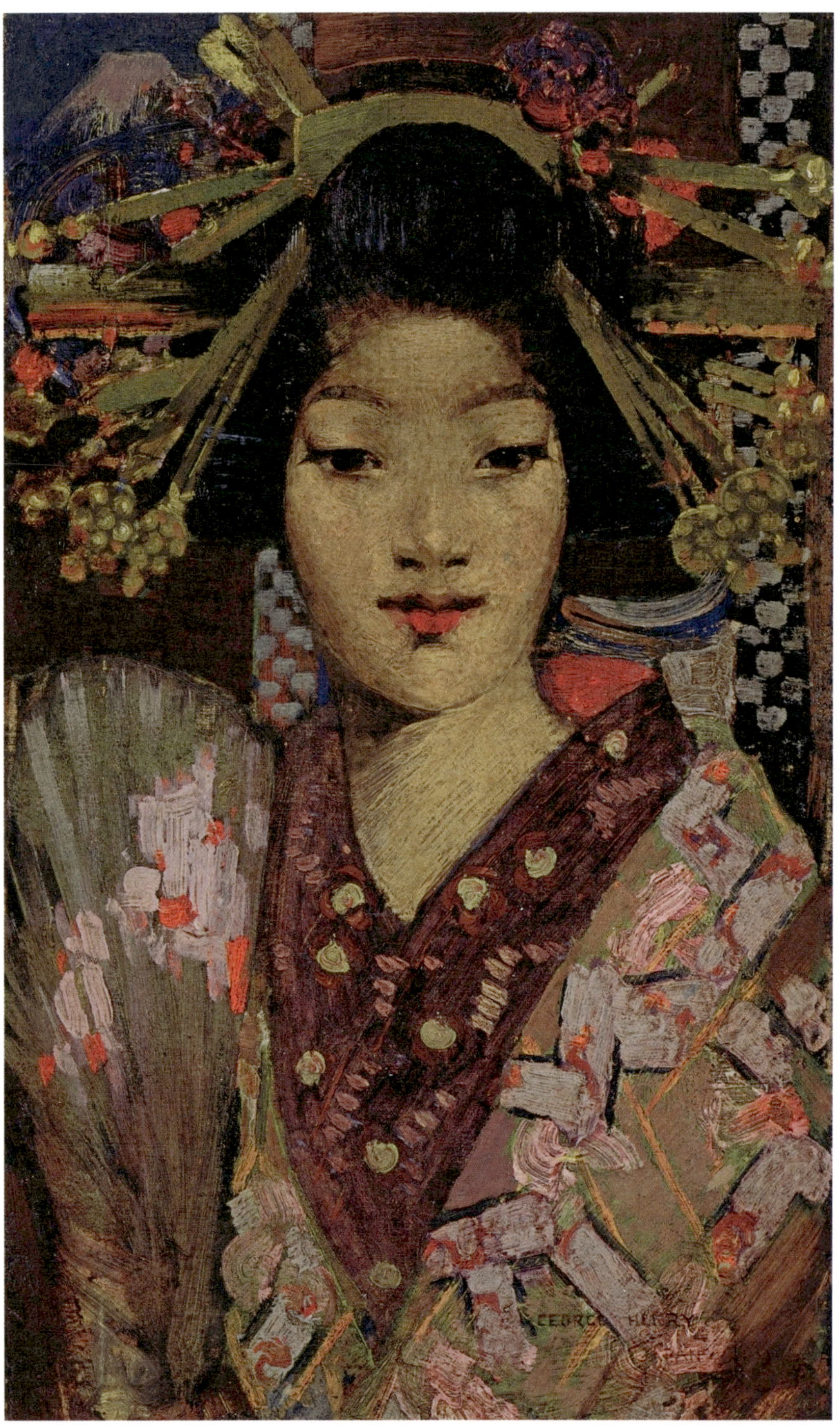

George Henry (1858–1943)
Oil on canvas, 53.3 x 32.8 cm (21 x 13 in)
• National Galleries of Scotland, Edinburgh

The Geisha Girl, 1894 This geisha girl is in the same direct composition as Gauld's *The New Bonnet* (*c.* 1893–94, *see* page 117) but, with the contrasting patterns of the kimono and fan, elaborate hair ornaments, Japanese screen and glimpse of Mount Fuji, far more ornamental.

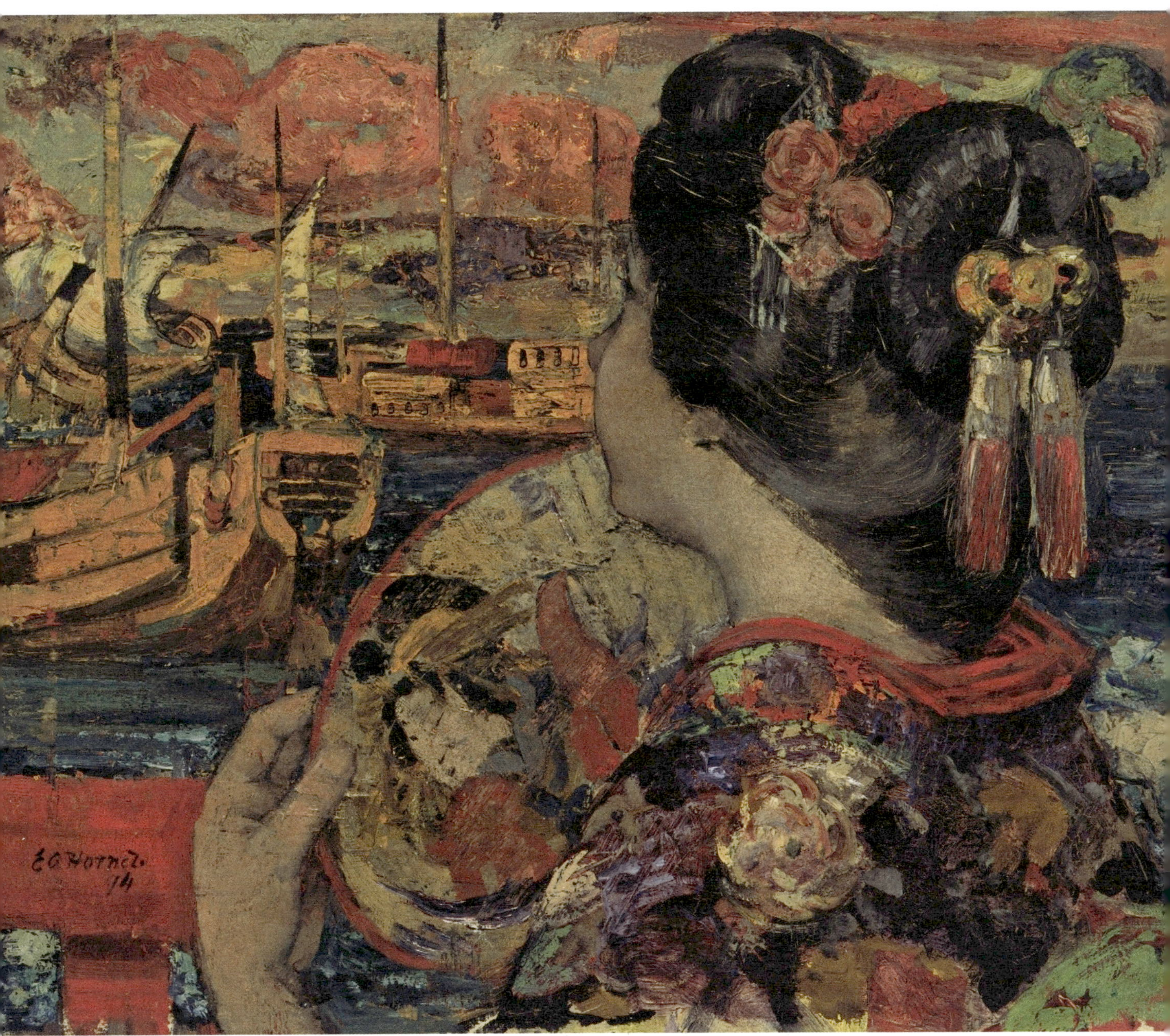

E.A. Hornel (1864–1933)
Oil on canvas laid on panel, 40.6 x 50.5 cm (16 x 19⅘ in)
• Yale Center for British Art, Connecticut

The Balcony, Yokohama, 1894 Hornel's Japanese paintings emphasize surface texture and pattern. This exotic image, with its asymmetrical composition and intense colours, features a young woman on a balcony in a patterned kimono and hair ornaments, watching boats on the water.

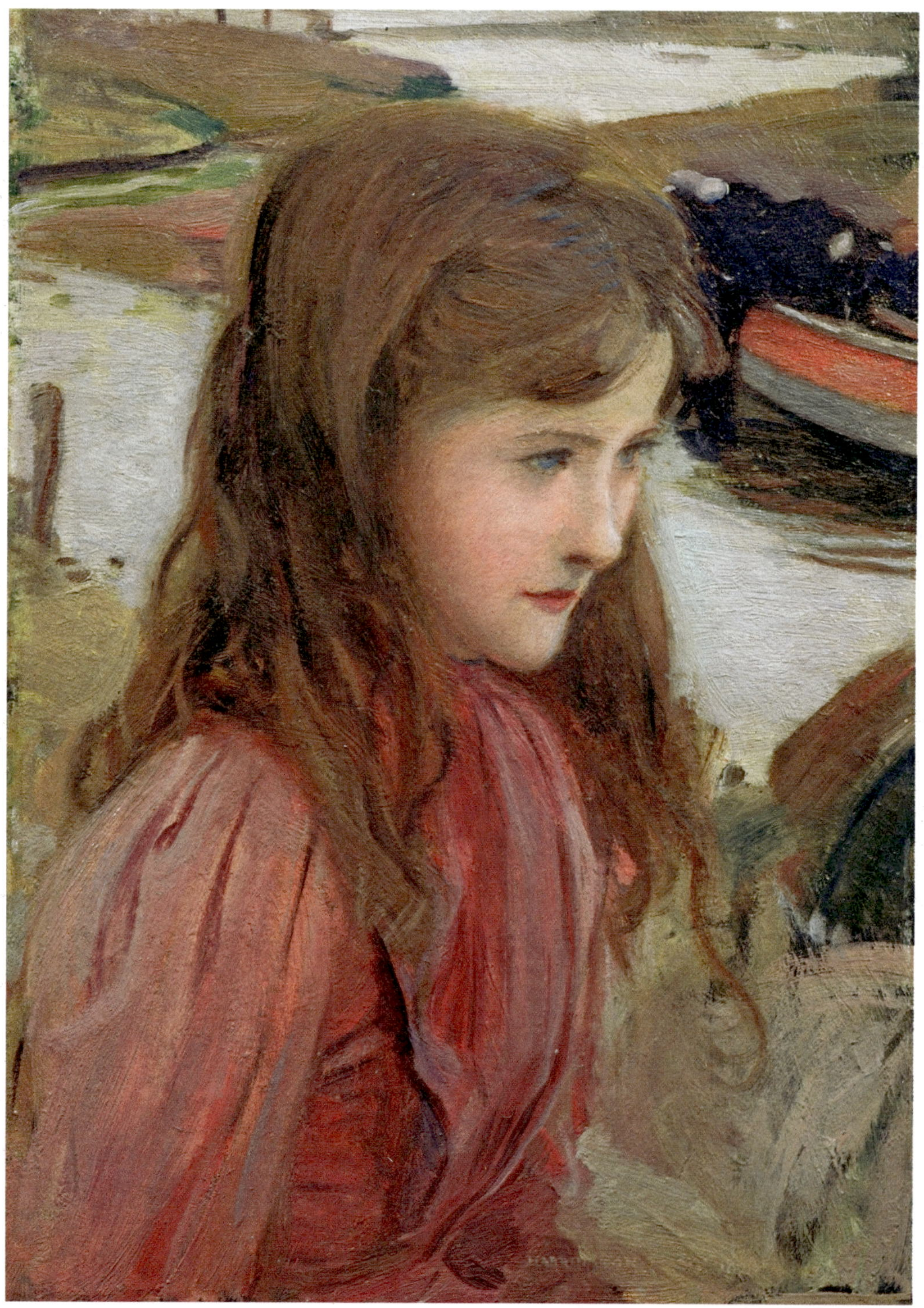

Harrington Mann (1864–1937)
Oil on board, 31.8 x 22.9 cm (12½ x 9 in)
• Private collection

Study of a Young Girl, 1898 After their first group exhibition outside Scotland, in London in May 1890, Harrington Mann was widely appreciated as a skilful portraitist and naturalistic landscape painter. This image of a Scottish girl with boats in the background mixes the two disciplines.

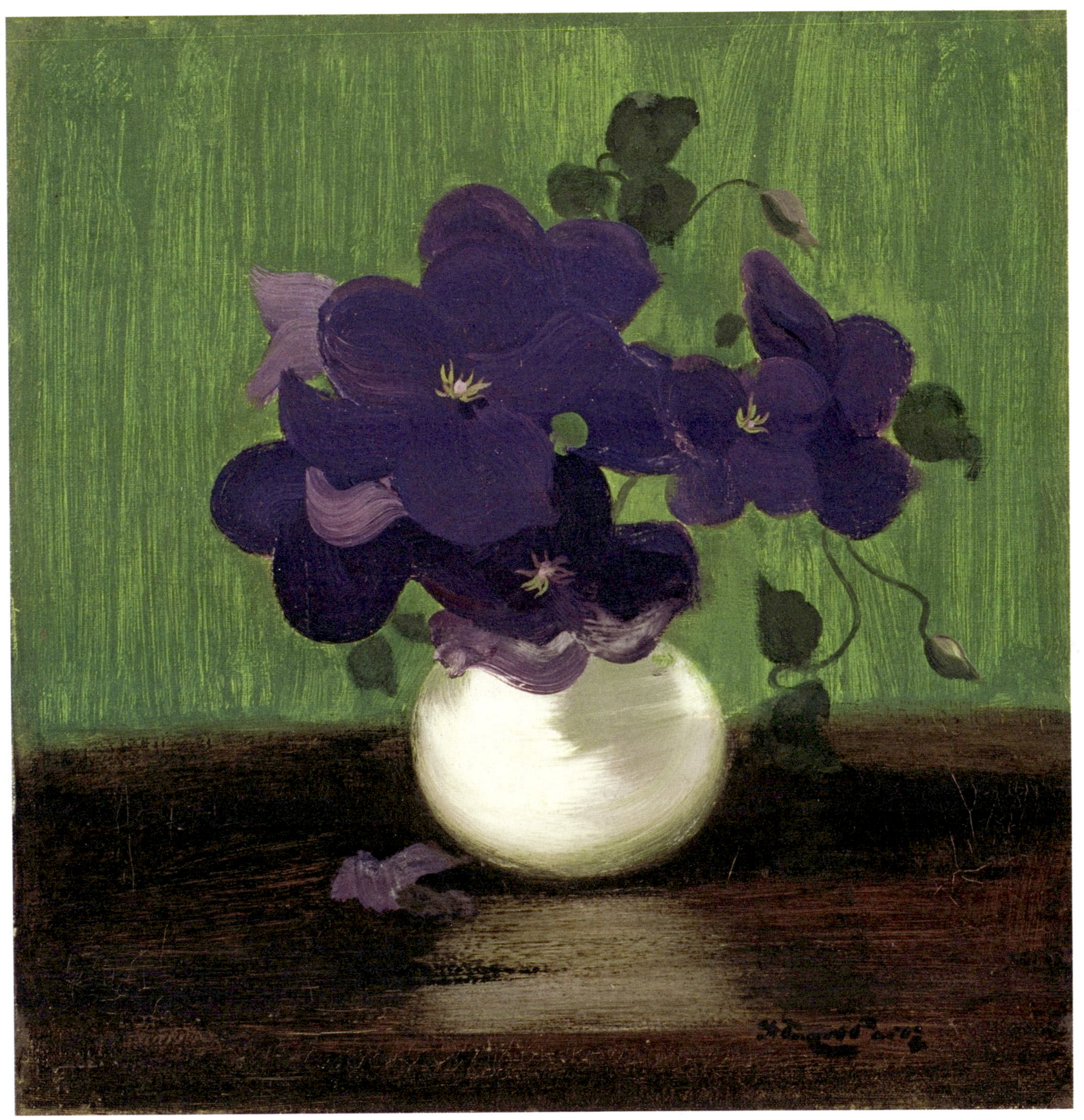

James Stuart Park (1862–1933)
Oil on canvas, 38 x 30 cm (15 x 11⅛ in)
• Private collection

Violets, 1900 Using thick, layered paint and rapid brushstrokes, Park specialized in flower paintings. Using strong, minimal colours, he suggests the textures and colours of these velvety violets, creating what appears to be a shallow space, with few details and smooth tonal contrasts.

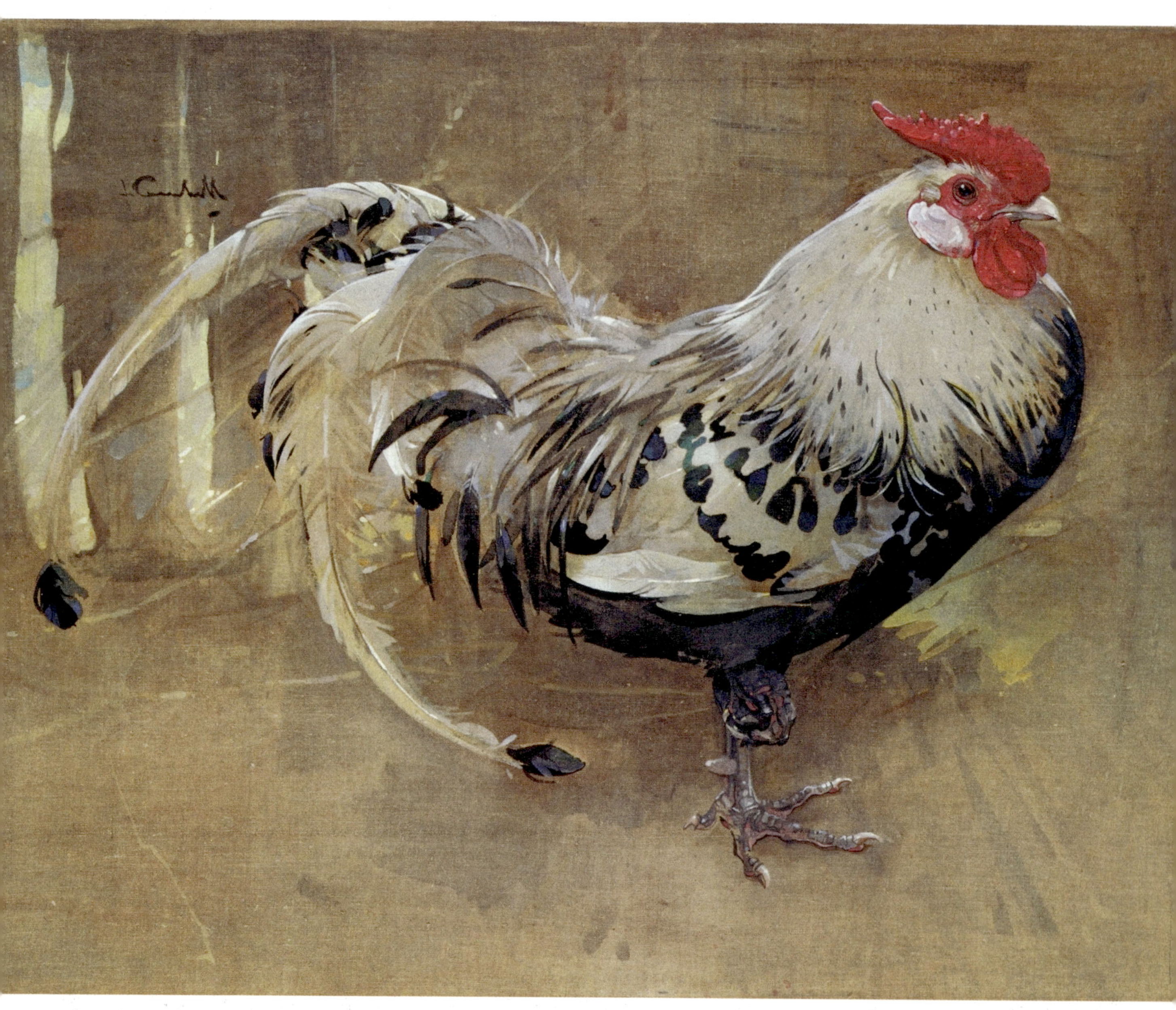

Joseph Crawhall (1861–1913)
Gouache on linen, 44.5 x 58.4 cm (17½ x 23 in)
• Private collection

Spangled Cock, 1903 An accomplished oil painter, Crawhall was also a master draughtsman and one of the finest watercolourists of his generation. Here, he builds up the effect of feathers layer by layer, using his remarkable memory to convey the colourful cockerel emerging from the plain background.

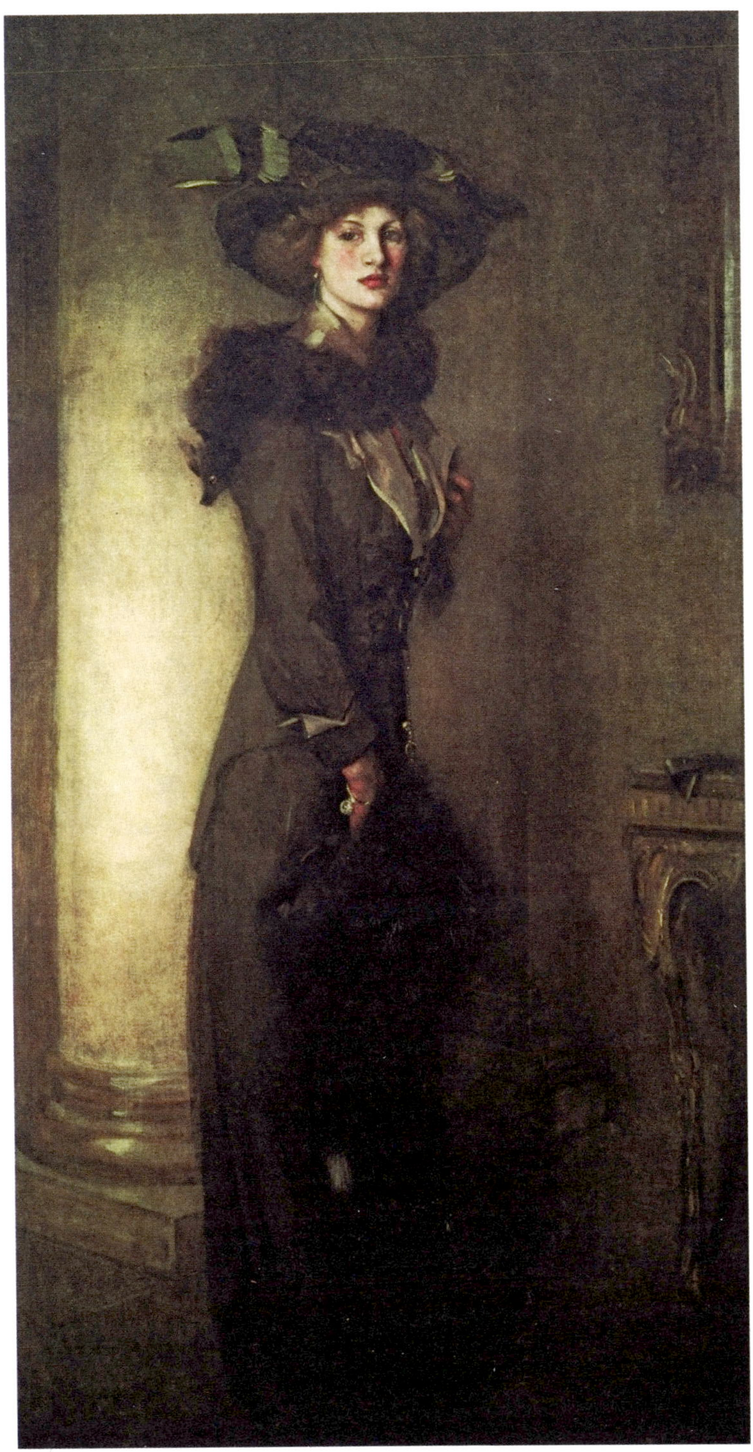

Edward Arthur Walton (1860–1922)
Oil on canvas, 200.5 x 106.5 cm (79 x 42 in)
• Private collection

The Beaver Hat, c. 1912 Clearly influenced by Whistler, with its subdued lighting and subtle tonal contrasts, this atmospheric portrait of a fashionable woman is an example of the Glasgow Boys' third phase, when some depicted the modern, wealthy middle classes, rather than the rural poor.

Indexes

Index of Works

Page numbers in *italics* indicate
illustration captions.

General Index

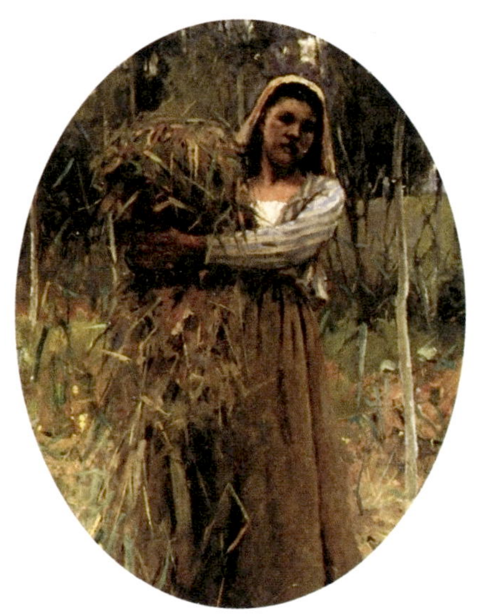

Masterpieces of Art
FLAME TREE PUBLISHING
A new series of carefully curated print and digital books covering the world's greatest art, artists and art movements.

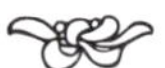